TRENDS IN 20TH CENTURY DRAMA

Trends in 20th Century Drama

A Survey since Ibsen and Shaw

by

Frederick Lumley

BARRIE and ROCKLIFF
LONDON

FIRST PUBLISHED 1956
SECOND (REVISED) EDITION 1960

Published by Barrie and Rockliff (Barrie Books Ltd.) 1960
2 Clement's Inn, Strand, London WC2

© Frederick Lumley 1960

MADE AND PRINTED IN GREAT BRITAIN BY
C. TINLING AND COMPANY LIMITED, LIVERPOOL,
LONDON AND PRESCOT.

This book is for
Ian and Vaudine

ACKNOWLEDGMENTS

THOSE critics who have become part of dramatic history appear to the young critic like the giant Atlas himself; they are our inheritance (though not responsible for our views) and yet it is not the done thing to canonise them in a list of acknowledgments. I do, however, acknowledge the debt I owe to contemporary critics and writers, and even here a list of all the sources of information collected over the years from reading about the theatre in newspapers, magazines, books and in conversation would be impossible. I have given a selected bibliography of those books which cover some of the subjects discussed in this volume and which may help to fill in the background.

No excuse is offered for the fairly long analysis of the leading plays of our dramatists in the following chapters. Telling 'the story' has become unfashionable since critics were forced to compress their notices during the war through the shortage of newsprint, but there is no reason why in a book a critic should shirk a major part of his job. Telling the story does not mean telling the whole story, but merely setting the atmosphere and selecting the incidents so that the reader can follow the criticism even if he does not know the play — and it would be unwise to assume that the reader is acquainted with all the plays discussed here. I have therefore made use of quotations from many plays, and for permission to include these quotations (and the translations where these have been used) I would like to thank the following:

Signor Enzo Scipioni and *Amministrazione degli eredi di L. Pirandello*, and E. P. Dutton, New York; the Office Artistique International for quotations from the plays of Jean Giraudoux; Librairie Gallimard, Paris, for extracts from Paul Claudel and Jean-Paul Sartre (Copyright by Librairie Gallimard); Messrs. Faber & Faber for T. S. Eliot quotations and for the quotation from *Casida de la Hinda*, published in Arturo Barca's *Lorca, the Poet and his People;* Mr. Roy Campbell and Miss Karin Alin, Stockholm (representing Trustees of the Garcia Lorca estate) for passage from *Blood Wedding;* New Directions, New York, for passage from *The House of Bernada Alba* published in *Three Tragedies;* Messrs. Methuen for passage from Jean Anouilh's *Colombe;* Messrs. Secker & Warburg for quotation from *Three Plays by Gabriel Marcel*, introduced and translated by Rosalind Heywood.

To my friends, and in particular to Mr. Iain Hamilton — who has given me encouragement at so many stages in the writing — my indebtedness is very great. I would like also to thank Mr. Richard O. Paterson for all his suggestions and Mr. Lothian Small, who has provided me with translations of Claudel and Giraudoux. Mr. Small's translations are those marked with an asterisk. Where translations are taken from other sources I have indicated the translator; those where no translator is named are my own responsibility.

And I do not, of course, ask friends to share my views; I stand to be judged alone.

F.L.

PREFACE TO THE REVISED EDITION

1956, when this book was first published, was a decisive year in the theatre. The majority of the continental playrights were still relatively unknown and unproduced in Britain and the United States, while the British theatre had sunk to an incredible impotency. It was an actor's theatre *par excellence* where plays were taken for granted and young writers had to wait. Since then much has changed. Continental writers, from Giraudoux to the *avant-garde* theatre of Beckett and Ionesco have been introduced—and found an enthusiastic public. At the same time ventures such as the Royal Court Theatre in London have discovered John Osborne and other young potential playwrights. Among established dramatists, Tennessee Williams has added to his prestige, the autobiographical cycle of O'Neill has been produced, and important plays have come from both expected and unexpected sources on both sides of the Atlantic and the Channel. These developments have meant a complete revision of the text, a modification here and there as well as a considerable expansion. The theme however remains the same; trends apparent in 1956 have continued, sometimes more pronounced, in the same direction. It is hoped that this revised edition will be of continued use to those who have already welcomed the first edition, and that it will appeal to all those interested in the living theatre.

F.L.

CONTENTS

ILLUSTRATIONS

INTRODUCTION

THE DRAMA SINCE IBSEN AND SHAW

TITLES of theatre books remain elusive and open to mis-interpretation; there are consequently more reasons than merely those of custom and convention why an author writing on modern drama should hasten at the outset to define his frontiers. We have reached a situation to-day when it is no longer sufficient to use the word 'theatre' by itself — we require explanatory adjectives such as 'commercial', 'art', 'experimental', 'literary', 'proletarian', 'religious', 'naturalistic', 'mystical'. . . while plays have either become 'well-made' (a term of derision!), *pièces à thèse*, plays for the actor, plays for the box-office, plays for the study, but never just plays, comedies or tragedies. Good theatre and good plays are no longer accepted as critical currency.

It is indeed necessary to state aims and purposes clearly, for this book attempts a study of good plays and good theatre covering a period stretching from the end of the 1914-1918 war, but more especially in the last quarter of a century. It is a theatre which gives 'expression' to our times (to use Ashley Duke's definition) rather than always a mere reflection of them. It is not our intention to survey the whole field of modern drama which emerged in the closing decades of the nineteenth century. Up to the nineteen-twenties the modern theatre is fully documented; what critic worth his *métier* has not had his say on the giants of the period — Ibsen, Strindberg, Shaw, Tchekhov, Synge? But it seems to me that in spite of the ever-increasing number of new books on the theatre, very few have even attempted to view the modern drama in perspective. Little attempt has been made to appraise the important figures of the last thirty years, and even such a distinguished dramatist as Jean Giraudoux was until recently ignored outside essays in specialist quarterlies. What work has been done is by American critics, and Eric Bentley's vigorous championship of the intellectual drama in his *The Playwright as Thinker* (published in Britain under the less dynamic

title, *The Modern Theatre*), although it was published over a decad
ago, remains one of the few books on the aesthetics of the moder
drama worth debating. This book, which in many cases adopts
rather different standpoint from Bentley's, is, like his, a 'preliminar
survey', a tentative canter over different ground, for we shall be exam
ining some of the dramatists excluded by Bentley's personal approach
But this survey has not been written in any way as a reply to Bentley'
views; some of them, such as his attack on the fallacy of the 'box-offic
never lies' proposition, deserve three resounding cheers; nor would an
lover of the theatre wish to deny the rightful place of Ibsen and Shaw
Arguments, of course, depend on temperament, and to this write
Bentley's approach to the theatre is not only an incomplete one, bu
even in his more recent theatrical essays (collected and published unde
the title *In Search of Theatre*) there remains this theoretic aloofness
though less marked than in *The Playwright as Thinker*.

Since the publication of Bentley's critique, various features of th
post-war disillusion have found expression in the drama. The dominan
and prevailing mood is uncertainty, the French *inquiétude,* the blin
groping for a way of life in a civilisation where crises have become
state of normality, where war may mean the annihilation of man —
these thoughts are ever present in both naturalist and anti-naturalis
camps. Yet this complete sense of bewilderment is not noticed, fo
example, in the social-purpose plays of Ibsen and finds no place in th
buoyant cock-sureness of Shaw. It reaches us suddenly, in full fury, i
the plays of Pirandello and Claudel, it extends from dramatist to drama
tist, Sartre, Salacrou, Lorca, O'Neill, T. S. Eliot — to name a few
since then. The restlessness in spirit also results in an incessant experi
ment for interpretation in form; the pendulum of the two opposin
camps swings back and forth. Thus the modern theatre presents u
with an enigmatic problem which disturbs our conscience and does no
necessarily comfort us with the hope of a solution.

This book does not attempt to be a history of the contemporary
drama (such histories tend in any case to become a list of titles, per
formances and dates) nor even an account of the stage during thi
period. We are not here recording performances seen, such as dramati
critics delight in compiling from their ephemeral notices. Still less ar
we interested in the slick who-dunnit, the sophisticated triangula
concoction or the sentimental musical which will send its tunes tinklin
over radio networks for a few weeks and then be as dated as the New
Look. We are not concerned with the theatre as light entertainment an

relaxation; this book is about the theatre judged as an art; a living theatre continuing the great tradition of dramatic literature. For we shall judge a dramatist by both the literary and dramatic quality of his work, remembering C. E. Montague's remarks that the two terms can be complementary, and are not necessarily opposed: "if one's own conception of literary quality and dramatic quality be confused and shallow, the distinction is a gaping one. If by literary quality you mean bookishness, and by dramatic quality you mean staginess, the antithesis between them may be striking. But in proportion as one examines and defines more exactly one's own conception of literary excellence on one side and of dramatic excellence on the other, one finds the assumed contrast and antagonism to be fading away into nothing."

Our playwrights are selected, then, not according to box-office tabulation, but for their ability to make the theatre live as an art; dramatists who will represent all that is best and worth while in our contemporary drama. We may agree to differ on who are the outstanding dramatists, but even if our candidates cannot qualify as outstanding they will not be on the dead level of mediocrity. Whatever their faults, they are stimulating and provocative, they refresh the imagination, make the mind think faster, invigorate the senses and appeal to our emotions and intellect. They do not belong to any one style, school or nation.

None of the dramatists we shall be discussing are uniform and shallow for should the theatre succumb to this way out, there could be no question of making it live. Our dramatists, whatever their conception of our world and however outrageously provocative they may be, view life as a contest of dramatic forces to be resolved according to an attitude of mind. This survey does not propose to present these dramatists in the way that histories of the drama invariably do, with an impartiality which imparts nothing. Those who have their own outlook should not attempt to conceal it, and should one be accused of being partial there is always the defence offered, I think it was, by Lord Hewitt, when he said that the only impartiality of which the human mind is capable comes from understanding neither side of the case. No, we shall not be impartial! Our partiality will itself be the result of an attitude of mind, a desire to identify what we see in the theatre with a philosophy of life which is neither excessive nor grossly distorted. While we shall always consider a play first from an aesthetic viewpoint, judging a play as a play is not the only consideration, and it is at this level we shall apply Baudelaire's critique: "In order to be fair, that's to say in order to fulfil its purpose, criticism must be partial, passionate, political, in other words, strong in an exclusive viewpoint, but a viewpoint which unfolds the widest horizons."

The playwrights I am not particularly tolerant with in this survey are those who choose the narrowest horizon, who see and depict life only in the grotesque phase of its sordidness, who distort it unsparingly so that the world of the living tradition of the great dramatists of the past is no longer recognisable; our new 'masters' have dug an unbridgeable ditch. It is the fashionable school for pessimism, which is such a powerful and negative force at the present time, that we shall assault, for it threatens to destroy the humanist framework so essential in both the theatre and world literature. It is to be hoped it is only a transient mood, and it would be rash to elevate the existential supermen to be equals with the great figures of modern drama.

There is no place in this book for the Soviet theatre or that of the Soviet satellites, since both attitude of mind and aesthetic considerations exclude political mumbo-jumbo. Art cannot prosper when subordinated to the reprobate intentions of propaganda and the imposition of socialist realism. Except for Afinogenev's *Distant Point* (and Afinogenev was himself in disgrace for many years when he might have been creatively productive) the Soviet drama is at a vastly lower ebb than even the second-rate pieces offered on Broadway or the West End, which do, after all, provide entertainment. It is a far cry from the proud days of Tchekhov, Stanislavsky, the Moscow Art Theatre, and even Gorky (who wrote his best plays in the pre-Revolutionary period). Russia is as removed culturally as politically from events on our side of the safety curtain. In place of progress she has imposed on her own artists the most frightening reaction, control by the central committee of the Communist Party to dictate to writers the plays they must write. No wonder the characters of Russian plays have become puppets reciting bureaucratic statistics! In sacrificing the human element the dramatist has become a hack journalist. The present plight of the Russian drama must be appalling, for in the post-Stalinist "thaw" grievances were given a temporary hearing, and the fact that works lacked humanity and writers individuality has been admitted at a Soviet writers' conference. But just how far any measure of freedom will be possible no longer gives grounds for hope; Pasternak dared to use art creatively, and his offence was all the greater not because he was against Communism, but above it. Who in Russia to-day will follow his example?

Viewed in perspective, the English theatre since Shaw has not, like the Russians, cut itself at its roots and withered, but by 1956 it had sunk to an incredible impotency and had almost ceased to play any creative rôle in world drama—although as an actors' theatre Britain was second to none. But playwrights had become servile to mediocrity and gentility, emotions were as damp as a London smog. Since Shaw (who for practical purposes ceased writing in the twenties) Eliot had been the only writer to be considered seriously, and even Eliot had shown more promise than fulfilment. For the rest, Rattigan, Priestley and Emlyn Williams were competent craftsmen, 'tailormakers', but hardly the white hopes necessary to revitalise the English theatre. There remained Christopher Fry, whose verse has melody and to some, ethereal delight. His style may be idiosyncratic, his themes unusual, but his plays have no destination, they neither reveal nor illuminate. He has not returned us to the Elizabethan spirit or passion, rather he has stuck firmly in the groove of modern polite comedy.

And then in 1956 the London theatre felt a stir once more, something was happening. The prolonged drawing-room slumber was over, at the Royal Court John Osborne kicked flying, in a frenzied rage, the whole clap-trap of traditional values. The muzzle is removed, the contrived polite conventions, the etiquette of what could and what could not be accepted in the theatre are brushed aside. The dust is still rising from where the walls collapsed, but Osborne does not yet show signs of becoming sufficiently a humanist to offer something in the way of reconstruction. Nor have the discovery of the plays of Beckett, Ionesco or Tennessee Williams given any signpost to the wanderings of young British playwrights, for the most part all too keen to imitate rather than create. Perhaps only Brecht has had a positive influence, though the result is a kind of synthesis which no Brechtian would approve of or accept. Nevertheless things are once again moving and out of the turbulence of anger, esotericism and despair the air may be cleared. Let us hope so, for the theatre cannot live by sensationalism alone.

Perhaps the years of doldrums in British drama may be explained as a result of the negative influence of Shaw, and the "very wrong influence", as Mr. Ronald Peacock has observed in his book *The Poet in the Theatre*, of the social-purpose plays of Ibsen. The 'deceptive' skill of Ibsen is only matched by the 'deceptive' skill of Shaw. Both writers could have no imitators, and both were to encourage hundreds of would-be imitators. Alas, none of their disciples had the mental genius of their masters. While it is true that even in *Ghosts* and *A Doll's House* Ibsen was always first a poet, and a reporter of social

B

conventions only secondly, it was nevertheless as a reporter that his plays attracted attention and, indeed, influence.

It is paradoxical that Ibsen and Shaw won so complete a victory for the play of ideas that, in the years that followed, imagination gave way to intellect. With lesser writers the English theatre became frigid and passionless. By 1921 Gordon Craig was complaining that "the dramatic art in England is excellent — only it is not dramatic — and there's no art in it". If we want to go to the theatre to be moved by drama, it will not be found in polite modern English theatre, we must look to the Continent, perhaps America, or else in our classics. Passion is on an equal footing with intellect in Pirandello. And how the Elizabethan drama was a theatre of passion!

Our view, then, is of world theatre. The theatre is an international art, yet it is especially noticeable in the modern theatre that the greatest dramatists are those who are intensely national; it is as if plays, through their nationality, attract international recognition. Even if no mention were made of a writer's nationality in this book, there would never be a moment's hesitation as to which nation he belonged. No one could be more Spanish than Lorca; French than Claudel, Giraudoux, Sartre, Anouilh; Italian than Pirandello; more American than Tennessee Williams or Miller; or more English than Eliot has become. Our dramatists epitomise their national temperament even when dealing with themes of universal application.

A survey of the theatre since Ibsen and Shaw proves that in spite of the worst excesses of commercialised entertainment and the growing eclipse of the individual in society, good theatre is neither dead nor dying (as it was in the nineteenth century); on the other hand there is no cause for complacency. The important dramatists of the period, Pirandello, Giraudoux, Claudel, Lorca, O'Neill, are dead. Yet they offer the dramatist of to-day greater scope for freedom and experiment than did Ibsen and Shaw.

The theatre, if it is to survive, must do so at the hands of the true artist and poet, not through the reforming zeal of political or religious missionaries. It must appeal to the audiences through sensitivity, enabling them to identify the world through the expressiveness and inspiration of poetic vision, or, if you prefer, poetic reality. The drama is not for any class or artistic clique; it is for the public, though it will inevitably appeal to its audience at different levels. It makes demands on an audience, and if the audience is not willing to give it its attention or ready to treat the theatre seriously, then the theatre can only stay alive through small art theatres until the public is ready to return to dramatic traditions. Should the theatre spoon-feed its public, should it stoop to the taste of the lowest common denominator, the theatre will deserve to die. But if it fights for its independence, sooner or later the public will tire of and reject the banality of the caterers, and will rediscover in the small art theatres the sources of originality and intelligence, a theatre where they are respected as equals and not talked down to like children. The better plays in London are invariably discovered in this way. The Vieux-Colombier tradition has spread to many Paris playhouses.

The only theatre that can live is one which is not afraid of life, which does not offer escape from moral responsibilities. The theatre must seek to give the public reasons for truth as against falsity, belief against doubt, good against evil; contraries give life to one another. Man cannot escape from thinking, as Sir Thomas Browne expressed it "of things long past and long to come; acquaint thyself with the choragium of the Stars and consider the vast expanse beyond them. Let intellectual Tubes give thee a glance of things which visive Organs reach not. Have a glimpse of incomprehensibles and Thoughts of things which Thoughts but tenderly touch." The theatre, through the communion between audience and actor, is in a better position than the other arts to make man experience the supreme moments of life, the heights of human achievements; it can plunge him into the depths of despair and rescue him, it can throw his prejudices into confusion and produce in him a state of enlightenment and ecstasy.

Here is the task of the dramatic poet and of good theatre. We shall consider in our first chapter the relationship between the theatre and society, the play and its public. Perhaps in this short introduction I have given a sufficient outline of some of the problems with which we shall be concerned, and the type of approach to be expected in the following chapters. I do not claim that the views reached in either the individual studies of dramatists or the book as a whole will be in any way original; but at least it was Goethe who said that you do not forfeit your originality because you recognise a truth which has already been recognised by others. The general reappraisal of modern dramatists, however, and their relation to the whole framework of the modern theatre will, I hope, lead to a better understanding of our living drama. It will also perhaps encourage support for those dramatists who do not choose the easy way of pleasing, who do not follow but lead, if necessary backwards to the traditions of the drama, rather than seek transient and facile success in the seduction of public taste.

ONE

CONTEMPORARY DRAMA AND LIFE

> "Stage presentations produce a sort of temporary half-faith, which the spectator encourages in himself, and supports by a voluntary contribution on his own part, because he knows that it is at all times in his power to see the thing as it really is."
>
> SAMUEL TAYLOR COLERIDGE

WHY do we go to the theatre? Why do playwrights exist and for whom do they write? In asking "What is Literature?" Jean-Paul Sartre has suggested than no one ever thought of such a leading question until he himself was ready to answer it; in the theatre, however, this subject has been debated throughout the ages. Was it not Hamlet who requested the players to be "well used", because "they are the abstracts and brief chronicles of the time: after your death you were better have a bad epitaph than their ill report while you live"? In the Elizabethan era reasons were also advanced why society should not go to the theatre, and why poets should not write plays; the drama was aesthetically condemned by Sir Philip Sidney and morally attacked by the Puritans. The modern drama is more than ever a forum for controversy over aesthetic considerations, while its frontiers have been attacked by mass entertainment media, faced as it is on the one side with the cinema and on the other with television. And even if the theatre is no longer the only target for charges of moral laxity, Britain at any rate still considers the services of the Lord Chamberlain necessary.

In recent years the theatre has almost ceased to be treated seriously — even Agate had to write his well-known essay on "Playgoing" for a series entitled "These Diversions". The golden rule of the theatre has become that the dramatist must please his public at all costs. Any critic who in his innocence still believes that a play must be judged first as an art, and that the artistic criterion does not always bend to the demands of the caterers, is told in patronising tones how unrealistic and snobbishly highbrow his attitude is. Did not Shakespeare write for the commercial theatre and please his public? This argument is a glorious example of the dangers of simplification and wishful thinking. Were the commercial pundits quite the same in those days? And even if we could equate our present theatrical set-up and public taste with those Elizabethan times, are we so certain that Shakespeare would be willing to serve his public at any price, if it meant sacrificing the creation of a work of art? Was it not a later generation that was to write a happy ending for *King Lear?*

With the exception of George Jean Nathan, Eric Bentley and a few other critics writing in America, the critics in the Anglo-Saxon world have not concerned themselves with asking questions about the state of the drama; indeed, they have taken the theatre so much for granted they have never considered it as mortal. We have either to turn, as so often we must in cultural matters, to the French critical citadel, or else return to the ideas and ideals propounded by Edward Gordon Craig in his book *The Art of the Theatre* (1905). Craig pleaded for a unity of production without which no theatrical achievement was possible. He appealed for the recognition of the fact that there is such a thing as the 'art of the theatre'. And above all he demanded imagination. In *The Theatre Advancing* (1921) he explained that imagination was "far more rapid than the inventions of modern science, far more powerful than anything in the world, it can pierce all that is material, no matter how dense; it leaps all divisions, no matter how wide. While it is the one thing needful to-day, it is the one thing disregarded." But his theories and advice went largely unheeded, when not rebuked, like all prophets in their own country; he was, however, to have a profound influence on the Continent, stimulating Max Reinhardt and Jacques Copeau in their early work. We shall not examine here the theories of Craig, which cannot be described satisfactorily in a short account and which do not in any case come within the scope of this book. Having paid this tribute to him for his pioneering work, for his courage in introducing new ideas and imagination into the art of the theatre, it is the modern French theories of drama and life that we shall now look to and consider.

There is, of course, no one dominating theory in French discussions of the theatre, but several diverging viewpoints. They all belong, however, to the anti-naturalist camp, and are concerned with the participation and communion between actors and audience in the theatre. They vary from the extreme vision, the dream of Copeau for a mass audience and spectacle, linked with the view that "there will only be a new theatre on the day when the audience will be able to whisper the words of the actor at the same time and with the same spirit as he", to the idea expressed by Georges Jamati that "a theatrical play must establish a union between our inner self and that of the author, his interpreters and his characters". This latter view has approximations to George Jean Nathan's belief that "one does not go to the theatre to see life and nature; one goes to see the particular way in which life and nature happen to look to a cultivated, imaginative and entertaining man who happens, in turn, to be a playwright".

The French theories, involving as they do to some extent the conception of magic and the importance of collective communion, have been vigorously challenged by Eric Bentley in an article in *Theatre Arts* (March, 1950)* — the French 'highbrow' theatre, which from Gaston Baty onwards becomes "a theatre of dreams, a consensus of opinion unfavourable to Naturalism and all realism, favourable to magic and other-worldly vision". Bentley pins down the word 'magic' and suggests that this may be interpreted on religious grounds and in fact is so interpreted, rather than on the aesthetic 'as if' contact. The theatre thus becomes associated with the concept 'more than a theatre', the existence of the supernatural, and Bentley goes on to assert that these mystical theories of the theatre have been fostered "by the modern flight from freedom, from decisions, and from the self". In creating a force which unites the audience as if in a dream, the theatre is in danger of a crime politically known as totalitarianism. From this stage a play can by-pass dramatic art and lead straight into a religious — or political — communion. Bentley attacks the idea of a theatre being more than a theatre under three headings, an historical heresy, a psychological perversion, and political fascism. He claims on the first accusation that the supporters of a mystical theatre demand that the theatre return to its origins and be in essence religious. On the second crime he likens the audience to "Hitler's storm troopers wildly losing their separate existence in a celebration of the Volk". All this leads to his third assumption that the audience would consist of individuals with identical opinions, which would, in practice, reduce it to either a Christian or a Marxist gathering.

The result of Bentley's polemics is so overwhelming that at first

* Reprinted in "In Search of Theatre.

sight anyone who has ever shown sympathy for these French theories feels like hiding his head for shame; perhaps after all only naturalistic theories are healthy. And, of course, when he applies this to certain aspects of a group of French theorists, notably Copeau, Henri Ghéon and Antonin Artaud, one realises that an element of fanaticism exists in their ideas. But Bentley so states his case against the whole current of the French theatre, linking Claudel with his argument, dismissing Giraudoux, that we get the impression that the entire state of the anti-naturalist theatre in France should be viewed with suspicion. True, the reaction against magic has led to Brecht's concept of "alienation" which we shall discuss later on. Meanwhile, it might be suggested that even a return to naturalism would be preferable to an overdose of this remedy. But if we do hold to the French anti-naturalist approach to imaginative theatre, why then should we surrender this view of theatre to find ourselves once more enmeshed in the laws of orthodox naturalism?

What defence has the anti-naturalist supporter? Bentley makes him walk the tight-rope between the angels and the deep blue sea. It is like a Labour supporter or Democrat suggesting to a Conservative or Republican that he should abandon his views for fear he goes too far to the Right and becomes a neo-Fascist, and *vice versa,* of course. Positions in the theatre, as in life, are never as simple as that.

It is very noticeable that in all his writings Bentley is never at home in trying to understand the French *esprit.* He is irritated by their lack of interest in other cultures and even accuses their mentality of being 'provincial'; yet he is well aware that no other nation has produced such a galaxy of great writers in the twentieth century, nor has any other nation been anywhere near so creatively fecund. Bentley himself does not want rigid naturalism, so it may be that his feelings towards moderate anti-naturalist theorists are rather like those of a Labour supporter viewing progressive Conservatives from cross benches. One is not enthusiastic about opponents' views, even if one admits their validity. Certainly Bentley does not make his exceptions clear in his general attack; he would agree, I believe, that a moderate approach both avoids fanaticism in any form and obeys artistic truths; but I doubt if, having admitted that, he would wish to accept them in their own rights, any more than he has done with Claudel and Giraudoux (many light years removed). It is Eugène Delacroix's old remark: "One is never understood, but one is admitted". Bentley makes it clear that he is not against religious and political subject matter provided it is judged as a "mere" play and not "more than a play". And he would doubtless accept T. S. Eliot's observation that "the 'greatness' of literature cannot be determined solely by literary standards; though we must remember that whether it is literature or not can be determined only by literary standards."

The gap between naturalist and anti-naturalist camps is not really so vast. All moderates agree with Bentley that a critic's duty is to say when a religious or political play can no longer be classed as a play but merely as a mechanical chant for their respective ideologies. The views, however, advanced by critics, must not sacrifice the creative elements of *mise en scène*, nor control emotions with such puritanical intellectuality as Bentley envisages. They should allow a religious conception of theatre which establishes an equilibrium between the forces of magic and those of sensibility and intelligence. Even when our mind is grasping the infinite, when we are sharing communion with our neighbours and the actors, we do so because we have gone to the theatre with a desire to believe in make-believe, and know we can at any time see it as it really is, or judge it afterwards as such. If we are unwilling to surrender our individuality on such occasions we surely miss the supreme moments of theatre; we live a play through communion; we judge it afterwards by intelligence. If a play is only to be judged as intellectual dialogue, far better to read the play. For a performance is to be felt, not thought.

If certain theorists have longed for a return to ceremonial spectacle, to mass-crowds rather than a play-going public, this has not achieved any importance, any more than a pageant is important. On the other hand there has been a revival of drama in France which evokes miracles and calls in the aid of dreams and imagination. In many instances the plays are religious, but they do not fall victim to the accusations raised by Bentley. In the first place the return to religion in France has not been a return to medieval mystery plays or the liturgy as practised by the Church. Religious drama has not sought the origins of the theatre, but has remained modern, secular and free. The audience does not worship. Even in Claudel, as critics have pointed out, the Pope is not always right, though the office of the Pope is of course respected. It is the idea that though one may criticise the President of the United States as President, one does not criticise the institution of 'the President'.

Anti-naturalist theatre does make an appeal to the intellect as well, indeed always, whereas we can recall many instances when the naturalist theatre makes no attempt to make such an appeal, but relies on all manner of preciosity and sugar icing, with lamentable results. The anti-naturalist theatre, on the other hand, seeks a means of creating poetic reality by extending the dramatic horizons by calling on the creative resources of the theatre. But this 'magical approach' is done inside, not outside, the auditorium. In other words, the audience inside the theatre *do* accept the 'rules of the game' as Henri Gouhier puts it, the belief in 'as if'; communion is made at this level, and not at the level of what the audience or, indeed, the author think as individuals in the street. Thus it is possible for an atheist to accept a Christian play because he has accepted the principle of collaboration voluntarily. But it goes beyond this. The play does not preach; it presents a dramatic conflict. We are not interested in the mere existence of a character; we do not accept Macbeth or Hamlet as individuals, but as part of a dramatic conflict which is given meaning when an appeal is made to life values and the play is given a religious or philosophical significance. Again in the words of Gouhier, we are willing to believe in the intervention of destiny, we are willing to accept the appearance of ghosts or the realisation of miracles, even though as individuals in the street we would no more believe in ghosts than in flying saucers.

Thus the audience is not composed of individuals who hold unanimous viewpoints; on the other hand an audience must not be antagonistic or hostile to the general outlook of the play. Should an individual feel so strongly on a certain subject that he cannot surrender his beliefs, if the 'as if' contact gives way to animosity, if there is no longer any sympathy between him and what is happening on the stage, he will no longer be able to share communion. Should this be the reaction of the audience as a whole, collective participation will give way to individual feelings and the audience will act as so many individuals. Ask any actor what that experience would mean.

Such a situation might be envisaged in the performance of a religious play in the presence of members of the Communist Party, though individually they might experience communion, if they really wished to, in an ordinary public performance. The question does not arise in the case of a Marxist theatre (though theoretically it could) since ideas are always so crudely and blatantly expressed that all sympathy is lost except among the faithful. Such plays preach to the converted and require an audience of militant supporters.

But supposing we have an audience which, though far from sharing identical opinions, has more or less a similar outlook on life, the same hopes and fears, and if not a common aspiration at any rate the same vision of the world. As M. Georges Jamati has observed in *Théâtre et la vie intérieure*, the greatest periods of drama are those where there is such agreement between people. It is then that "the great dramatist gives expression to hopes which are in the air, he draws them, models them, portrays them. It is at that moment that genius reveals itself, like the voice of collective sentiment."

Perhaps we can extend this general vision of the world to include an audience who are agreed on certain fundamentals but who agree to differ about political parties and religious denominations. In our age it must be possible for an audience of Protestants, Catholics, Jews, atheists, all shades of political opinion from radical to reactionary, to enjoy communion, given the will to co-operate. The rest is up to the dramatist and the interpretation of his ideas — the appeal made to the sensibilities of the collective consciousness of an audience. In this connection the French theatre can rely on making this appeal through language and poetry. Not just poetry brought into the theatre, but poetry of the theatre. The importance of language has been discarded in the English-speaking theatre; it is our theatre's loss. Louis Jouvet, in his *Perspectives du Théâtre Français*, tells how, when his company was in South America during the war, he asked a young Colombian student how the public could react with such force when the sole medium of communication was a language which they could not understand. The Colombian student replied that he believed that he understood perfectly. "But", Jouvet asked him, "you don't know any French?" "That's true, sir, but I don't know any Latin either and I understand the Mass perfectly." Jouvet concluded that the aim of the theatre was not to make itself understood but to make it felt that it was through the prestige of a language alone, in the writing, that the theatre reached its highest efficacy.

Such is the ability of communion in the theatre. It can cross language barriers, it can make an audience which does not understand a word lose itself in voluntary participation. It is wrong, however, to infer that this collective consciousness of an audience is the same thing as that of a religious ceremony. This is the great talking point among the French theorists, from Copeau and Jean Vilar on the one hand, who wish the theatre to be a great spectacle, and those who draw a distinction between the public and the crowd, the theatre and the meeting-place. An admirable symposium has been published under the title *Théâtre et Collectivité* which discusses the whole problem of dramatic communion at length under such headings as "Communion in the Theatre"; "The Public and the Crowd"; "The Public of the Mystery Plays"; "The Dramatist and the Public"; "Leisure Activities and the Theatre", and so on. These are papers which were read at the second and third sessions of the Centre of Philosophical and Technical Studies of the Theatre held at the Sorbonne in March, 1950, and March, 1951, by a number of well-known figures in French academic as well as theatrical and literary life, including Henri Gouhier, Jean Vilar (director of the Théâtre National Populaire), Georges Jamati, Etienne Souriau and André Villiers.

One of the most interesting aspects of this book is the clarification of the modern French attitude to Copeau's idea for a great religious ceremony. Whenever this was discussed the idea was declared outside the limits of dramatic communion proper. Henri Gouhier, for example, suggested that there might be two types of communion, communion properly dramatic and communion where the audience were not only spectators, but also participants. Another writer, quoting Gide, exclaims "The danger of the crowd is that it's always hungry". As for communion proper, Gouhier stresses the co-existence of two worlds in the theatre. We know that Tartuffe exists on the stage, but we know also that Jouvet is playing him. Jouvet also exists, and for that matter we know that the décor is by Braque. The theory is far from original, but it is so obvious and important to the conception of communion that it does well to underline it.

We have discussed religious theatre; where does the political theatre enter? M. Jamati, realising that it often occupies a similar position to that of religious theatre, asks why a play of political propaganda puts us in a bad humour, when even atheists can feel the greatness of religious theatre. The answer, of course, is that the *pièce à thèse* generally lacks imagination, and only succeeds when it humanises its characters. The religious theatre, on the other hand, is safeguarded by the force of myths; moreover, it generally has a lyrical richness allied to a dramatic conflict which enables it to escape from purely religious dogmas. Propaganda can also result in a worth-while play, but only if it escapes or goes beyond the frontiers of propaganda, and is thus at a disadvantage.

What is the result when we apply these theories to the state of world theatre, such as it is? One thing is certain — if the theatre is to wake up, its salvation lies inside and not outside its walls. It is not to be found, for example, in an attempt to change society. A revolution such as occurred in Russia or her satellites would only keep the corpse of the theatre artificially alive; a large number of the classics would be proscribed, while false gods and falser values would be introduced. If not in revolution, then what about education? It is a fact that the classical education given in French schools, together with the place of philosophy in the school curriculum, enables French writers to approach their audience on a rather different level to that in other countries, and it is reassuring to notice the attention the French playgoer pays to what the Anglo-Saxon would dismiss as 'words, words, words'. The difficulty is that the conception, in Britain at any rate, of spreading education, expecting limited resources to go a long way, does not contribute in helping make the arts flourish.

It seems to me that the theatre can only live through personal discovery, and that discovery by the public will only be worth while if the theatre rediscovers the beauty of poetry and the power of imagination. Poetry is referred to in the widest meaning of the word, poetic vision. But this vision to-day is more likely, in my opinion, to be found in a non-naturalistic type of theatre; a theatre where dream, fantasy, illusion exist, but not as a means of escape; a theatre where they have significance and identification with the world in which we live.

The theatre at the moment is symptomatic of the malaise of society. Whereas in the Soviet Union it has no hope of flourishing, it could flourish in the West, given half a chance. But since the theatre does not offer escape, it is difficult for it to come to terms with an age of evasion. Part of the theatre gives up the fight and attempts to catch up with the whims of public taste — the larger part. But this is a jet age. The living theatre, on the other hand, cannot escape from life. It must rely on the few, who believe in the theatre even though, to tell the brutal truth, it is a wearisome patient who seems to have lost interest in living. It asks, instead, to be respected for the glory of its classical achievements. But the faithful followers are determined to restore her to life and attempt, as Harold Clurman puts it, to discover those methods that would truly convey our interest in the life of our times through the theatre.

FROM PIRANDELLO TO GIRAUDOUX

OUR first study, that of Luigi Pirandello, may seem at a cursory glance in direct opposition to the French theories of the drama and the anti-naturalist school, and that his *teatro dello specchio* (theatre of the mirror), with its emphasis on the drama of the intellect rather than of passions, would firmly establish the claims of the naturalist over the anti-naturalist camps. Exactly the opposite has taken place. Pirandello's exploration through the mask and face technique, with its different planes of illusion and reality, has led directly into the anti-naturalistic camp. It was Jean Giraudoux who was to adopt a theatre of contrasts to explore an imaginary universe which has similarities with our own, only it reflects to an imperfect world the mirror of the ideal. The anti-naturalist trend was to extend further to writers such as Jean Anouilh, and also to the existential school. It is as if Pirandello, himself discarding the limitations of naturalism, discovered in his cerebral drama the field of magical illusion, but, bound to the torments of this world, he never attempted exploration. Perhaps the differences between Pirandello and the anti-naturalists who followed him are not so striking as are the similarities. In the modern theatre, whether in the *teatro dello specchio* style, or the dream world of Giraudoux, or the nostalgic vision of Anouilh, the modern dramatist wishes to intervene directly in our life and thoughts. As such, playgoing becomes an integral part of our existence.

TWO

THE MASK AND FACE OF LUIGI PIRANDELLO

"No man can justly censure or condemn another, because indeed no man truly knows another."

SIR THOMAS BROWNE

"What do we really know of other people? Who they are . . . how they are . . . what they do . . . why they do it . . ."

PIRANDELLO, Così È (se vi pare)

H E who has been born a character, Pirandello tells us, can alone afford to laugh at death, for his being does not change from day to day. Those characters, interviewed by their creator (so the story goes) on Sunday mornings, including the six who were discarded, live on and suffer within the 'immutable bounds' of their creation, the struggle between objective truth and subjective logic, the absolute and the relative, the real and the illusory, the mask and the face. What is important to remember at the outset is that these characters are a mirror not to the world, nor to any literary fashion, but to Pirandello's own life; they are his apology for and justification of his profound pessimism.

For Pirandello is a dominant pessimist; everything is purely transitory, reality only exists at a given moment of time, the flash of a camera or a gun. Nothing will stem the tide of physical destruction, the heart beats a slow funeral march which makes our hopes of to-morrow the lost chances of yesterday. Again and again Pirandello expounds the motivation for his pessimism in his plays, until the drama of action becomes a scientific investigation of the human mind, or cerebral theatre. The audience is asked to give attention to the complexities of inner contradiction, to follow involved explanations which are so seductive that the critic is apt to become exponent, and merely quote rather than comment. It is always easier to accept the resignation of pessimists rather than search for your own judgment, for there is a vogue and school for pessimism to-day which may offer a facile solution, but fails to convince. Pirandello, on the other hand, is one of the few modern writers whose pessimism does convince; his pessimism, however, does not spring from a surfeit of hate, or from the fact that this is the worst of possible worlds; it is because his eyes sadden at seeing so much that is beautiful and yet so irrelevant to the human façade, with its bruises and scars. There is no doubt that Pirandello would, alas, second Schopenhauer's belief that if you knocked at the graves of the dead and offered them a return to life, they would shake their heads. No one would expect Pirandello to wish his life over again.

More than any other modern writer, Pirandello's work can only be appreciated fully as a parallel to his life. He was born at Girgenti in Sicily in 1867, seven years after the union of Sicily with Italy. His father Stefano, a rich owner of sulphur mines on the island, was a violent figure who defied even the powerful Mafia. His mother was a docile and long-suffering wife who accepted her cruel life after being abandoned by her husband for another woman. The silent suffering of his mother must have affected Pirandello's own behaviour in his pitiful marriage. The whole environment of Sicily, an island which had scarcely emerged from the Middle Ages, the contrasts between rich and poor, the chiaroscuro of the landscape, the balance between life and death — whether by starvation, disease, childbirth, or the Mafia — must have permanently moulded the outlook of the young Pirandello. His whole theatre is a theatre of contrasts.

After studying at Palermo, Pirandello was sent when he was eighteen to the University of Rome, but a clash with some of the professors (Pirandello had inherited his father's independence) over teaching methods made it advisable for him to leave, and he took his doctor's degree instead at Bonn in Germany. Already he had started writing poems and short stories about Sicilian life, and on his return from Germany he decided to devote his life to writing fiction. He lived among a group of other young writers and artists, and became a fierce opponent of D'Annunzio and the school which was in fashion in Italy at that time. Because of this his name remained unknown, and none of his work found publication for several years.

In 1894 Pirandello's father arranged a marriage for him with the daughter of his business partner. Although he had never met the girl, Antonietta Portulano, they were married and they settled in Rome on an allowance given by Pirandello's father. For a few years life was uneventful, and three children were born of the marriage. Then in 1904 came disaster. The family fortunes were lost, and this coincided with the mental collapse of his wife. Her form of madness took the shape of unreasonable jealousy, and even though Pirandello stayed at home in his free hours (he had been forced to take a school-teacher's post) she continued to hurl abuse at him and make accusations of unfaithfulness. His life became so much a prison that he began to see in his mind another character, the one described by his wife, and so the world between madness and reality, and reality and illusion came into existence. Pirandello stayed by her side, although his mind acted as a dam to the torrent of her fury, and was powerless against the irrationality of her accusations. Life became a daily torture, in which the only outlet he could escape to was in his writing. Isolated from his friends, isolated mentally from his wife, he flung himself into a frenzy of activity, where the depth of his tragedy was reflected. The 1914-1918 war added to his difficulties and his wife's illness. Their elder son was taken a prisoner of war, their younger was ill in a military camp, and their daughter tried to commit suicide. In 1918 relief came with the death of his wife.

It was during the war that Pirandello had turned to the theatre, and from 1918 onwards he devoted himself to a prodigious output of plays. Fame came slowly in its wake, until in 1921 he became a world celebrity with the production of *Six Characters in Search of an Author*. In 1925 his elder son founded an arts theatre in Rome, and asked his father to become artistic director. Pirandello accepted, and invested a considerable fortune in the project. He hoped that Rome would be able to assume the leadership in modern drama, and had the theatre succeeded, there is every reason to believe that a vigorous school would have been founded. But with its financial failure Pirandello was again a poor man, and felt little inclination to stay on in Italy. Instead he travelled, directing his plays over the world — it mattered little to him whether it was London, Paris, Prague, Berlin, Vienna, Budapest, New York or South America. In 1934 he received the Nobel Prize. He then returned to Rome, where the final tragedy overtook him on 19 December, 1936.

It is hard to draw a dividing line between the real and illusory worlds of Pirandello; certainly the illusory never surpasses the horror of the

C

real. Pirandello does not seek escape from his suffering in some false dream world, nor does he remain a victim of human misery; rather it may be said that he attempts to transplant his purgatory to the level of tragedy. His theatre does not lend itself to a label. He has been accused of absenting himself from life, of deserting naturalism for the abstract mosaic of cerebral drama; he has been accused of being too much a naturalist with the failings of a naturalist, not having the powers of poetry and imagination to prove his thesis wrong; he has been dismissed as a trick-comedy writer; still others have branded him with the decadent 'twenties. It is Pirandello himself in a truly Shavian manner who makes the director in *Six Characters* say of his work; "Ridiculous, do you call it? What can I do if no good plays come from France and we are reduced to put on the stage plays by Pirandello which require a 'highbrow' to understand them, and never satisfy either the actors, the critics, or the public?"

Although his pessimism is unquenchable, his plays do not exploit pessimism. There is a mask over life, and this mask often causes wild hilarity. The more you laugh, the deeper the tragedy. It is through laughter, irony, inconsistencies between the mask and the face, that Pirandello unfolds his drama. His technical skill is unfailing, his dialogue, so tense and abrupt, ideal for his purpose. His characters are not lovable, Pirandello has not a great love for people. They are ordinary individuals, good and bad. Like the Six Characters, some are fully drawn, others merely suggested. Often the dialectics of the problem prevent their appearing to us until the mask is withdrawn and they suddenly emerge as individuals — for Pirandello is a great individualist.

He has a philosophy, but he does not insist. This is how he sees life, but for every individual truth is something different. He believes in the triumph of pessimism, it is instinctive in his nature, his honesty, that his characters suffer and do not rise above their immediate anxiety. But then truth is what each of us makes of it. "We believe ourselves one person," he tells us, "but it is true to say that we are many persons, many according to the possibilities of being which exist within us. We are one for this and another for that person — always diverse and yet filled with the illusion that our personality is always the same for all." There is something reminiscent here of Strindberg's views on naturalistic drama, where incidents in life are caused by a whole series of motives, and the spectator merely selects the one "his own intellect finds the easiest to grasp, or the one which brings most credit to his powers of discernment." But Pirandello's method extends in quite a different context the Strindbergian point of departure. Strindberg's 'incidents' become for Pirandello 'abstractions', and the idea of resolving inner contradictions through dialectical reasoning bears little relation to what Strindberg attempted in his 'naturalistic tragedy'.

Pirandello, however, started out in the tradition of naturalism, and gradually deserted it when his experiments led him to choose the introspective drama of the individual in its place, or the *teatro dello specchio* (theatre of the mirror) as he called it. If some of his characters are naturalistically conceived, in that they accept the ordinary conventions of life and conform to a *modus vivendi*, other characters aspire to eccentricity; they belong not to the naturalistic theatre, but to the theatre of the grotesque. Essentially Pirandello's characters are puppets answering to the workings of his mind. The production must therefore be stylised, in the Italian *commedia dell' arte* tradition, and it is worth remembering that Pirandello collected his plays under the title *Maschere Nude* ("naked masks") and not "faces". To interpret these masks the actor must both work within the tradition and have the ability of turning passions into a drama of the intellect.

No solutions are posed, the question mark is never answered. In *Right You Are (If You Think You Are)* all the different explanations, although each is contradictory, may be taken as correct, since truth is what you make it. It is as if Pirandello says, "Please leave us all in peace", a reassertion of the rights of the individual against the interference of others. Those who imagine Pirandello to be some kind of theatrical psychoanalyst and disciple of Freud have completely misunderstood the premise of his theatre. To be left alone in uncertainty, in the knowledge that everything is uncertain and insecure, aware that our mechanism is running down — again we must return to his pessimism, which is always in spate. The crying need is for a certainty, a faith which would give him courage to face his pessimism, but God, to Pirandello, is negative, he is powerless and cannot rescue suffering humanity. Pirandello sees the frailty of man like Claudel, only without the latter's religious security. For Pirandello, life is a "second of illumination" and all is over. His religious play *Lazzaro* is not on the level of his better work, although he has taken for the theme that of a scientist who brings back to life a dead man. The religious discussions are vague and conventional, and Pirandello soon prefers to turn to the idealisation of healthy farming life with its honest labour and unsophisticated pleasures. Life after death is also the theme of *The Life I*

Gave You (*La Vita che ti diedi*) when Donn'Anna refuses to believe her son is dead: "Not even you can tell me that my child is dead", she insists. "You say that God took him back with Him ... Don't you feel that God is not there as long as he wishes to abide here, in me, in us; not only for ourselves but also that all those who have gone away may continue to live?" And later on she explains: "God wants my son to continue to live. Not of course the life that He gave him here, but that which I have always given him! This cannot be taken away from him as long as life endures in me." Death can be conquered by an illusion, but this is a poor substitute for the 'eternal' lives of the characters a soul may create. Perhaps for Pirandello religious belief, like other truths, varies according to the concealed consciousness of the individual; but we feel the fear of Pirandello's own isolation.

Yes, Pirandello suffers from obsessions, his plays are exaggerations, sometimes over-subtle and always variations (but what brilliant variations!) on a repetitive theme. Nevertheless, the position Pirandello occupies at the cross-roads of modern drama and the influence his works have had on younger writers place him in importance as one of the giants of the modern theatre. While he was still writing, the idea of different planes of reality had, consciously or subconsciously, been taken by Jean Giraudoux as the style so admirably suited to his anti-naturalistic interpretation of life. For Giraudoux (whose work we shall consider in detail in the next chapter) chose to set his plays in an imaginary framework, but one full of significance, presenting a symbolic picture, a fantasy and dream world which has similarities to our own — only with a difference, that it is a world that might have been if mankind had but remembered the meaning of those human virtues of love, hope, forgiveness and understanding. It is a world which still can be if we have faith in man. Giraudoux had faith in man, and his optimism (not a facile optimism, but balanced realism) might almost have been written in reply to the pessimism of Pirandello. It is the philosophy that this writer, at any rate, would prefer to accept, but oh how hard it is to counteract the overwhelming power of Pirandello!

More recently we find the influence of Pirandello very markedly in the plays of Jean Anouilh, and also in the works of the existentialists, both the Christian and atheistic branches. In Anouilh, both in the *pièces roses* and the more recent savage farces where their mask-like characters turn ridicule to pathos, the mood of Pirandello is often caught in a less intellectual and profound way. *Léocadia* ("Time Remembered" in London production), for example, with its theme of the image of an illusory past, recalls immediately Pirandello's *As You Desire Me*. A list of all the writers who have followed in Pirandello's wake would lead to tabulation — they range from Ugo Betti in Italy, Priestley in England, to Thornton Wilder and Tennessee Williams in the United States. The chances are that the list will continue to grow year by year, for Pirandello revealed the loneliness of the individual who does not want to be one of a crowd, the slave of the super-man (against whom Pirandello had rebelled in his youth) whether he be in the uniform of the commissar, the fascist dictator, or the managerial revolutionary of James Burnham.

Pirandello has emerged as a figure who has given new life to the theatre at a time when the sources of naturalism had ceased to excite; whether the new direction of the drama will again turn full circle and return to naturalism, time alone will tell. The French theatre is always happiest when it turns its back on naturalism. The American drama, the youngest drama, has still to come to maturity. But it is interesting to note that one of its leading playwrights, Tennessee Williams, stated recently that he considered Giraudoux the most important modern dramatist, while any observer can see he has studied his Pirandello very carefully. What could be closer to Pirandello than the following example, the opening lines of *The Glass Menagerie*, written thirty-three years after *Six Characters*?

> Yes, I have tricks in my pocket, I have things up my sleeve. But I am the opposite of the stage magician. He gives you illusion that has the appearance of truth. I give you the truth in the pleasant disguise of illusion.

Pirandello's mask continues to be borrowed. To tell the truth, he never had need of it, because what is unique in Pirandello's own personality is that there is no difference between his mask and his face. *Ecce homo!*

*

The early plays of Pirandello are merely sketches with a Sicilian setting, dramatised from his short stories. The first work worth considering is also an adaptation of an earlier story, *Pensarci, Giacomino* ("Think of It, Giacomino"), where we hear the familiar themes of Pirandello's future work as if in a kind of overture. The story concerns an old schoolmaster, Professor Toti, who instead of retiring and receiving his pension decides to stay on teaching, marry a young wife, and thus force the government to pay her the pension when he dies; in this way he will cost the government a lot of money, do the girl a good turn, and give himself a few years of happiness. He regards it purely as a charitable deed. The girl he marries is Lillina, who is expecting a child through her affair with Giacomino. Toti has no intention of interfering, rather he encourages the lovers. Everywhere the neighbours say the situation is scandalous, but Toti is only concerned with keeping Giacomino beside Lillina, and seeing that he does not marry someone else before his own death. If everyone is happy, let the scandal-mongers mind their own business.

The next play, *Right You Are* (*If You Think You Are*), written in 1916, is one of the most important of Pirandello's works. As in *Think of It, Giacomino,* the message seems to be live and let live. It is a tragedy, a revolt against wanton interference by others with what we wish to keep to ourselves, our hidden truths. What, then, is the tragic situation in the play? The answer is that we don't know. A certain Signor Ponza has newly arrived in a town with his wife, and taken a small room in the attic of a building. Next door, in a luxurious apartment, lives Signor Ponza's mother-in-law, Signora Frola. The mystery arises when Signor Ponza tells us that his wife is his second marriage, he having lost his first wife in an earthquake some time ago; Signora Frola, on the other hand, claims that her daughter is not dead, but that Signor Ponza refuses to let her see her. Daily she makes the journey to Signor Ponza's flat and, refused admission, she contents herself by gazing at her daughter's silhouette. This scandalous situation sets the whole town talking, and curiosity mounts as strangers turn detectives. Both Signor Ponza and Signora Frola accuse each other of madness. Signora Frola admits that for a year her daughter went to a sanatorium, and on her return Signor Ponza refused to recognise her as his wife, and insisted on going through the wedding ceremony again. Ponza then admits to pretending madness in order that Signora Frola should keep her illusions. At this stage the *raisonneur* of the play, Laudisi, turns ironically to the assembly and exclaims, "There you are, ladies and gentlemen, the truth is discovered." The only thing to do, people decide, is to ask Signora Ponza herself. And here is her answer:

SIGNORA PONZA   And what can you want of me now, after all this, ladies and gentlemen? In our lives, as you see, there is something which must remain concealed.

Otherwise the remedy which our love for each other has found cannot prevail.

PREFECT   (*with tears in his eyes*) We surely are anxious to respect your sorrow, madam, but we must know, and we want you to tell . . .

SIGNORA PONZA   What? The truth? The truth is simply this. I am the daughter of Signora Frola, and I am the second wife of Signor Ponza. Yes, and — for myself, I am nobody, I am nobody . . .

PREFECT   Ah, but no, madam, for yourself . . . you must be . . . either the one or the other.

SIGNORA PONZA   Not at all, not at all, sir! No, for myself I am . . . whoever you choose to have me.

In *Il Piacere dell' Onestà* ("The Pleasure of Respectability"), written the following year, the mask breaks down before the force of life. The Marquis Fabio Collo, separated from his wife, meets an attractive society girl Agata Renni and seduces her. To avoid scandal and save appearances, the Marquis and Agata's mother decide that a legal husband must be found for Agata, but a husband for form's sake only, merely to protect honour. They call upon the services of Angelo Baldovino, an impoverished intellectual, who accepts the rôle. Baldovino, however, has no intention of being made use of and demands that, in playing his part as husband, Agata should play hers as wife, and, since honour must be respected, cease her affair with Fabio. Fabio, desperate to get rid of Baldovino, plans a ruse whereby Baldovino will appear to have misappropriated money, but Baldovino avoids the trap. He can no longer carry on playing his part of being a puppet husband, for he has genuinely fallen in love with Agata. He, therefore, having proved his innocence, asks Fabio to ruin him and he will go away. This is no longer convenient for the others, since honour must still be protected. Baldovino is determined to go, when Agata, who had gradually come to think of Baldovino as her husband, tells him that she will go with him. Now that he can drop the mask and be her husband, Baldovino consents to stay.

In *The Pleasure of Respectability* there is quite a social satire to be found in the poor intellectual who does not sell his honour, whereas the rich believe that honour can be bought and does not need to be practised. Honour is also the theme of *Il Giuoco delle Parti* ("The Game as He Played It"), but viewed from a different angle. This time the husband, Leone Galla, has resigned himself to the behaviour of his unfaithful wife, Silia, whose sensuous nature delights in tormenting her many lovers. Silia's latest lover is Guido, but what infuriates her is that Leone could not care less. Silia asks Guido whether they cannot think of a way to kill Leone. Chance offers them an opportunity when she invites passing revellers into the house and sends her servant to tell the neighbours that she has been assaulted. Guido hides in the next room. Leone, for his honour, will have to fight a duel, and the man chosen for the insult is a renowned swordsman. Leone calmly agrees, and takes Guido for his second. But now the tables are turned: on the day of the duel Leone tells Guido that he has done the challenging; Guido, to all intents the real husband, must do the fighting, especially as he had been in the house when the insult happened. No match for Leone's cerebral logic, Guido fights and is killed.

There is intense bitterness and irony in Pirandello's next play *L'Uomo, la Bestia e la Virtù* ("Man, Beast and Virtue"); it is both his most naturalistic, most aggressive and perhaps his least appealing play. The plot involves a teacher, Signor Paolino, who is horrified by the hypocrisy of people and the stupidity of his pupils. The mother of one of his pupils, Signora Perrella, is his mistress and she is going to have a baby. Her husband, a sea captain, brutal, selfish, intolerant, only comes home for a day between long voyages, and then never looks at his wife. If only he would make love to her on his next visit, Signora Perrella's virtue would be saved, but she knows that this is impossible. At last Paolino finds a way to save her by asking the chemist, a man he had previously denounced as a hypocrite, to make a love potion to place inside a cake the captain would eat. The trick works and her reputation is saved. The Machiavellian world leaves an unpleasant impression, when virtue, in order to be saved, requires that Paolino, the man who has placed virtue in danger, should further through a trick see his loved one made virtuous again in the arms of the beast.

Pirandello then turned to the *teatro dello specchio*, and in *Tutto per bene* ("All for the Best") he has drawn in the character of Martino Lori a disillusioned, tragic figure we shall not easily forget. For Lori, who for years had worshipped the memory of his wife and had given all his love on earth to his only daughter, suddenly has the truth revealed to him so that all his hopes, illusions, the meaning of life itself are shattered. One look in the mirror and he sees his past as others have seen it, he sees that his life has been a mockery.

The play centres on the big scene, the *coup de théâtre* which was so important to playwrights of the old school, in this case between Lori and his daughter Palma. Palma enters the drawing-room where Lori is sitting in the dark, and mistakes him for Senator Manfroni, a rich man who has taken a fatherly interest in her which has gone to the extent of arranging a good marriage for her and giving her a handsome dowry. Lori has never questioned his motives, but sometimes feels the way his daughter cruelly dismisses him and transfers her affection to the senator. Palma calls out "father" and then seeing Lori, immediately shrinks away from him. When Lori asks her why she behaves like this, she tells him outright that she is tired of his 'acting' the part of her father. For of course Manfroni is her real father. Everyone else except Lori already knew this, and believed that Lori was merely acting the part (and greatly over-acting) of his devotion to his wife's memory, to the extent of going daily, in all weathers, to the cemetery to put flowers on her grave; always, in other words, acting false grief. At the moment of truth, Lori finds life unbearable. He thinks of revenge, but there is nothing that he can do that would not make things look even more ridiculous. He must go on acting the part, only with the mask off. His only consolation is that Palma, who had previously scorned his affection, now feels truly sorry for him and lends him her sympathy. Perhaps it is "all for the best".

The next play from Pirandello was his famous *Sei Personaggi in Cerca d'Autore* ("Six Characters in Search of an Author") where, at the height of his powers, he examines the very essentials of dramatic creation, the theatre, and life. The play, a most profound study, can be judged on several planes, from the satirical comment it has to make on the artificiality of theatrical production to a metaphysical enquiry into the nature of aesthetics. Perfect art can never be perfect reality, rather, the more perfect the illusion the more removed it is from reality. Neither the humdrum reality of every-day life, nor the slick professional interpretation of fiction can be accepted. The only fusion between reality and art would lie in Pirandello's own imagination, and it is for this purpose that he creates his own six characters. They correspond neither to the real nor to the theatrical delusion, for they are the instruments of creative inspiration. Already in a short story entitled "The Tragedy of a Character" he had developed his thesis for the play. "Nature", he tells us, "uses the instrument of human fantasy in order to follow her high creative purpose. A character in a play comes to life just as a tree, as a stone, as water, as a butterfly, as a woman." The " six characters" are a direct result of the human fantasy translating life in terms of art. Pirandello reveals the intense suffering of their creation compared with the stock romantic figures they become when actors take over. How admirably has Pirandello made this a drama both of passion and of intellect! The plot of the play is conveyed in the title, a play of characters where each character, consumed by the passion of his own consciousness, is driven to confession, by acting his own shame and tragedy on the stage.

The stage is not set for a play. The audience, on entering the theatre, see the theatre in its raw essentials, stage, footlights, props at sixes and sevens, stage hands and carpenters at work . . . the theatre without its greasepaint or glamour. Actors arrive in small groups, then the producer and finally the leading lady. The cast, thus assembled, start rehearsing Pirandello's *Il Giuoco delle Parti*, which seems to be giving them great trouble. A theatre usherette enters followed by the Six Characters. In his stage directions, Pirandello emphasises: "The characters must not appear as phantoms, but as created realities, immutable creatures of fantasy. They are more real and consistent than the voluble actors."

The Characters consist of the father (who also acts as the spokesman for the others), a man about fifty; the mother, appearing crushed beneath "an intolerable weight of shame and sorrow"; the step-daughter, aged eighteen, attractive, vivacious and impudent in manner; a gawkish younger brother of fourteen; a little girl about four; and the son, a taciturn youth of twenty-two who stands aloof from the rest and wishes to take no part in the proceedings. Evidently he is the character the author has not conceived very clearly in his mind. All the characters are dressed in black (except the baby girl, who wears a black sash over a white dress); the mother wears a heavy veil and never raises her eyes from the ground.

The producer, angry that his rehearsal should be interrupted, asks them what they want. The father replies they are looking for an author, any author. "But there's no author here, because we aren't rehearsing a new play", the producer replies. At this the step-daughter pushes her way forward and exclaims: "All the better, all the better. Let your new play be in us." The producer asks them if they are playing a practical joke, but has to believe the father's answer that they carry in them "a heart-rending drama" — "which could be your fortune", the step-daughter adds. "Where is your script?" the producer enquires. "The drama", the reply comes, "is in us, and we are impatient to represent it: our inner passion drives us to this." The characters plead that instinct makes them desire to live, if not for eternity, at least for their hour upon the stage. So the producer is persuaded; after all, their drama could not be worse than the one they are rehearsing. He orders a shorthand writer to take down their dialogue and instructs his actors to pay attention so that they should interpret the scene after the characters have acted it.

The story of the Six Characters is a drama of a divided family, tormented by the shame which has befallen them. The play within the play seizes us with its reality, until we forget the actors sitting on the stage like an Elizabethan audience. The father is a highly intelligent man who has married a woman of the people, kindly and homely, but unable to rise to her partner's intellect. She found sympathy with her husband's secretary, and when the father discovered this, he sent her away with her lover, keeping for himself their only son. Living with the secretary, the mother had three illegitimate children, the step-daughter, the boy of fourteen and the little girl aged four. The father, after he had sent his wife away, felt as lonely as he had in her company; only no longer did their son, her son, mean so much to him. But the years passed. During this time, following the death of the secretary, the mother had to bring up her three children in bitter poverty. Having to start work, she found sewing to do for Madame Pace, a fashionable establishment. The step-daughter, no longer a child but aged eighteen, used to visit Madame Pace's establishment with this work for her mother; but there was also another sort of establishment at Madame Pace's, it was the same sort of house as Madame Tellier's. It was there one night that the step-daughter met the father, and, not recognising each other, she was about to give her body to him when the scream of the mother saved them from disgrace. The father, to make amends, took the family under his protection where they are living out the complicated pattern of their shame; ahead lies a tragic despair. The mother has been completely crushed by the event, and her only happiness is denied her, because her legitimate son refuses to hear her tragedy or have anything to do with them. He suffers the same unhappy solitude as his father; the father complains bitterly that one moment of weakness has turned him into a character which is not him; the step-daughter, however, sees only the sensual, hypocritical old man in the father, and she also turns her hatred on his son, for his secrecy. There remain the little girl and the adolescent boy. One day, while playing in the garden the little girl drowns in a pond, and the boy, who can stand life no longer, draws a revolver and shoots himself. Reality reaches a parallel with the event (only slightly dramatised) of what happened in Pirandello's own family.

The characters arrange the stage so as to resemble as closely as possible reality. Both the father and step-daughter remonstrate against the type acting of the actors who interpret their scene, but the producer defends his actors:

> You're not going to pretend that you can act? Do you suppose the spirit of the piece is in you? . . . Not at all, your soul or whatever you like to call it takes shape here. The actors give body and form to it, voice and gesture. And my actors — I may tell you — have given expression to much more lofty material than this little drama of yours, which may or may not hold up on the stage. But if it does, the merit of it, believe me, will be due to my actors.

They continue with their drama. The step-daughter wishes to live the scene of her shame by revealing the brutal truth. She will undo her dress and corset, and feel the repugnance, let the reality of the horror be seen. But the producer hastily reminds her that such things are not allowed on the stage. She finally agrees merely to have her arms bare, so that she can watch a vein throbbing which on that night reminded her of the sin she committed in the father's power. "Scream, mother, scream as you did then", she cries. The producer sees the dramatic curtain line.

And so the play is acted, until the final revolver shot brings the actors face to face with the reality of death.

LEADING LADY	He is dead! Poor boy . . . dead, what a thing to happen.
LEADING ACTOR	Dead my foot. Just fiction. Quite unconvincing.
SOME ACTORS	Fiction? It's reality, reality. He *is* dead.
OTHER ACTORS	No, it's just the end, the end of the story.
THE FATHER	But what an end. Reality, reality, gentlemen, reality.
THE PRODUCER	Fiction, reality, to the devil with the lot. Lights, lights. I've never known such a happening. I've lost a whole day's rehearsal.

The subject of dramatic illusion is also dealt with in *Ciascuno al suo Modo* ("Each in His Own Way"), where after each act two real characters in the audience, from whom the author took the idea of the play, are infuriated at seeing their own sad lives thus represented in the theatre. They interrupt the play when the woman leaps on to the stage and slaps the actress; confusion breaks out in the theatre and Pirandello tells us there is yet another act, but the play cannot go on any longer.

Also following up his ideas in *Six Characters*, Pirandello wrote *Questa sera si recita a soggetto* ("To-night We Improvise") in 1930, where again the playwright demonstrates his material. The contrasts are the same, the reality of the characters compared with the artifice of the stage conventions, and again the producer, inflated with his own importance, is the target of Pirandello's satire. The author expresses again some of his essential ideas, but, alas, the Six Characters are missing, and without characters of their intensity he is unable to keep the perfect balance between the dramatic and the intellectual which he achieved in *Six Characters*. This goes for many of Pirandello's less important works, which are always worth reading, and are never without those brilliant flashes of insight into the mind and the equally marked precision of his exposition; we shall only discuss one more of his plays, *Enrico IV*, which may be considered both as Pirandello's *chef-d'oeuvre*, and as the outstanding tragedy in the modern theatre — indeed, critics have called *Enrico IV* "a twentieth-century *Hamlet*".

Enrico IV is not, however, a tragedy in the classical sense, for as Giraudoux notes, tragedy and comedy are interwoven in the modern drama. The tragic vision, however, is that of a soul who relinquished the real world twenty years previously, when he became mad. On regaining his sanity, he finds that he can no longer return to take up his life where he left off. He is condemned to his solitude, his lunacy, his masquerade, his despair, "now, of necessity, for ever". It is a realisation of how life filters away while we breathe, and suggests that in madness alone can one find shelter for the omnipotent reality. In the character of Enrico IV — a giant who towers above Pirandello's other characters — we have a genuinely tragic creation, for whom "the time is out of joint", as it was for Hamlet, and whose tragedy also becomes a 'tragedy of reflection'. *Enrico IV* was not Pirandello's final work in the theatre, but in no other play did Pirandello give so poignantly his summing-up on life. It is as if through Enrico IV he is speaking to each of us, individually, his hidden thoughts.

We are in the Italian countryside of to-day, in a castle where everything appears as if it were an illusion of the eleventh century. All the courtiers wear the costumes of the eleventh century, except one who is dressed in French court costume of the fifteenth. He is the new courtier who, having applied for the job, learnt up all about Henry IV of France instead of the Emperor Henry IV of Germany, some 400 years earlier. So he has to learn his part all over again. Such is the introduction we are given to this strange world; the action of the play, which started twenty years earlier, is already in a state of crisis when the curtain rises. Twenty years previously, we learn, a rich young Italian gentleman was disguised as Enrico IV for a pageant. He was riding with Matilde Spina with whom he was in love, but who in turn was the lover of a mutual friend, Belcredi. During the procession Belcredi pricked Enrico's horse, which reared up and threw him head first. Enrico got up, and everybody thought he had had a lucky escape. But it soon became evident that Enrico was no longer acting; he believed he was indeed the Emperor. Instead of being sent to an asylum, being a wealthy man, his friends set him up in a castle, surrounded with courtiers groomed for their parts. So life passed, and after twelve years of madness Enrico regained his sanity. But here lies the tragedy: how could he take up his former life again? He became the grim observer of his own drama; he "preferred to stay mad, to live my madness with the most lucid consciousness and thus avenge myself of the brutality of a stone that struck my head . . . I filled this solitude, squalid and empty as it appeared to me when I opened my eyes, with the colour and splendour of that distant day of carnival."

The day comes when Matilde Spina returns, accompanied by Belcredi, her daughter Frida, Frida's fiancé, and a mental doctor, in the hope that they might still cure Enrico of his madness. There is a striking contrast in how the years have passed . . . how Matilde has aged from the portrait of her on the wall, made twenty years before, while Frida is exactly like her mother was then. Enrico appears; he also has aged, dyed his hair in a ridiculous fashion. He makes some uncomfortable remarks to his visitors on growing old, and then at the sight of his old enemy, Belcredi, he can no longer wear his mask.

The doctor (Pirandello dislikes the certainty of his scientific theories and pat answers) believes that Enrico is really mad, but Matilde believes that he is conscious of the mask he wears and wishes to be freed from it. The doctor has a plan, to confront him with Frida, instead of her mother Matilde, dress her as Matilde was dressed on the day, and place her beside the portrait. The doctor hopes the sudden confusion of seeing her will restore to his mind a conception of time and set it going once again "like a watch which has stopped at a certain hour". When Enrico does see Frida, terror seizes him; he believes that this is madness in reality — and then he understands the trick. Matilde and Belcredi try to persuade him to return with them but Enrico is not interested. Stung with fury — Frida is the girl he loved — he seizes her and as Belcredi rushes forward to take Frida from him, Enrico draws his sword and kills him. He can never now return to the world. The masquerade must continue, the mask must be worn ... until death.

In *Enrico IV* we have Pirandello's most complete achievement, where man is alone in his solitude, where the life-force continues to reproduce humanity, but where age overtakes the individual and only illusions remain. There is much in Pirandello of the *théâtre de silence*; the unexpressed is often equal to what is actually said. It is a theatre of poetic vision, not of spoken poetry. A one-sided vision, but of genuine sincerity. It was the inconsistencies of life that troubled Pirandello, for he recognised that life must be consistent. "If life moved eternally it would never acquire consistency; if it acquired consistence, it would never move; and yet life must have both consistency and motion." Here, in Pirandello's own words, lies the mystery of life and a key to his theatre — as far as any key can be found to understand the 'own special world' of another human mind.

THREE

A DRAMATIST OF OPTIMISM:
JEAN GIRAUDOUX

"Evidemment, la vie est ratée, mais c'est très, très bien,
la vie."

Electre

THE inconsistencies of life were for Pirandello as impossible as
the marble blocks Sisyphus had daily to roll up the hill in the
world of shades; the world of Jean Giraudoux accepts their
existence and resolves their contradiction by leading us into an imaginary universe where everything is made consistent. For the despair of
uncertainty is substituted the hope of uncertainty; for the dialectics of
cerebral theatre is substituted the spur of French logic. Giraudoux, like
Cocteau's Orpheus, breaks the mirror of the *teatro dello specchio* to
find the logical conclusion. We are in a theatre of contrasts more than
ever, but logical imagination is substituted for nightmares; man rediscovers faith in his fellow-men, and the audience are reminded that
though this is only fantasy, it is also only common sense. It is human to
be foolish, but it is human also to have hope in the future, to believe
that dreams may become reality. "Granted that life is a blunder, how
very, very good life is", exclaims the gardener in *Electre*. "Granted", he
continues, "that things never go well, that nothing ever turns out
right, now and then you must confess that things turn out admirably
... not for me ... or rather, for me ..."

How far we are from the world of Pirandello! Life is not to be
dreaded from day to day as the final tragedy approaches, it is to be
lived fully as an adventure story culminating in the greatest adventure
of all. When Giraudoux's most beautiful heroine is drawn towards the
labyrinth of death and suicide, she is rescued by a humdrum citizen —

LUIGI PIRANDELLO

JEAN GIRAUDOUX

French civil servant — who argues the case for life. For the road to death he offers her is the "slow, gradual, but certain" road of life. Life has its pattern, and confusion only enters when it is permitted. The rigorous rejection of naturalism by Giraudoux was something which Pirandello had hesitated to attempt, though the frontiers between illusion and a make-believe parallel of reality merely require for transition an attitude of mind. If Pirandello's experiments disturbed the very foundations of naturalism, Giraudoux's return to the opposite camp has been followed by all the important French contemporary dramatists, though strange bedfellows they make in any camp!

Before we consider the theatre of Giraudoux in detail, perhaps this is the place to give a brief outline of the state of the French drama and stage before and immediately after the first world war, and in particular pay homage to the work done by Jacques Copeau, Louis Jouvet, Charles Dullin, Gaston Baty, and Georges and Ludmilla Pitoëff, *metteurs en scène* who have transformed the French stage from one of its lowest ebbs for generations to its highest achievements since the great classical period of the seventeenth century.

The first decade of this century was not a happy one for the French theatre. The fervid activity in the European theatre generally — with London playgoers finally awakened from their nineteenth-century slumber (Ibsen had already knocked at their door) by Shaw's iconoclasm, Strindberg experimenting in his 'naturalistic tragedy', and Tchekhov presented by the Moscow Art Theatre — these events found little or no reflection on the Parisian stage during *la belle époque*. Any discussion, therefore, on the very significant renaissance of the French drama during the last thirty years must stress that prior to 1914 the French was the most closed and backward theatre in Europe, and that it is only comparatively recently that the French playgoer has taken his theatre seriously enough to expect plays which are his intellectual equal. To-day, indeed, one might well wonder whether certain plays do not make demands beyond the level of any average audience.

There is no denying that in the *théâtre d'amour* of Georges de Porto Riche, the *comédies de salon* of Henri Bernstein, or the superficial optimism of Alfred Capus and others, entertainment was to be had. But, for the most part, dramatists during *la belle époque* either had to content themselves with artificial trivialities or become disciples of Zola's new naturalism (Zola refused to recognise Strindberg as a disciple). Unfortunately, however much naturalism was to prosper in other countries, it has always been alien to the genius of the French

D

character. Not even the great Antoine, who founded the *théâtre libre* in revolt against the conventions of *la belle époque*, was able to enforce naturalism as the alternative. His experiments had their utility in that they provoked men like Jacques Copeau to bring back the magic and imagination to the French theatre. Realism and naturalism was the wrong turning, the new drama in France lay in the discovery of the old traditions. As Jean Cocteau said of Antoine, "The Montgolfiers also had genius, but they retarded by a hundred years the progress of aviation" (the Montgolfier brothers experimented with the first air balloons at the end of the eighteenth century). Nor were the dramatists of the new school to become internationally known like other European naturalists; even the best of them, Henri Becque (far, far removed from the crudities of Zola), does not come across to-day without a certain monotone (very evident in a recent production of *La Parisienne* at the Comédie Française), while social documentary writers such as Eugène Brieux offer plain boredom. The truth is that naturalism does not find roots in the great and living tradition of French drama; the 'common-sense' dictates of naturalism forbid a logical conclusion, while the brilliance of so many French logical conclusions is that they discard the narrow horizon of common sense.

However stubbornly self-satisfied the French theatre may have been at the outbreak of the first world war, it could not shut its eyes completely to the work being done by men like Stanislavski at the Moscow Art Theatre, Adolphe Appia in Switzerland, or Edward Gordon Craig in England. In 1913 Jacques Copeau (1878–1949), a man of letters who had founded the Nouvelle Revue Française, put into practice a number of their ideas (and developed his own theories in their wake) when he formed his company at the Théâtre du Vieux-Colombier. Copeau saw the theatre in the hands of speculators and wished to return it into the hands of creative workers. He sought to harmonise all the elements of production, discipline his players and banish anything which might distract or deform the pure conception of the poetry and language of the play. His was the gift of a creative animation of the whole field of *mise en scène*. The theatre was not a copy or 'slice' of life, but an interpretation of an escape to the supreme moments of our being.

The war put a temporary end to Copeau's work, and the French theatre reached the limits of banality. With the peace, however, Paris was ready to assume the rôle of intellectual capital of the world. The time had come for little art theatres. Though Copeau closed his own theatre in 1924 and retired to the country, taking his actors with him, two young members of his company had already launched out on their own: Louis Jouvet and Charles Dullin; in 1921 Charles Dullin founded his company and moved the following year to the present Atelier Theatre in the Place Dancourt; in 1922 Jouvet found his home at the Comédie des Champs-Elysées. Jouvet may be said to have created there a modern theatre repertoire, while Dullin, after a few years, explained "My ideas on the theatre have changed a lot. They can be summed up in one sentence: when I began I wanted to make the Atelier a school for actors, to-day I would like to make it a school for authors."

Both Jouvet and Dullin believed in the anti-naturalistic theatre. For Jouvet the theatre was shrouded in mystery. Dullin attempted to create a 'Western style' of theatre as complete as the Eastern. He wished to find the sources and make the drama live again. His style was simple, but from it all elements of naturalism were banished. He placed special emphasis on music as an accompaniment to the acting, for, like rhythm, it accentuates the imagination of the play. In other words, Dullin sought a stylised theatre, which bourgeois naturalism had almost caused to disappear and which he recreated in a return to tradition and a return to poetry. The classics, consequently, always occupied the major part of Dullin's repertoire, but among modern dramatists he introduced Pirandello to France, produced Cocteau and Salacrou, and later the first play of Jean-Paul Sartre, *Les Mouches* (produced at the Théâtre de Sarah Bernhardt in 1943).

Among the other "animators of theatre" (to use Robert Brasillach's title of his excellent study of the French stage in the inter-war years) the names of Georges and Ludmilla Pitoëff and Gaston Baty must be mentioned, though an examination of their work would require a book in itself. Baty's theories were to respect the text, but to express the whole text so as to "translate what words alone cannot translate". Beyond the text commences "another zone, a zone of mystery, silence, what we call atmosphere, environment, climate . . ."

It is these names that have enabled the renaissance of the French drama to take place; it is only in the individual work of animators that any hope can be nursed for world drama. It is in the so-called art theatre, or *avant-garde*, that we find true theatre; neither commercial theatres (in to-day's unhappy economics) nor national theatres (with the experience of the greatest of all national theatres, the Comédie Française) can take their place. But these little theatres would be useless unless they were identified, as well as with producer and actors, with a dramatist. In the Paris theatres during the inter-war years, you chose your theatre as you chose the book of your favourite poet. And when in 1928 Jouvet made his greatest discovery of all, when he presented the first play of Jean Giraudoux (then known only as a novelist), he made certain that Giraudoux would not be known merely as a dramatic author, but as a member of his company, turning out plays as required. Such was the beginning of a partnership broken only by the war and Giraudoux's death; the result was a victory for Jouvet and his players, for the little theatre, and for French drama. It may be said that with the plays of Giraudoux, and the subsequent discovery by the public of Claudel (whose works written before the first world war were known only by a small circle of admirers until the second), the French theatre has rediscovered its soul.

*

Jean Giraudoux was born at Bellac, a French country town in the department of Haute-Vienne, in 1882, and died on 31 January, 1944, the year of the liberation of the France he loved so dearly. By profession he was as much civil servant as writer, and spent most of his active life in government service. Somehow the two tasks never conflicted, though he did find himself in the paradoxical position of being head of the propaganda ministry in 1939, "Cassandre à la Propagande" as Aragon described the situation. After the fall of France he refused the position of French ambassador to Greece under the Vichy régime.

Giraudoux was always first in life, he never took second place in anything. At school he was naturally always at the top of his class, he was first in the Concours Général, in the Concours des Chancelleries, and, more surprising for a brilliant scholar, first in sports in university running. At the age of forty-six Giraudoux turned to the theatre, and with his first play he became the leading dramatist of his generation.

It was as if he had a mission to perform that Giraudoux saw the theatre. He explained his crusade thus: "The play is the only form of moral or artistic education of a nation. It is the only evening course available for adults and the aged, the only means whereby the most humble and least literate members of the public can find personal contact with the highest conflicts, and create for themselves an unde-nominational religion, a liturgy and its saints, sentiments and passions. Some people dream, but for those who do not dream there is the theatre."

In the realisation of his dream world Giraudoux found his magician n Jouvet, but it was not without the doubts of a mortal that Jouvet contemplated the manuscript of *Siegfried,* which Giraudoux had adapted from his novel *Siegfried et le Limousin.*

At first the play was considerably too long, and throughout rehearsals Jouvet requested important cuts to be made, with which Giraudoux always did his best to comply. It was the language of the play, however, that most people feared, for here Giraudoux deliberately made no compromise. The dialogue of a novelist is written to be read not spoken, and Giraudoux was a French novelist *par excellence.* Whereas the theatre so often requires the short, elliptical phrase, Giraudoux's style is complex, his sentences are loaded with subordinate clauses in which he allows his thoughts to wander far and wide throughout the domains of the universe. His is the magical language of poetry which, allied with his philosophical ideas and wit, is far removed from the conversation of every-day life.

The rôle of the writer in the theatre, Giraudoux believed, was to reintroduce style. He explained himself: "Our age no longer asks writers merely for books — every street corner is littered with them — what above all else it appeals for is language. The writer does not have, like the jester to some fortunate king, to search for scars and criticise in novels and plays, for after all, criticism can be as contemptible as flattery. Our age asks that the writer should reveal his mark of which he is the sole trustee — style. That is what we need to-day in the theatre." In Giraudoux the French theatre found a stylist with grace and nobility, of a quality with which perhaps only the language of Marivaux can be compared. Giraudoux is essentially polite theatre, the drama of the spoken word rather than action, of conflict through thought, never through histrionics. It is the recesses of the human mind that Giraudoux seeks to explore, and thus what problems he presents to any translator! How can one render a delicate prose style where every word has been carefully selected, into a relatively formless language like English? And even if this can be done without seeming highly artificial, how can a British and American audience, not accustomed like French audiences to following complexity of thought as a substitute for action, be persuaded to listen to Giraudoux? The answer is that so far those plays of his which have been presented in Britain and America have tended to be adaptations rather than translations. Many of these have been less than adequate even as adaptations, and have missed completely the poetry of the original.

Maurice Valency, who adapted *La Folle de Chaillot* for its Broadway production, has explained the translator's dilemma in an article in *Theatre Arts*. He points out the difference between importing a French play and a bottle of reliable French vintage. Not every play can change habitat without some adjustment. Mr. Valency believes that in cases where photographic accuracy is impossible, it is better for a translator to be himself creative and render an impressionistic version. Unfortunately there is a strong belief that Anglo-Saxon audiences will not listen to long-drawn-out speeches, and Valency laments that "the predominance of white over black in a page of typescript" is "very persuasive in managerial circles". The point is, in other words, that since the audience prefer short snappy dialogue, and it is the audience who pay the box-office, then it is the old story of the man who pays calling the tune. Whatever the flaws in the reasoning, managements do fall for it, and that is why a different Giraudoux is known in London and Broadway than in Paris.

There is yet another reason why the works of Giraudoux took a long time to reach London and Broadway, where the triumph of naturalism has so completely won the day. The theatre of Giraudoux is neither realistic nor is it altogether unrealistic. Intellect and imagination walk hand in hand, for the destination is not the never-never land of Barrie. In all Giraudoux's plays one can identify situations of real life, but they have a resemblance only; they are familiar, but there is a differentiation. If, for example, some of his characters make us think of Hitler and Mussolini, we know that they are not meant to represent Hitler and Mussolini. Giraudoux was too great an artist for that. What his plays have is a moral signification, and he selects those problems which have a capital importance for our own time and civilisation.

Giraudoux is an idealist, but he does not believe in miracles. He has confidence in man and prefers to leave him to search for his own solutions through debate and an appeal to the intellect. He does not believe that we live in the best of possible worlds, but he does not exclude the possibility that we could live in the best of possible worlds. His universe magnifies beauty, because he knows that it is an alternative to ugliness; the one would not exist without the other. Perhaps he remembers the verdict of Socrates — "Evils, Theodorus, can never pass away, for there must always remain something which is antagonistic to good." The antithesis of words, and the play on these words in the dialogue, is to be found throughout Giraudoux's plays. In *La Guerre de Troie n'aura pas lieu* the play is on the words 'guerre/paix'; in *Amphitryon* 38 the play is on the words 'jour/nuit'; it is on 'vie/mort' in *Intermezzo* and 'vice/vertu' in *Sodome et Gomorrhe*. In *La Folle de Chaillot*, Irma, the Parisian dishwasher, has a soliloquy in which she invokes the following examples: "I detest the ugly, I adore the beautiful"; "I detest the wicked, I adore kindness"; "I detest the evening, I adore the morning"; "I detest the devil, I adore God"; "I adore freedom I detest slavery"; "I don't much like women, I adore men"; "I adore life, I detest death".

In his strange land of reality and make-believe, Giraudoux brings together both human beings and those who are not subject to human laws. Frequently the humans lack those human virtues of love, forgiveness, understanding which the non-human characters may display, but in the end these are only human failings which can be redressed. Many questions are asked which are as perplexing as the songs of the Sirens, but no definite answers are attempted. Young girls can retain their youth and beauty for eternity, or turn into the mad old hags of Chaillot, and we may live in a world where the mad old hags are the sane inhabitants. The only certainty is death and everlasting life, which, indeed, is the riddle of the universe.

Many modern writers have been moved, like Giraudoux, to ask what is the place of man in life, and although most have given more excessive interpretations than Giraudoux, none has been a greater humanist. Life is neither a tragedy nor a comedy. Laughter can follow tears and laughter can lead to tears. All the threads are interwoven in the modern theatre, as a character observes in *Siegfried*. This, then, is the point of departure for Giraudoux's study of life, where there are no borders between laughter and tears, no frontiers between dreams and reality, and where always we can see our vision of the ideal in terms of the real world.

It is very noticeable that in his first play Giraudoux expounds some of his essential ideas. The theme of *Siegfried*, which is both a psychological study of mental disintegration and at the same time a symbolic picture of Franco-German relations, haunted Giraudoux for many years, and formed material for a number of novels as well as his play. His approach has been widely commended. "There is no better introduction to the Franco-German problem," Louis Joxe affirms, "for it is not as a technician but as a man and less as a historian than as a psychologist that he [Giraudoux] succeeds."

The theme presents a remarkable situation. A French writer, Jacques Forestier, disappears on the battlefield, and everyone, including his friend Geneviève, assumes that he has been killed. In fact he has been struck with total amnesia, picked up by the Germans without any means of identification as to nationality, and taken to be German. He is re-educated by a nurse in all the German myths and culture. When the play opens he has risen to be a prominent political figure, a determined, vigorous leader who offers Germany hope and salvation from her moral and economic chaos. One German, however, suspects that "Siegfried" is French, and recognises in his writing and oratory the lyrical style which was precisely that of Forestier. He arranges for Geneviève and Robineau, a friend who knew him well, to come over from France and identify him. The discovery of his origin and the decision Siegfried must make forms the conflict of the play.

Siegfried, then, is a play of a struggle, a struggle in the mind of one man who admires France and is attracted by Germany, and is repelled by the faults of both countries. It is a struggle tormented by the prospect of war, and in his condemnation of fighting, dictatorship and military rule Giraudoux prepares the ground for ideas which he was to develop more fully in *La Guerre de Troie n'aura pas lieu.*

Siegfried chooses France, but he does not choose France as against the alternative of choosing Germany. Giraudoux preserves on the Franco-German struggle an optimism which, alas, though it was to be betrayed, is nevertheless still valid to-day. In the conflict between the two nations he finds less antagonism than parallelism, and if he condemns, it is the anonymous forces which prevent the two people living side by side in peace.

Consider the first meeting of two friends, Zelten, a German, and Robineau, a Frenchman, for the first time since the war:

ROBINEAU   . . . Well, what have you been up to these last twelve years, Zelten? You who so loved Springtime and music, joy and peace, what have you been up to?

ZELTEN   Waging war! War on thirty-five nations. Waging battle only on one . . . And what about you, old Goggles, the easy-going common man of the Royal and Imperial Libraries, tell me, my most dear friend, what have you been up to these last twelve years?

ROBINEAU   Waging war! On you . . .[1]

Neither of the characters is a principal in the play, yet this short scene must surely be one of the most touching in contemporary drama.

[1] See original on p. 291.

Coming at the beginning of the play it makes the subsequent entry of Siegfried less dramatic, and if Giraudoux had been more of a technician he would certainly have reserved it for a more important stage or curtain in the play.

It is in the last act, set in the customs house on the Franco-German frontier, that Giraudoux makes Siegfried argue his decision to two German generals, who put the case for his staying in Germany. The customs house is itself symbolic, divided in two by a *ligne idéale*, the German half being well laid out, brightly painted, tidy and clean, centrally heated and, of course, thoroughly organised for customs procedure; the French side is shabby, untidy, offers neither comfort nor routine, and depends on the individual whims of the customs official as much as the room depends on an individual oil stove for heating. One should add that there is an aggressive Corsican official with cigarette behind the ear to put the finishing touches.

The German general, Ledinger, addresses Siegfried:

LEDINGER   Come back with us, my friend. You are unwell. You are losing weight. Come back.

SIEGFRIED   Yes, Ledinger, I have lost weight. But quite as great as that loss is the grandeur of the gift I have been bearing these recent nights. A convalescent in my condition is truly more in need of the most modest homeland. If one be cut off suddenly from Germany and given responsibility for France, the laws of equilibrium would have to be properly upset for him not to feel it. I may tell you that only the day before yesterday I had it in mind to disappear, to seek asylum in some third country, one I should have chosen as far as possible for its having no neighbours, no enemies, no monuments to the dead to unveil, no dead. A country without war in the past, without war in the future . . . But the more I hunted for it on the map the more I felt my attachment to nations which suffer and feel compassion — the more clearly I realised my mission.[1]

The tension mounts. The generals ask Siegfried if he cannot be persuaded to change his mind or, if not, whether they cannot announce that Siegfried has been killed in an accident. Thus he could become

[1] See original on p. 291.

Forestier again, and the glory of Siegfried would be able to live for the German people. Siegfried refuses, and Ledinger asks him if he really prefers to live as it were under two shadows. The reply is:

SIEGFRIED   I shall live, simply that. Siegfried and Forestier will live side by side. I shall endeavour to bear becomingly the two names and the two destinies which happen to be mine. A human life is not a worm. Cutting it in two is not enough to let each part become a separate existence. Nor are there any sufferings so opposed, experiences so inimical, that they cannot fuse one day into a single life; for the heart of man remains the mightiest crucible of all. Before long maybe that faded memory, those homelands lost and found, that unawareness and awareness in which alike I suffer and delight, will make one coherent pattern, one single existence. That within one human soul, where the most contradictory virtues and vices cohabit, the word German and the word French should be the only ones unwilling to come to terms would surely be much too much. I, for one, am unwilling to dig trenches within my own being. I shall not enter France as the last prisoner let out of Germany's gaols. I shall enter as the first to benefit from a new learning or a new heart . . . Farewell. There is your engine whistling. Siegfried and Forestier bids you farewell.[1]

So Siegfried crosses the *ligne idéale*, to France, where only Geneviève remembers him. But we know that Siegfried will not resume the life of Jacques Forestier as if nothing had happened. Geneviève in the play now loves Siegfried as much as Jacques, and we feel that together they see before them the chance of a new life which could be the dawn of a new age.

Siegfried is not Giraudoux's masterpiece, but in no other play can we identify the author so closely with his leading character. If in its construction *Siegfried* is far from being a 'well-made' play, such as we expect from less gifted professional playwrights, it is because mere mechanics did not interest Giraudoux. It was through his style that Giraudoux was able to transform his characters into symbols of human destiny.

[1] See original on p. 291.

It is, however, by an author's second play that one judges a play-wright, and *Siegfried*, after all, had been treated first as a novel. The test came eighteen months later, on 8 November, 1929, when Girau-doux produced *Amphitryon* 38 — so called because Giraudoux esti-mated that thirty-seven writers had dealt with the same Greek legend before him in the theatre (it has been suggested that seventy-five would be just as good a guess). In *Amphitryon* 38 the course is set for a light-hearted adventure in the company of gods and men; the theme is the test of human fidelity; the story of Jupiter's plan to seduce the faithful Alcmena has an irresistible appeal. Once again style distinguishes the play and is itself sparkling with gaiety to suit the mood of Greek high spirits. In the background, however, we hear the rumbling and echoes of war — Giraudoux's ever-present obsession.

We are first introduced to two gods, Jupiter and Mercury, looking at the shadows of Alcmena and Amphitryon. From this amusing start we learn that Jupiter wishes to love Alcmena himself, and asks Mercury how he can obtain her consent. Jupiter explains it must be a human plan rather than a divine one, for he does not want to miss the finest moment in human love — her consent. The trouble is that Jupiter knows that Alcmena only loves her husband Amphitryon. Mercury replies that Jupiter must borrow the shape and form of Amphitryon, and that in order to remove Amphitryon from the scene they should make a war break out. Then Jupiter, in the guise of her husband, would be able to call on Alcmena pretending that he had slipped away from the army to pass the night secretly with his wife. Such is the human plan the gods adopt.

So no sooner has a trumpeter read a declaration of peace (peace is shortly to be defined as that period between two wars) than a giant warrior, no doubt symbolising war, announces that the Athenians have crossed the frontier. Everything goes according to plan; Amphitryon takes his leave of Alcmena, Jupiter assumes his form, knocks at the door, and is eventually admitted as Amphitryon.

A scene of high comedy follows in Act II. The following morning they wake up when the sun is already high in the sky.

JUPITER   What a divine night.

But Alcmena takes exception to the word 'divine'. She suggests 'perfect', 'charming', best of all 'agreeable'.

JUPITER   Then it was the most agreeable of all our nights, wasn't
             it, by far?
ALCMENA   That depends . . .

After considerable coquetry on this point Alcmena concedes:

> if you want an adjective for this night, my dear, I would
> say that it was conjugal. It had a feeling of security which
> bewildered me.

Soon Alcmena is having another argument which pricks Jupiter's pride,
for it is none other than failing to show any interest or admiration in
Jupiter himself. Jupiter cannot understand why she has no wish to be
honoured, why she does not long to be able to walk through the air or
over the water, to understand the meaning of other worlds (Alcmena
replies that her neighbours have never interested her). As for being
immortal, what is the good of that? Jupiter tells her she wouldn't die,
but Alcmena only shudders at the prospect of eternal life. She believes
it is treachery for a human to become immortal, and Jupiter has to
acknowledge her stubborness by admitting to Mercury that she is the
first being who is really human that he has ever met. He has much to
tell Mercury:

> her life [Alcmena's] is a prism where the common in-
> heritance of gods and men, courage, love, passion,
> spends itself in truly human qualities, steadfastness,
> gentleness, devotion, over which we have no control.

Of course he has fallen seriously in love with her, and announces that
her future son would be his favourite son. Fresh complications have
meanwhile arisen, for Mercury, according to the custom and thinking
that Jupiter would like to spend another night with Alcmena, this time
without disguise, has announced to the whole universe that Jupiter is
to visit Alcmena to honour her with a son. When Mercury asks Jupiter
what he now wants, Jupiter replies "that Alcmena should remain faithful to her husband and give herself to Jupiter".

But the meeting between Alcmena and Jupiter is not as Jupiter had
anticipated. For Alcmena has her own proposition to make:

ALCMENA   You can taste love with others. But I would like to create between us a union both more fragrant and powerful; alone of all women I can offer it to you. I do.

JUPITER   And it is?
ALCMENA   Friendship.
JUPITER   Friendship! What is this word? Explain yourself. It's the first time I've heard it.

The situation is saved; all ends as Jupiter, Alcmena, Amphitryon and the audience wish it to end. "He only wanted to test us," Alcmena tells her husband.

It was with his third play *Judith*, which Jouvet produced in 1931, that Giraudoux met his first theatre failure, a failure which came to him as a double disappointment, since the play had undoubted literary quality and the character of Judith, "la plus belle et la plus pure des filles d'Israël", was his first complex feminine study.

Why, then, did the play fail? Giraudoux wrote afterwards in his *L'Impromptu de Paris* that "le mot comprendre n'existe pas au théâtre", but one cannot help thinking that Giraudoux was expecting too much from his audience in asking them to follow the subtle psychological transformations of Judith and at the same time to understand the rich assortment of his many themes — first the war, then destiny, original sin, relations between man and God, fatality, feminine pride, jealousy, etc. . . . As far as the construction of the play goes *Judith* marks a distinct improvement in Giraudoux's technique, and while following the biblical story the author has made several changes to aid the dramatic intensity of the play.

The play opens with the news of a Jewish military defeat. The enemy is at the gates, and it is decided that a Jewish woman should go and offer herself to Holophernes, and by cunning kill him. Judith offers herself, and sets out on her dangerous mission, while Jean, who is in love with Judith, sends a prostitute, Suzanne, to try and reach Holophernes first.

Judith goes to satisfy her feminine instinct, and face to face with Holophernes she knows she is betraying her God. Suzanne does not succeed in her mission, because destiny has deemed otherwise. To Holophernes Judith may be just another woman, but Judith, who has only flirted with men up to now, has never known a man. "The duel Judith-Holophernes has become that of a brown body and a fair one", is Judith's summing-up.

The Jews are told of Judith's treachery, and Jean arrives at the camp for vengeance, when he discovers in amazement that Judith has killed Holophernes. The Jews interpret this as a sign that she has been faithful to God and her country. In fact she had loved him and in a perverse frenzy of love she had killed him. "Judith la putain", the guard mutters. But Judith suddenly accepts the decision of destiny, demands that the guard should be killed, and declares that "St. Judith is ready" for the triumphant procession.

A tragedy indeed is this sudden *volte-face* of Judith, for it is very difficult to reconcile her attitude with her previous behaviour. There is much to admire in the play, but the failure of the public to accept it is not really so baffling. Whether they would give a different verdict to-day remains a question mark; Jean-Louis Barrault proposes to revive it some day, so time alone will tell.

With *Intermezzo* (produced 27 February, 1933) we are in the French countryside of our own time, in a little town where strange events are happening and where unknown spirits are said to be terrorising the population. For instance, in the monthly municipal lottery the first prize goes to the poorest person in the district instead of going as usual to the local millionaire, the young champion wins the motor-bicycle, no one votes in the local elections, and the inhabitants answer the census in such a truthful way as to bring blushes to the mayor's cheeks and make it impossible for him to return the questionnaires to headquarters. And all this because a ghost has come to haunt the town.

We would be wrong, however, to imagine that Giraudoux only meant the play to be a superficially amusing ghost story; there exists quite another level, where we can view life from two sides at the same time; there is the positive side, as depicted by the bureaucratic inspector, the bourgeois twin sisters, the controller of weights and measures, with his feet firmly planted on the ground but not incapable of poetic feeling and understanding; on the other side is the negative picture, the enemies of life, where the ghost hypnotises the imagination of the young and beautiful village schoolmistress Isabelle in search of the unknown and forbidden questions, which can be learnt only by being in love with death.

Once caught in this passionate labyrinth the living have great difficulty in rescuing Isabelle, but each of them tries in his own way. The controller, who is himself in love with Isabelle, tries to plead with her in the eloquence of a lover — almost with success. But Isabelle still cannot resist the ghost when he comes to keep his nightly rendezvous.

There is nothing for it but that the controller should defeat the ghost by arguing the case for life. Isabelle is torn between two worlds, affected deeply by the controller's love for her, but tormented by the divine secret which, of course, the ghost will only disclose to her alone. Soon the ghost realises that she is not willing to leave her world for his, and withdrawing his offer he vanishes. Isabelle rushes after him and falls in a faint.

The inspector, the controller, the chemist each discusses how to bring her back to life. It is the little girls of the village school who understand perfectly the situation and solution. The chemist explains their remedy: "The only message, the only artificial circulation that we can practise in this case is to reconcile her sleeping consciousness with the noise of every-day life. It's not a matter of leading her back to herself, but to us." And so with the voluble chatter and idle gossip of the company, the choir of little girls' voices, Isabelle returns to life, the town returns to normal, and the millionaire wins the lottery as usual.

Intermezzo is a highly original play, a delightful meander in the realms of fantasy where Giraudoux could give full play to his imagination. One must add that it is an exceedingly difficult play to act. The first period of Giraudoux's writing came to an end with *Intermezzo* (even the title hints at this); in his next play he turned to his ever-present dread of war, which coincided with the ever-mounting tension in Europe at the coming to power of Hitler. *La Guerre de Troie n'aura pas lieu*, produced in 1935 (*Tiger at the Gates* in the Fry translation, London, 1955), is one of the greatest pacifist plays in literature. We are in Troy in 1935, for, with all the classical setting, we realise the fading hopes of the inter-war years — "The whole universe knows it, we're going to fight", as it is expressed in the second act. The opening dialogue explains the theme:

ANDROMACHE	The Trojan war won't take place, Cassandra.
CASSANDRA	I'll wager you on that, Andromache.
ANDROMACHE	The Greek envoy is all right. We shall receive him cordially, wrap his dear little Helen up carefully, and give her back to him.
CASSANDRA	We shall receive him with insults. We shall not return Helen. And the Trojan war will be on.
ANDROMACHE	It would, if there wasn't a Hector.

Hector is a general against war, a fighter turned pacifist; he believes battles stupid and senseless; but on his side there are those who believe any compromise would besmirch their country's honour and see in pacifism cowardice and betrayal. The war won't break out if Helen can be persuaded to return, and Helen has no desire to stay or go. She will do whatever people want her to do. The talks between Hector and Ulysses, the diplomatic representatives of the two sides, may seek a treaty to safeguard peace, but they cannot promise that their people will respect their policies. Chauvinism and primitive desires for vengeance are powerful instigators of war. And even Hector gives way to the momentary impulse when reasoning with Ulysses seems impossible: "Well, the die then is cast, Ulysses. Go away and fight. My hatred of war is only matched with the incontrollable desire to kill." Surely the most terrible words ever spoken by a pacifist.

La Guerre de Troie is a simply constructed, single-purpose play which moves rapidly towards its tragic fate. Giraudoux for the first time allows pessimism to influence him; he sees war as inevitable as long as some men (but not all) are what they are.

In *Electre*, presented 13 May, 1937, Giraudoux gives us his most complete work in the theatre, a tragedy following the classical design, with intensity and depth, written in a style which reaches the height of his poetic powers. It is a difficult play to read, and its long soliloquies make infinite demands on an audience and actors, but we are in a world where greatness is visible.

Once again Giraudoux goes to Greek mythology for his plot, and adapts it to suit his purpose. Orestes returns from exile to the palace of Agamemnon, his father, who is dead. He meets his sister Electra and learns that his mother Clytemnestra is the lover of King Aegisthus, who followed Agamemnon on the throne. Electra hates her mother, and when she has proof that she is Aegisthus's lover she at once suspects that her mother took part in the murder of her father. Her soul thirsts for the truth, it becomes an obsession. Orestes is the weaker, and finds it hard to understand the strength of Electra's bitterness. Once she has proof, it is Orestes who is to do the deed. Meanwhile the city has been attacked by the Corinthians; Aegisthus is the only person who can save the city. Electra no longer cares, she does not want the city saved by someone with stained hands. Orestes kills Aegisthus and his mother, and at last Electra is content. The city goes up in flames and falls to the enemy, but Electra has satisfied her intense egotism. "I have my conscience, I have Orestes, I have justice, I have everything", she exclaims. The Furies in the play warn her that she is now the guilty

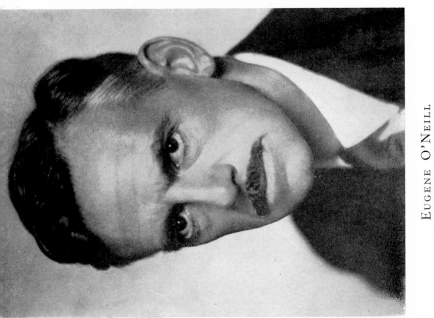

Eugene O'Neill

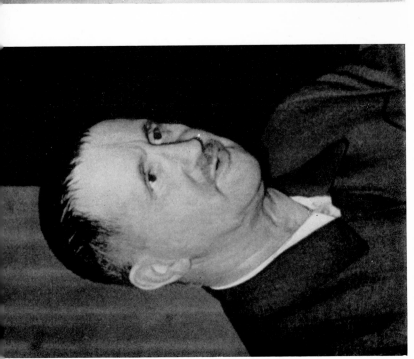

Bertholt Brecht

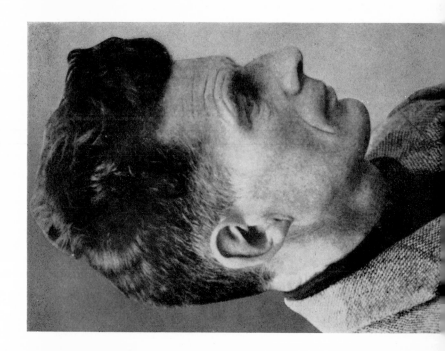

(*Above*) GRAHAM GREENE

(*Left*) SAMUEL BECKETT

ne, that she will never see Orestes again. Still Electra insists that she
as done right, for out of the flames of destruction she sees the birth of
new city. She sees the dawn.

Giraudoux makes three innovations in the classical legend. First of all
e introduces the Furies in the form of three little girls, the cheeky
tle schoolgirls of *Intermezzo* — they make fun of the palace gardener
a front of a visitor with such impudent remarks as "if flowers are to
mell sweet, gardeners must have a nasty odour". But there is a mystery
bout them; the gardener does not know where they have come from,
nd he can almost see them growing taller while he looks at them.
Then they know everything that has happened in the past (including
many things no one else knows) and seem to know the future with
qual certainty.

Throughout the action of the play the Furies grow until in the final
cene they are adults, the same age and size as Electra. They act as a
Greek Chorus, offering a malicious commentary on events and fore-
asting disaster. One can say that the play itself grows to full maturity
long with the symbolic Furies.

There is also a second character introduced who acts as a Chorus,
his time a beggar, who remains an obscure character and never reveals
is identity to us. Thirdly, we have the character of the gardener, who
s to marry Electra and so keep her out of harm's way (a plan of
Aegisthus's). But Electra is herself disposed to marry the gardener, since
he feels the need for a mother, and as the gardener says, he "was the
only man, absolutely the only man who could be a kind of mother".
The gardener is also a poet in his own way, and represents the qualities
of joy and love. He therefore disappears from the play at the end of
he first half, making a personal farewell 'lamento' to the audience.

For his next play, *Ondine*, presented on 27 April, 1939, Giraudoux
vas to return to Germany to borrow a fairy tale written by Frédéric
de la Motte Fouqué, but the subject is also another aspect of that
reated in *Intermezzo*; relations are broken between an individual soul
n the shape of a young mermaid and the soul of the universe to which
he belongs. A handsome German knight-errant, Hans von Wittenstein zu Wittenstein, meets Ondine in a fisherman's hut in the heart of
a Rhineland forest. Hans is a singularly prosaic knight, with little
magination; Ondine, who does not share the same destiny as a mortal,
s a portrait of youth, beauty, truth, innocence and fidelity. She immediately falls in love with the manly features of Hans, while Hans,
although he is engaged to a Countess Bertha, is prepared to forget

E

Bertha and marry Ondine. In obtaining permission from the King of the
Ondines to marry Hans, however, Ondine has to make a bargain:
should Hans ever be unfaithful to her he will die and Ondine, returning
to the ondine universe, will forget all about him.

Hans is anxious to introduce his wife to Court life, and the pomposity
of the Court scene enables Giraudoux to poke fun at human flattery,
pride, jealousy, and so on — manners unknown and incomprehensible
to Ondine. Here it is obvious that Ondine is a misfit. She knows immediately that she cannot hold Hans faithful. After a last attempt
Ondine leaves him and in desperation spreads the rumour that she has
been unfaithful first. The King of the Ondines knows the truth, and in
vain Ondine pleads with him:

KING OF THE ONDINES	The end draws near, Ondine.
ONDINE	Do not kill him.
KING	Our pact says we must. He's deceived you.
ONDINE	Yes, he's deceived me. Yes, I wanted to make you believe that I deceived him first. But do not judge the sentiments of men by our ondine standards. Often men who deceive love their wives. Often those who deceive are the most faithful . . .

The King shakes his head and tells her she is talking almost like a
woman. He is inexorable in his demands. Hans dies and Ondine no
longer recognises him. "How I would have loved him", are her farewell words as she leaves behind Hans' dead body.

Ondine, I think, should be considered Giraudoux's achievement in
the feminine ideal; he shows through Ondine, a woman who is more
than a woman, the impossibility for men to understand perfection.
What a misfortune it is to be merely human! In characters such as
Ondine it is not Giraudoux's intention to make a psychological study
of a woman; characters become rather symbols of virtues and vices
which act as masques, as in the drama of ancient Greece. There is, for
example, little differentiation of character between Geneviève,
Alcmena, Isabelle, Andromache and Ondine; we are introduced to the
same young woman revealing Giraudoux's conception of fidelity in a
world where love (in order to be faithful) is an essential condition.

Ondine, as we have noted, was produced in the spring of 1939. It
was to be the last play of the Jouvet-Giraudoux partnership; within a

w months Europe was at war, a year later France was under German
ccupation and it looked as though the whole free world was doomed.
iraudoux saw his hopes of an 'eternal friendship' between France and
ermany shattered; Jouvet, forbidden, it is said, to play Giraudoux, left
ith his company for South America. When he returned to Paris after
he liberation Giraudoux was dead.

It was perhaps inevitable that during the last period of his life
Giraudoux should lose some of his former optimism; no sensitive
riter could have remained uninfluenced by the times in which he
ved. Three full-length plays were written before his death early in
944; one notices a slightly different Giraudoux in all of them. In
odome et Gomorrhe, presented in October, 1943, under the Nazi
ccupation, an apprehensive fear that the destruction of the world is at
and seizes the imagination of Giraudoux; in *La Folle de Chaillot*, pre-
ented by Jouvet in December, 1945, we notice an element of bitterness
nd a failing of theatrical force never evident in his earlier work;
inally in his last play, *Pour Lucrèce*, presented by the company of
Madeleine Renaud and Jean-Louis Barrault in October, 1953 (nearly
en years after the death of Giraudoux and two after that of Jouvet),
he pervading note is despair for a purity which is to be found in this
vorld only in a flash of lightning every ten years. The play was
resented in London in 1958 under the title *Duet of Angels*.

There are many features to admire in all these plays; we recognise at
nce the unmistakable tones of the Giraudoux symphony, those
diosyncratic leaps into fantasy and poetry which are his genius and
which, of all his contemporaries, he alone could accomplish. But
somehow the symphony never reaches the world of *Intermezzo* or
Ondine or the impeccable crescendo in *Electre*. Is the answer to be
found in the absence of Jouvet? Giraudoux himself acknowledged his
debt in these words: "The actor is not only an interpreter, he is an
nspirer; he is the living mannequin through whom many authors quite
naturally personify a vision which is still vague; and the great actor is
a great inspirer."

The theme of *Sodome et Gomorrhe* is the relations between man,
woman and destiny. The message of God is that he wishes man and
woman to be united, to be a couple, an ideal couple, so that "you don't
think either of the husband or the wife. He is there, she is there.
That's all." But men, in their arrogance and stupidity, do not want this.
They wish to have an exchange of man and woman, and this fatal mis-
conception of the principle of love is the cause of all their misery.

Jean and Lia fail to stay united, and both retire to live with their own sex. Fire and destruction ravage the earth, but Jean keeps on pretending that all is well with the men, while Lia insists that all the women are happy. Thus the world is destroyed and humanity and civilisation reduced to ashes. It is alarming to think that the play, written before the use of the atom bomb, has grown in topicality — a justification, no doubt, for its excessive pessimism.

La Folle de Chaillot is an attack on another aspect of modern society, the unprincipled selfishness of exploiters against ordinary decent folk. The play is far from being a dull, doctrinaire, political satire. The Madwoman of Chaillot lives in a fantastic make-believe world of her own, and through her the harsh symbolic realism of the exploiters and their shady deals are contrasted with a dreamland where only such people as those who love honesty, beauty and the world are allowed.

The scene is the café, Chez Francis. The prospector tells a baron whose name he wants for 'respectability' reasons on the board of his newly formed company, that he has discovered oil in the least prospected place in the world — in Paris. Because the authorities have refused him permission to drill for oil and destroy the centre of the city, he plans to blow up the city architect's office. But the young man they entrusted to throw the bomb fails in his duty (he tried to commit suicide instead); the Madwoman takes him under her protection and learns from him about the evil people who are everywhere in the modern world.

To the Madwoman the solution is simple. She sends the prospector a bottle of petrol with a letter saying she has found this liquid in her cellar and invites him (and all his friends) to call and inspect her discovery. This, as she anticipates, brings along all the evil men, as well as some representatives of the press (Giraudoux once worked in a government press office), and three of their mistresses. She shows them all down into her cellar, where a staircase vanishes mysteriously into the underworld and whence there is no return. When Irma, the café dishwasher, asks where they have all gone, the Madwoman tells her: "Vanished. They were wicked. The wicked evaporate." Though there may be no such sane conclusion, though we can no longer believe like the Madwoman that the good of course inherit the earth, in a simpler and less sophisticated world how the Madwoman would be praised for her logic!

La Folle de Chaillot is not altogether a satisfactory play. With *Pour Lucrèce*, Giraudoux's last play (he finished it in 1943 after

odome et Gomorrhe), we have a more theatrically effective work, not
without those inimitable flashes of the exceptional but flashes also of an
irony and an unaccustomed bitterness. In taking the tragedy of
Lucretia, wife of Tarquinius Collatinus, whose beauty and virtues
inflamed the passion of Sextus and incited him to rape her (which led
Lucretia to commit suicide), Giraudoux has made a number of important variations in his treatment — the theme is one of his favourites,
the purity of love. First he transplants the action from Rome to a city
with only a Roman heritage, Aix-en-Provence; the period is of an
empire, but not that of the Roman Empire. In choosing the period of
Napoleon III Giraudoux enables this age-old theme to be identified in
a more modern, but not contemporary setting.

From the rise of the curtain we know this is tragedy, an all but
Racinian tragedy. The action is already far advanced in a state of crisis
at our first introduction to Lucile Blanchard (his Lucretia); within
twenty-four hours in the play she is the victim of her virtue; we sense
that Destiny is against her life, but her reasons for taking it are her
own. As she sips her ice in a café on the Cours Mirabeau, the wife of
the newly appointed imperial attorney at Aix has already as great a
reputation for fidelity and virtue as her husband has for severity; already she is surrounded by enemies. She came to a city of love, and
found that in the first month no man in Aix loved anyone else but her.
At the end of this month Aix had become, through her morality, a city
of original sin. She could not hide her utter contempt for the easy living,
for women like Paola, women who loved and lived for promiscuity.

Paola is the evil force of the play. She is as hot in temper as in sex;
harmless until hurt, until her husband learns through Lucile that she is
not an angel. Then her flood of revenge knows no mercy, nothing will
stem it. She is the most dangerous and the most eloquent woman in
Provence. She accuses Lucile of being quite another character from
what she pretends to be, a person who loves men but not her husband.
"Whether your virtue be the domino of holiness or lust, no matter.
You're all right within, buttoned up to the neck. But the day will come
when the buttons will burst . . ." It remains for Paola to slip a sleeping
drug into Lucile's glass, and in her unconsciousness to arrange her
body on a slightly disordered bed so that when she wakes up she will
believe the buttons have burst — and by none other than the Don
Juan of Aix, Count Marcellus.

The second act develops the intrigue. Marcellus is killed in a duel
fought with Paola's husband (he was a former lover of Paola) without

denying that he raped Lucile. In the last act Paola is all but triumphan
Lucile's husband has returned and far from listening sympathetically t
his wife's confession of the trick that has been played on her, orders he
out of the house. And by now, even though Lucile knows that she ha
not been raped, she prefers to keep the truth to herself. She admits tha
she doesn't love her husband, and when Paola prepares to celebrat
her victory, Lucile replies:

LUCILE   No last resort? What a mistake! There it is in my ow
          hands, my last resort. When you said a moment ago tha
          I was beaten, I could laugh at you, for it was there already
          It came to me from a little girl, of my own name, my ow
          age who, when she was ten years old, took an oath neve
          to acknowledge evil, and vowed to herself to prove, a
          the cost of her life if need be, that the world is a nobl
          place and human beings pure. This earth has become fo
          her a vile place stripped of all, this life only degradation
          that does not matter, it is not true; for she still honour
          her vow.[1]

The last words fall to Barbette, the sorceress of the play, who closes
the play with a tribute and a lament:

BARBETTE You have been violated all right. But not by Marcellus.
          That kind is curable. Half a hundred have been cured
          You quite thought so yourself. You got over it. But wha
          you can't get over is the stupidity of men, the grossness o
          men, the wickedness of men. That came to you all of a
          sudden. It was too much. A gentle being like you dies
          of it.[2]

The language of the play does much to conceal some of the obvious
failings, in the last act in particular. Can we really imagine that the
husband would be so utterly unsympathetic? — and it is even harder to
believe that Paola's husband would not have told the truth outright
and in no uncertain manner. We have a sense of deception unworthy
of Giraudoux.

There are those who accuse Giraudoux of being a literary dilettante
in the theatre, presumably either those who do not hold so highly the

[1] See original on p. 292.
[2] See original on p. 292.

purpose of the drama, or the existentialists, who see their paradise threatened by the influence of Giraudoux's universe, and who have therefore taken the critique of Giraudoux by their lord and master Sartre to heart. But all important writers have had their critics — Pirandello was responsible for riots in the streets of Rome and duels in Milan — and Giraudoux has had fewer than most. His reputation to-day in France stands exceedingly high, his plays have entered into the repertoires of the new provincial dramatic centres, and the possibility of Jouvet's prophecy that "if the language of Racine is still spoken in France in 200 years, the plays of Giraudoux will still be performed" should not lightly be dismissed. For Giraudoux believes in good theatre, the theatre of the great dramatists. And Giraudoux's success has been as remarkable as his plays were unorthodox and his ideas unlimited. He can have no imitators. Yet he does point a direction in which young writers can follow, he has led them to a point of departure from where they can advance. Just as Pirandello experimented gradually away from the naturalist camp, Giraudoux has succeeded in turning the semi-circle in theatrical fashions and has freed the theatre from the stifling atmosphere of naturalism. With his impressionistic interpretation of life Giraudoux has shown how the world we live in can respond to the poetic sweep of imagination. His way is always towards a less sophisticated universe, and his creation of this little world which is more than a world, inhabited by characters which are more than human, is the testament of faith which Giraudoux has bequeathed to a world in doubt.

THE MUSE WHO IS GRACE—A NOTE
ON PAUL CLAUDEL

PAUL CLAUDEL is first a poet and only secondly a dramatist. The reason is not because he lacks dramatic power — power is what attracts us most in Claudel's work — but because when he wrote his theatre between 1890 and 1924 the public was not ready for a return to religious drama, or indeed for plays which appeared to be 'difficult' at all. Not until the middle of the second world war, when Jean-Louis Barrault presented *Le Soulier de Satin* at the Comédie Française, did the public recognise the existence of a poet who was soon to be acknowledged as one of the great figures in French literature. Like Pirandello, Claudel sees everything connected with man threatened and transitory, nothing human can be saved from destruction and death. The development of Claudel's career was the development of his own faith from the time of his conversion to Catholicism, and we follow his progress from the violence of a Paradise lost in a transitional play like *Partage de Midi*, to Paradise regained, with the culmination of his thought in *Le Soulier de Satin*. Claudel invokes the mystical element in his plays; where reason ceases to throw light he uses a symbol to take its place. He reintegrates his characters into this symbolism, and through the powers of the mystical he can change a soul from darkness to light. Claudel's plays are not simple mystery plays, but plays to counter the Reformation, and to counter it in a style which demands attention. His plays offend many in their harsh, uncompromising Catholicism, for Claudel, never at any time a willing listener to the arguments of the other side, is a writer who insists; as Gide writes in his *Journal:* "When he talks, it is as if something were released within him; he proceeds by sudden affirmations and maintains a hostile tone even when you share his opinion." He requires an effort to be understood, but his work repays study both for the richness of his language and the sweep of his imagination. Here we have poetry as a means of divine communication.

FOUR

THE DISCOVERY OF PAUL CLAUDEL

"Le combat spirituel est aussi brutal que la bataille d'hommes."

ARTHUR RIMBAUD

IN the contemporary theatre, especially the French theatre, religion once again plays a vital rôle; believers and atheists, both sides contribute to and passionately disturb our living drama. This preoccupation with religious themes is a development of great significance; it certainly cannot be called a return to religious drama, since for the first time plays of a religious nature are being presented by a secular theatre. Instead of addressing our spiritual beliefs, an appeal is made to our intelligence and our doubts. Though certain of the plays of Claudel, *The Tidings Brought to Mary* for example, take us back to the Middle Ages, they do not follow the pattern of the medieval mystery play. The mystery plays were essentially ceremonials to be performed before a mass-crowd sometimes as large as those seen to-day at major sporting events; they were the work of several hands; they were not concerned with originality. It was, moreover, an audience of believers, sometimes resembling "a cathedral in motion". To-day, on the other hand, Christian playwrights turn from divine problems to directly human aspirations, viewing man from the vulnerable side of uncertainty, his hope and despair, light and darkness, the trial of strength between saints and the devil, the conflict between the divine and the diabolical.

Claudel, then, is a great Catholic writer. But can he be great to those who cannot accept the Catholic faith, and to those who feel that the acceptance of its dogmas imposes too severe a restriction on the freedom of thought of any author to allow for greatness? It might be suggested that such a view, itself sincere, denies the possibility of a

Catholic writer to be himself sincere. For a writer such as Claudel, it is his spiritual faith which completes the unity of his existence. His work is a record of man's struggle through successive stages towards the peace which comes with the "délivrance aux âmes captives" — the end of the pilgrimage of life. Claudel sees his faith as a source of light and hope in a world where darkness prevails. In his Paradise rediscovered, "the human soul", he wrote at the end of his life, "is something which is able to catch fire, in fact that was what it was created for, and when that takes place, or as we say 'the spirit descends on her', she manifests such joy, gives forth such a cry . . . that there is no other word except enthusiasm to describe it."

The appreciation of this enthusiasm, whether in its final stage in the "communication with God through poetry", or in man's earlier conflict between the call of the flesh and the vocation of the soul, can be of the greatest interest to non-Catholics as well. Claudel's plays yield themselves to anyone provided they are approached with the necessary tolerance to submerge one's own beliefs. They should be understood as a Catholic draws inspiration from the great paintings of the Renaissance. Obviously, those who would never set foot in Saint Peter's, or the materialists of the Anglo-Saxon school who view 'Popery' in the same light as the 'Wee Frees' in the Highlands, are not the audience for Claudel. Even those with open minds will require to initiate themselves into the meaning of his symbols which act as a key to his expression if they wish to appreciate the real significance of the struggle his characters fight against sin and temptation. Claudel's is a difficult drama even for Catholics; his plays never allow departure from the terrible reality of punishment for those who break the rules, and there is the necessity to be superhuman not to yield to the forbidden. Claudel's plays are intensely rewarding for those who wish to explore them. More than anything, it is his power which sweeps us along with him. He is, as Jean Vilar says, writing in *La Revue Théâtrale* (October, 1946): "The only contemporary dramatic poet who is able to invigorate us is a Catholic poet, enclosed in a confessional world against which all other religions, philosophies and the modern beliefs of mankind combine to assail." Claudel's ambitions are vast, he describes the setting of *Le Soulier de Satin*, for example, as being the world. He wishes to explore the whole range of human experience, and the only difficulty is to find the means of communicating our perception. He demands that an audience should complete what it sees by imagination; in other words, he asks for the collaboration of the audience. But just as his plays are intolerant and exacting he can incite the tempesr of others. For this reason naturalist critics with a strong anti-Catholic bias are not likely to accept the world which Claudel introduces into his plays.

There is also the language problem, where it is almost impossible to give an adequate rendering in translation of the strange force of Claudel's poetry. In his penetrating study, *Maria Cross*, of the imaginative patterns in a group of modern Catholic writers, Mr. Donat O'Donnell draws attention to the symbolism which acts as a 'currency' in the interpretation of the meaning of Claudel's work, and to two words, 'gold' and 'water', in particular. As Mr. O'Donnell explains in his essay, the French 'or' (gold) has a significance quite different for French ears to that which it has for English-speaking people. 'Or', in French, immediately suggests 'corps' and 'morts', which have clear associations with the idea of communion and death which are the signposts of Claudel's writing. Water can be found to have similar associations with 'la mer' and 'la mère', or the adjective 'amère' (bitter) and the similar sounds of 'l'amour' and 'la mort'. How can these be expressed in English? The result surely is that the power of Claudel's poetry is never so direct, so forceful in another language, and this may be as great a difficulty in the appreciation of his work outside France as is the religious content, which is not nearly such an insuperable barrier.

Though Claudel wrote the majority of his plays without a view to stage production, he had an intensely dramatic aptitude for the theatre, and if only, like Giraudoux, he had found his Jouvet, he would have been as great a dramatist as poet. Consider, for example, the insight he gives into the theatre in the following speech from *L'Echange* (1933):

The theatre. You don't know what it is? Really?
There's the stage and the auditorium — the house.
It all being enclosed, people come there in the evening and sit
        down row behind row, watching.
. . . They are watching the curtain in front of the stage.
And what there is behind once it rises.
And then something happens on the stage as if it were the real
        thing.
. . . I watch them, and the house becomes nothing but live flesh
        clothed
Packed like flies from floor to ceiling.
And I see hundreds of white faces.

Man grows bored and the ignorance he was born with sticks to
    him
And not knowing a thing about how it begins or ends, that's what
    makes him go to the theatre.
And he is looking at himself, with his hands resting on his knees.
And he cries and he laughs, and he hasn't the least desire to go
    away.
And I have a look too and I know the box-office man is there
        Who knows that to-morrow
His books will be checked, and the unfaithful mother
        Whose child has just taken ill
And the man who has just committed a theft for the first time,
And the one who has done nothing all day.
And they are all watching and listening as though they were
    asleep.[1]

Had he had an opportunity of seeing the immediate effects of his plays
on an audience as he wrote them, Claudel would have been a greater
dramatist, but he could not have given us plays of greater dramatic
content or literary value. When he died in 1955, he was the last of a
generation which produced a number of outstanding figures in French
literature. To-day one fears this golden age is finished.

Paul Claudel was born in 1868 at Villeneuve-sur-Frère, in Aisne, a
countryside which was to teach him in his childhood the reality of
being ever close to the land, and give him a feeling of the freshness of
nature which is to be found everywhere in his poetry. Just as a painter
learns to contemplate a landscape, so Claudel drew inspiration from his
own meditations. He was fourteen when he came to live in Paris and
attend the Lycée Louis-le-Grand. At this time he had abandoned his
early religious instruction, and believed — "what most of the so-called
cultured people believed at that time" — in a materialistic goal.
Little by little he fell into a state of despair. He tells how over many
months he had watched his grandfather consumed by a cancer of the
stomach, and he was haunted by the fear of death.

The revelation came to him on Christmas Day, 1886, when, for
nothing better to do, he attended Christmas Mass at Notre Dame. He
found the service somewhat ordinary, but decided to stay on for
Vespers. He writes: "And it was then that the event took place which
was to dominate my whole life. In one instant my heart was touched and

[1] See original on p. 292.

I believed. I believed with such a strength of adherence, with such a profound conviction, that there was no room for any sort of doubt. And since then all books, all the hazards of a troubled life, have been incapable of shaking my faith, or in truth, of touching it."

But though Claudel had, as it were, made his 'divine' conversion, he had still to make his spiritual one, which was to be a hard struggle. For he was plunged into a new world, a world repugnant to all his previously held convictions. He disliked priests. He had not a single Catholic friend. He did not dare to announce his conversion even to his family. During this period he attended the Ecole du Droit and the Ecole des Sciences Politiques and entered the French diplomatic service.

Religion became his dominant interest. He found comfort in the works of Arthur Rimbaud. Pascal answered many of his doubts. He read anew the Bible. But it was *La Somme Théologique* of St. Thomas Aquinas that was to enable him to make his spiritual conversion. He found there a key which enabled him to construct almost a grammatical interpretation of the universe. It is not our purpose here to examine in more than a brief outline the religious thought and development of Claudel, such as is essential to any understanding of his drama. The Catholicism of Claudel is that divine truth is outside us. God exists whether we wish him to or not. Man is not the source of religion.

We must not accuse Claudel of diminishing the dramatic intensity of his plays as he becomes more at peace with his own mind. Though his earlier plays are different in mood from his later works (Jean-Louis Barrault has called *Tête d'Or* his 'sap'; *Partage de Midi* his 'ordeal' and *Le Soulier de Satin* his 'synthesis'), the world of Claudel remains a dark world, where everything related to the flesh is threatened and salvation can only be found by transcending earthly things and seeking the message of God. His characters are on trial. They struggle with their minds and their flesh and find that a human being cannot be the supreme end of another human being. The quintessence of Claudel has been explained in some notes published in "*Cahiers de la compagnie Madeleine Renaud — Jean-Louis Barrault*" (1953) where Claudel gives us quite a new key to himself and his writings:

The mind . . . yes . . . but egotism, avarice, being hard, dry vain — the things God most detests.
The flesh? True, the need of the other one, being a slave to the other and recognising that the other cannot be reached, something not unlike hell.

But above the flesh there is the super-, the trans-flesh — there is
the heart which too is flesh, that heart which has made us and
knows more about it than we do. If God placed it in our bosom it
is so that it may find its echo in some other person's.

In 1893 Claudel left for his first post as vice-consul at Boston in the
United States. From 1895–1909 he occupied different posts in central
and southern China. In 1909 he was sent to Austria as consul in
Prague, and in 1914 he found himself Consul-General at Hamburg on
the outbreak of war. During the war he was in Italy, Brazil, and at the
time of the armistice was Minister in Denmark. In 1921 he was appointed French ambassador in Tokyo, in 1927 he became ambassador
to the United States, and in 1933 he was ambassador in Brussels. And
yet he managed to combine this active career with a no less active
career as a writer. Neither career seems to have imposed on the other
it might almost be said that he gained from being absent from France
in that he never came under the influence of any school; Claudel was
his own 'maître'. No wonder he infuriated those who believed that he
was wasting his talent as a diplomat, no wonder Antonin Artaud one
day announced after a performance of one of the acts of *Partage de
Midi*, "The act we have just presented to you is by Paul Claudel, poet,
ambassador and traitor."

*

Claudel was twenty when he wrote his first play, *Tête d'Or*. "A
twenty one is afraid of nothing", he apologised to Jean-Louis Barrault
when he refused to grant him permission to present the play. "It is no
because the play lacks sincerity. Good heavens no! It has too much
But it is precisely this sincerity — crude, clumsy, horribly naïve —
which makes me shudder." Nevertheless, *Tête d'Or* is a remarkable
first play, and one of the important plays Claudel wrote. It was to be
Baurrault's choice for the opening of the Odeon under his directorship
in October 1959.

Tête d'Or is a young adventurer, so called because of the golden
colour of his hair. He believes he is a law unto himself, and respect
neither law nor religion. Having saved his country from defeat by
taking command of the army and driving out the enemy, he now feel
that he has the right, through his strength, to overthrow the government. This he does, and proclaims himself King. He presents himself a

leader who will lead the nation to conquest; he does not offer peace
nd security. The old King is killed, and he drives the beautiful
'rincess, who represents beauty and joy, into exile. Tête d'Or then
eads his army over the whole of Europe and to the frontiers of Asia.
Everywhere he is victorious. He has one last battle to fight, in which he
s mortally wounded. Everything has been in vain. Before he dies he
ears a cry of anguish, and sees crucified to a tree the Princess he had
Iriven from her country. She pardons him, and they die side by side.
The soldiers return, having won a futile victory.

Here Claudel introduces the first temptation of man, that of power
nd possession. But no matter what success a dictator may achieve, he
s doomed to failure, for no man can seek to rule the earth. In his next
lay, *La Ville*, this barren victory is followed by redemption. Avare
s a man like Tête d'Or, seeking power through violence and destruc-
ion. Coeuvre is a poet restlessly seeking for art, and refuses to join
he side of Avare and Lala, Coeuvre's wife, who has deserted him.
instead he finds his answer in entering the Church and devoting his life
o the service of God. In the last act Coeuvre has become a bishop.
Avare, although he has achieved power, cannot rebuild the havoc he
as caused. He hands over his power to the Prince Ivors, the son of
Coeuvre and Lala. The young prince receives his conversion from
Coeuvre — the new city will be built not by the negative forces of life
out with the spiritual faith which gives continuity . . .

The construction of this early work leaves much to be desired and
annot be said to be theatrically effective, even when given such an
xcellent production as that of Jean Vilar and his Théâtre National
Populaire. Instead of dramatic tension mounting act by act, the drama
n *La Ville* subsides and gives way to sermon. The young Claudel
as revealed for us in this play many of his important ideas — ideas
hat he was to develop in his subsequent work more effectively. Yet
even here he has mastered the use of a poetic language which is always
admirable. But the dramatic content is not in harmony, and the play
acks the power that is so marked in Claudel's better work. As it is,
he play lends itself better to reading than to performance.

L'Echange (1893–1894) is a very different type of play, much smaller
n dimensions, human and bourgeois in appeal, and yet with an ab-
orbing dramatic conflict which raises the play to Claudelian tragedy.
An American, Louis Lane, soon finds that he has no time for his French
oride Marthe, and is willing to 'exchange' her for a pocketful of dollars
vith a rich American, Thomas Pollock Nageoire. She is, after all, his

property. Marthe believes in the beauty and dignity of marriage; s]
will not leave Louis. An actress, Léchy Elbernon, reveals to Marthe th
she is already Louis's mistress. But Léchy, who loves Louis, know
herself how slight her hold is over him, and threatens that she will ki
him should he desert her. She begs Marthe to help her prevent thi
Marthe refuses, for what is to be must be. Louis is murdered.

L'Echange presents character studies drawn more to types than (
interest as individuals, but the play holds an audience. It might almo
be regarded as an exercise in play-writing, a model for instructio
before embarking on *Partage de Midi*, where Claudel reaches th
summit of his art.

"You know that I never wanted to discuss *Partage de Midi* for th
theatre," Claudel wrote to Jean-Louis Barrault, "and that I have lon
ago recalled from circulation all the copies of the first edition. It is a
ordeal which I suffered so strongly from in my youth that its effec
have accompanied me all my life. Even to-day the play lives . . . wha
prevents me to-day is a kind of shame 'there are cries that a man has ne
the right to utter. *Partage de Midi* is such a cry.' It embarrasses me as
I were naked."

The subject of *Partage de Midi* is the limitations of love. In this or
play Claudel places all the chances and all the obstacles of life. Th
characters do not seek a conjugal love, but that of a satisfied passio
The argument is both banal and complicated, but that has little cor
sequence. Claudel admits this in the preface to the 1949 edition of th
play: "Nothing apparently could be more commonplace that the two
fold theme this drama is built around; that of adultery — husband an
wife and lover — and that of the conflict between religious vocatio
and the call of the flesh. Nothing more commonplace but at the sam
time nothing of so long standing and I would almost venture to say –
nothing more sacred. For the idea of that conflict between the La
and Grace (in the most varied and unexpected forms), between God an
man, between man and woman, runs right through the Old Testamer
stories richest in significance."

From the rise of the curtain we sense an atmosphere of conflict whic
is rare, we are gripped almost with an element of terror. We are on
vessel bound for China, it is midday and the ship is somewhere in th
middle of the Indian Ocean. There are four characters. Ysé, a youn
and beautiful wife of a prosaic trader De Ciz, meets Mesa, an intense
unhappy man who has a noble and spiritual disposition. On boar
there is also Amalric, a forthright man and something of an adventure

He knew Ysé before she was married, and is trying to have an affair with her. Ysé, however, rejects his advances, for she is attracted to Mesa.

So the four of them meet in blazing solitude. It is "midday in the heavens, midday in the centre of our lives". For midday is the central hour, the moment in life when one attains what one seeks. It is an instantaneous moment of obligatory choice. It can be one of chosing between dream and action. It is the supreme moment of freedom. It is the most difficult moment in life, for it is the moment when man is the farthest removed from God. It is the moment when he has to bear the heaviest responsibility, the responsibility of the direction of his soul.

Ysé senses in Mesa something strange and beyond her comprehension. "You don't understand me", Mesa tells her. "I understand that you are unhappy." She has tempted him, and Mesa is willing to become her lover. But Ysé suddenly becomes frightened. There is something wrong in her loving a mind like Mesa's. She tells him:

Ysé   No, no, you must not love me.
      No, Mesa, you must not love me.
      It would not be right at all.
      You know that I am a poor weak woman.
      Remain the Mesa I need.

.   .   .

Tell me you will not love me. Say: Ysé, I will not love you.[1]

The second act takes place in the European cemetery of Hong Kong. Mesa and Ysé are to meet again and be left alone together, for De Ciz has to go away for a month. Ysé knows that the temptation will be too powerful for her to resist, and implores her husband not to leave her, but in vain. Alone with Mesa, Ysé gives herself to him: "I am yours, I am not holding back, you may do as you wish." But their passion is joyless, because they know that their love is a theft; a sense of guilt is between their union.

Ysé   And what are the others to us? Since you are unique and I
      am unique

See original on p. 293.

And your voice stirs my very entrails like a cry that canno
  be borne
And I rise up towards you with difficulty, a thing enormous
  massive, blind, silent and filled with desire.
But what we desire is not at all to create, but to destroy and oh
Nothing exists any more but you and me, or in you but me
  or in me but being possessed by you, madness and tenderness
  rage to destroy you, no longer hampered
Detestably by those garments of flesh, and those cruel teetl
  in my heart,
Not cruel at all!
Ah it is not happiness I bring you, but your death and with i
  mine.[1]

A year passes. This tragic love has brought happiness to neithe
Mesa nor Ysé. She decides to escape from this passion which resemble
death. She escapes to Amalric's plantation on the mainland, and bearing
Mesa's child, becomes Amalric's mistress.

Mesa searches everywhere for her and eventually traces her. She is i
great danger, for there has been a rising of the Chinese, and the Euro
peans are being massacred. In order to prevent their being taken aliv
Amalric has laid a charge under the house so that they will not fall int
Chinese hands. While Amalric and Ysé are preparing themselves fo
death, Mesa arrives with the means to save Ysé. De Ciz is dead, he ha
a pass through the Chinese lines, and they can marry. But, seeing Ysé
he reproaches her, asks why she has betrayed him thus; she remain
silent. Mesa speaks:

MESA Tell me, Ysé, it is no longer the midday sun's full blaze.
        You remember that Ocean of ours?
        But the lamp of the grave is shining on your cheek, and you
          ear, and the corner of your brow
        And reflected in your eyes, your eyes in the mirror . . .
                      He blows out the lamp
        The lamp's little flame is out. And extinguished at the same time
        The last sunshine of our love, that great mid-August sun
        Where we said our last adieu in the light devouring, separating
          us, as we desperately

[1] See original on p. 266.

Signalled to one another across the widening distance.
Adieu, Ysé, you did not know me at all! That great treasure
  I bear within me
You were not able to uproot
To transplant, I was not able to give it. It is not my fault.
Oh yes! It is our fault and our punishment.
  I ought to have given everything,
And that is what you have not forgiven.

                                                    Silence.[1]

Amalric enters. By her silence Mesa learns that Ysé prefers to stay with
Amalric. The two men fight, and Mesa is injured. Amalric takes Mesa's
two passes and Ysé has to make her choice. She choses Amalric and,
preparing to leave with him, strangles her child by Mesa. She believes
he has made her choice, but at the last minute she returns to the
condemned house. She has decided on certain death with Mesa rather
than life with Amalric. At the frontier between life and eternity they
discover the realisation of love. It is not the midday union, but the
midnight union which has made this possible. The title, *Partage de
Midi*, is thus symbolic.

His next play, *L'Otage* (1908–1909), is the first part of a trilogy, of
which *Le Pain dur* and *Le Père humilié* are the other two plays, covering the period between 1812 and 1871. *L'Otage* covers the post-
revolutionary years 1812–1814, but it would be wrong to view the play
purely as a historical drama condemning the French Revolution. The
story introduces Sygne de Coûfontaine, a girl from a noble family who
were executed at the Revolution, who has with difficulty managed to
restore the family property. Her cousin Georges, the only other
member of the family who escaped, is attracted to her through the
mutual pride of the family and distress at what has happened. They
pledge their engagement. Through Georges Sygne becomes the
possessor of a vital secret, that the man he has asked her to protect in
her house is none other than the Pope, whom Georges has rescued from
imprisonment. Toussaint Turelure, the Republican prefect of the
district, the executioner of the parents of both Georges and Sygne,
guesses the identity of their guest and presents Sygne with a choice
which is to her none less than martyrdom. Ambitious to possess what
Sygne has so diligently restored, he demands that she should marry
him. Should she refuse, the Pope will be sent back into captivity.

See original on p. 266.

Sygne, although at first unwilling to make this sacrifice, eventuall
submits and breaking off her engagement to Georges she agrees
marry Turelure. She prefers to be true to her religion at the cost of h
own honour. From this stage on she ceases to care about life, her min
in unconscious, her spirit extinguished. She exists. The play ends on
stroke of irony, Georges has been forced to seek Turelure's suppo:
some years later for the restoration of the monarchy, and thus con
promises his own honour. In attempting to kill Turelure the bull
hits Sygne, and Georges and Sygne both die. Claudel has provided tw
endings to this play, one in which Sygne dies at peace with the Churc
by pardoning Turelure, the other in which she dies defiant. If religio
demands the first ending, the play demands the latter.

The marriage of Mesa and Ysé had taken place on the frontiers c
eternity, but it was a barren marriage. The marriage between Sygr
and Turelure had filled Sygne's life with disgust; it was inhuman an
could only engender hatred. In *L'Annonce faite à Marie* (1912, bein
the final version of *La Jeune Fille Violaine*, which dates back to 189
and 1898 in first and second versions respectively) Violaine has to sacr
fice everything in this world through no fault of her own. The darkne:
which separates her from Jacques is only removed in their final meetin
before her death; for the first time they understand each other in perfe
accord.

The Tidings Brought to Mary is a mystery play which admirab
conveys the atmosphere of the Middle Ages, an age of faith, but also c
suffering and darkness, of fate and destruction. We find in this symbol
play an avalanche of human misery which descends on characters i
equipped to struggle against it without an appeal to God's mercy. Th
good suffer with the evil, Violaine is a victim for her holiness, and h:
to suffer a terrible ordeal and fate for her compassion. Mara, her siste
who knows only jealousy, hatred, revenge, suffers less but finds n
happiness when she achieves her ambitions.

In the prologue Violaine forgives Pierre de Craon, an architect wh
once made an attempt on Violaine's honour, but who has since bee
smitten with leprosy. Moved by sympathy, Violaine gives him a kis
Her father, Anne Vecors, master of Combernon, announces that he
going on a pilgrimage to the Holy Land, and hands over his esta
during his absence to Jacques, to whom he also betrothes his daughte
Violaine. No sooner has he gone than Mara, his younger daughte
who is secretly in love with Jacques, says that she will kill herself shou
the marriage ever take place. Moreover, she has seen Violaine kiss th

eper. She does not need to carry out her threat, however, since Violaine as contracted the disease and is banished to die in the distant woods. Mara is able to marry Jacques and a daughter is born to them, Aubaine.

Some years later Aubaine dies, and Mara decides to seek Violaine, now a blind and holy recluse, and beg her to work a miracle. At first Violaine refuses, saying she is not a saint, but she yields and Aubaine is reborn. The child has now been given Violaine's eyes, which causes Mara a fresh wave of jealousy. Realising that Jacques still remembers his love for Violaine, Mara kills her sister.

Such a brief outline is quite inadequate to give an impression of the quality of the play, through the richness of Claudel's poetry, or indeed suggest the emotions it disturbs. With *Le Soulier de Satin* it becomes impossible, for this vastly complex play — indeed, not one play but several related — is beyond the limits of a satisfactory synopsis. We shall therefore discuss some of the situations and the ideas rather than deal with this, Claudel's testament of life, which contains all that is essential in the evolution of his poetry and vision. Before we consider *Le Soulier de Satin*, let us mention in passing the remaining plays of Claudel, which include *Le Pain dur* and *Le Père humilié* of the *L'Otage* trilogy; *Le Livre de Christophe Colomb* (1927); and two short comedies, *L'Ours et la Lune* (1917) and *Protée* (second version, 1926. One writer has compared this satire as being close in *esprit* to Giraudoux's writing). These plays, however, add little to the body of Claudel's works, though that is not to say they should be dismissed. *Le Pain dur*, in particular, is among the most effective of Claudel's plays from the dramatic point of view. It is a natural sequel to *L'Otage* with Turelure remaining as avid as before both for money and love. We see how he hates his son because he reminds him of Sygne, and we watch the development of this hatred until the son is driven to make an attempt on his father's life.

In *Le Père humilié* we meet the next generation, Pensée, a beautiful girl who has been born blind as if she were paying for her parents' sins. Pensée is not specially religious, but she falls in love with Orian, who feels the spiritual 'call'. We see the familiar Claudelian theme unfold, this time against a definite historical setting which plays a leading rôle in the plot. Orian is willing to renounce everything for Pensée, but the Franco-Prussian war breaks out. He has a duty to do, and Pensée persuades him to go to the front. He never returns.

Le Livre de Christophe Colomb is interesting for the possibilities it offers for an imaginative *mise en scène*. The book is published with an introductory essay on "Drama and Music", delivered at Yale in 1930 where Claudel explained some of his basic ideas for making the theatre more than a theatre. He believes that instead of a static set we should allow pictures, suggested by poetry and music, to appear on a screen which would open a road to dreams, remembrances and imagination. "Why," he asks, "when a flood of music, action, and poetry entrance the minds of an audience, reply with a false heaven as crude and trivial as a café mural? Why not utilise the screen as a magic mirror where all sorts of shades and suggestions more or less vague and designs may pass, follow, and eliminate each other. Why not open the door of that troubled world where the idea gives birth to sensation and where the ghost of the future unites with the shadow of the past?"

If Paul Claudel had been born a generation later, he would doubtless have set himself the task of "discovering the formula", as he puts it, to unite the new arts with the old, and embody them within the framework of the living theatre. For his greatest work, *Le Soulier de Satin* offers the severest test for any producer; it is total theatre and requires all the resources of the modern theatre — and more. The play is not divided into acts, but into 'Days' of uncertain duration. The full text which took Claudel over five years to write, is published in two volumes, but an abbreviated version was used for the Comédie Française production in 1943.

"The scene of this play is the world," Claudel writes, "and more especially Spain at the close of the sixteenth, unless it be the opening of the seventeenth century." The play roams far and wide, its mood changes from that of medieval mystery to classical tragedy, and at times it has an element of the ducking-stool of farce; each scene is a marked contrast ("it is essential", notes Claudel, in a word to producers, "that the scenes follow each other without the least interruption"). But we must not suppose that *Le Soulier de Satin* is an abstract work, on the contrary, nothing is obscure and the purpose and direction are never hidden. We are, it is true, very far from the real world, and it would be foolish to consider the events that take place as if they were true. That is not the significance of the work. It is concerned with the invisible, what takes place inside the mind, and Claudel uses symbolism in a concrete sense to enter there.

The subject of *Le Soulier de Satin* has been described as a resumé of *Tête d'Or* and the conclusion of *Partage de Midi;* whereas *Partage de Midi* is a transitional play in Claudel's career, *Le Soulier de Satin* affirms vigorously and clearly. Human love and divine passion; the fusion of two beings into a single whole. Carnal love is weaker than the union of souls; the love of the body may be strong, but that of the mind is always more powerful. Just as Tristan loved Yseult, Mesa Ysé, so Rodrigue in *Le Soulier de Satin* loves Prouhèze, because they were made for one another. We are concerned, however, not only with the desire to love, but desires under many forms, power, possession, envy. To all these there is only the Christian solution.

Rodrigue and Dona Prouhèze in *Le Soulier de Satin* replace Mesa and Ysé in *Partage de Midi*. Rodrigue is like Tête d'Or, full of ambition. Dona Prouhèze has already met Rodrigue, and although she has only seen him for a short time she knows that she loves him. But since she is married, it is a love without hope. Rodrigue, for his part, knows that nothing can extinguish his love for her. As he explains:

> And can you imagine the body capable alone of kindling in mine
> such deep desire?
> What I love is not what in her can melt away, flee me, be absent
> and cease one day to love me, it is the very cause of her, what
> brings forth beneath my kisses life, it is not death!
> If she learned from me that she is not born for death, if of her I
> ask her immortality, that star which, unknowing, at her core
> she is,
> ... Ah, how then could she refuse me?
> It is not what in her is cloudy, mixed, unsure, that I would ask,
> what is perishable, neutral, inert,
> It is the stark naked being, the pure life,
> It is that love, strong as I am when filled with desire like a great
> raw flame, like laughter in my face
> Ah, might she give it to me (I droop and night is closing over
> my eyes)
> Might she give it to me, yet she must not give it to me,
> Never will her body, dear though it be, give me contentment
> enough,
> Never except through one another shall we succeed in over-
> coming death.
> Out of orange mingled with violet comes the purest red.[1]

Rodrigue is wounded, and other difficulties are placed in their way. Prouhèze's husband decides that the best way to enable his wife to

See original on p. 267.

resist temptation is to place in her way a greater temptation. He arranges for her to assume command of a North African garrison, with as her lieutenant a Don Camille, who makes no secret of his fierce love for Prouhèze.

After some years Prouhèze's husband dies, and she immediately sends a letter to Rodrigue. This gets mislaid, and only reaches him after ten years. Meanwhile for reasons other than love Prouhèze marries Don Camille, so that when Rodrigue eventually arrives it is too late. Prouhèze meets him on board his ship in what is one of the most moving scenes of the play. She refuses to escape with him from Don Camille, for she has given her word that she will return — although she knows that certain death awaits her at the fort, which is to be blown up in order to forestall an attack by the Moors. For Prouhèze realises that she can never love Rodrigue on earth:

PROUHÈZE   Would you have had me then, noble Rodrigue, let you
            hold an adulteress in your arms?
            And later, after Don Pélage's death, launch that appeal
            to you
            Who, it were better perhaps, should not hear it.
            I should only have been a woman soon to die on your
            heart and not that undying star for whom you thirst.[1]

Rodrigue is about to prevent her leaving, but she challenges him to say one word and she will stay. He cannot prevent her going.

The love of Rodrigue and Prouhèze, it must be remembered, is only a part of *Le Soulier de Satin*, although it is of integral importance to the dramatic conflict. In a work of the magnitude of *Le Soulier* we cannot help noticing Claudel's faults (especially in the Fourth Day), but we feel that compared with the conception of the play and the clarity of its expression, the occasional momentary lapses unworthy of such a subject do not destroy it, but are themselves destroyed. Whatever may be the task of a critic to analyse a play, *Le Soulier de Satin* inspires enthusiasm or nothing.

Critics are inevitably divided about Claudel, but then, like everybody, critics like to ride their Dada's and hobby-horses, and it would be a dull world if everybody was infinitely and insincerely polite. But it is not the critics who have discovered Claudel, it is Claudel who has discovered his public. André Gide once wrote that though the public

[1] See original on p. 294.

hinks that it chooses its authors, it is in fact the artist who chooses his public. This is certainly the case of Claudel, who had already written the majority of his plays before he had secured one performance in the theatre. Even after Copeau had presented *L'Annonce faite à Marie* in 1912, and *L'Echange* and *L'Otage* before the 1914 war, it was not until forty years later that the French public had come to treat its theatre seriously enough to admit religious and philosophical subject matter. As for production outside France, a Claudel play is fragile, however universal his theme may be. *L'Otage* is perhaps his best-known play in Britain, and recently has proved admirably suited for radio. But the language difficulty together with the idiosyncratic methods of Claudelian craftsmanship and spiritual expression prevent his plays ever being widely appreciated outside France, just as Shaw and even Ibsen have never quite fitted into the French *esprit*. Claudel will always be one of the major French poets, and in his creation of plays which restore the place of religion in the modern theatre he has introduced something which is entirely new in French dramatic literature.

FIVE

T. S. ELIOT AS DRAMATIST

"To my mind, the drama took a wrong turning when the demand for realism led it to abandon the ornament of verse."

SOMERSET MAUGHAM, *The Summing Up* (1938)

"If the poetic drama is to reconquer its place, it must, in my opinion, enter into overt competition with prose drama."

T. S. ELIOT, *Poetry and Drama*

ALTHOUGH Eliot comes from another generation than Claudel, and his environment and character are so completely different from that of the great French master, his point of departure as a dramatist traces a parallel course to that which Claudel was attempting in his plays thirty or forty years previously. There are the same liturgical echoes of ritual and the same search for a poetical language which would come to terms with the balanced rhythm of a sentence and be able to lead from ordinary conversational idiom to the rhetoric of chant and the intimacy of poetry. Religion also plays a major rôle in Eliot's drama, and he approaches the theme of 'sin and expiation' with a religious zeal as urgent as in Claudel's own works. These similarities are often overlooked in the different direction Eliot has subsequently turned since *Murder in the Cathedral* and *The Family Reunion* and in the concessions he has made to the demands of naturalistic theatre. The work of Claudel and Eliot cannot be compared, the one in terms of the other. Both are among the greatest poets of their age, but whereas Claudel was primarily a poet and only viewed the theatre as a medium for his poetical expression whether audiences were there, ready to accept his work, or not, Eliot is a poet who has turned dramatist, willing o "discipline his poetry" and put it "on a very thin diet in order to adapt it to the needs of the stage". He hopes "there may be a later stage, when (and if) the understanding of theatrical technique has become second nature, at which he can dare to make more liberal use of poetry and take greater liberties with ordinary colloquial speech".[1] In the meantime Eliot has gone more than half-way to meet the public, accustomed as it is to the conventions of polite naturalistic comedy, and he has been accepted as a popular dramatist. Claudel remained a poet and had to wait nearly half a century for recognition by play-goers; Eliot, on the strength of five plays has become one of the most discussed dramatist of the age.

Here we have the major difference in temperament of the two poets. The one goes his own way regardless, the other is determined to intervene directly and "bring poetry into the world in which the audience lives". Claudel does not restrict his inspiration; Eliot is a conservative, too consciously a critic to wander an inch from the theories of drama he so carefully propounds beforehand. The best criticism of Eliot's plays has been written by Eliot himself, and few theoreticians have proved their views so convincingly in practice. Eliot, a great poet, has become both master and pupil of dramatic theory, yet however important his plays have been, he has still to give us his *chef-d'oeuvre*. His best play, *Murder in the Cathedral*, is noble in its theme and treatment, but lacks the natural abundance of creative genius. His cold, austere intellectuality is apparent in all his plays, and the more his plays have moved from spiritual to secular, the more onerous this has become in making his plays acceptable; if *The Cocktail Party* remains abstract, *The Confidential Clerk* aims to introduce human characters but not even *The Elder Statesman*, described as his "most human play", succeeds. Presented realistically, no wonder a play like *The Confidential Clerk* was roughly handled when it was performed at the first Festival International d'Art Dramatique in Paris in 1954. It is not surprising that *Le Monde* compared it to "a pyramid of happenings as unlikely as they are artificial", while *Le Figaro* said that "one has the impression of opening the door of a refrigerator". Eliot in this play would seem to have become a naturalistic poet, where naturalism has won and every vestige of poetry has, as planned, been removed. Lorca, it is true, did the same in *The House of Bernarda Alba*, where he claimed that there was not "a jot of poetry" to be found; but Lorca radiated his play with

Poetry and Drama.

an intense and personal poetic vision, which in his present theatrical timidity Eliot seems unable to achieve.

The journey Eliot has made from *Murder in the Cathedral* to *The Elder Statesman* has been essential to his development, and others may benefit from his experience. Yet this writer believes it to have been a mistaken direction, for in diluting his poetry Eliot has removed the power which, above all others, he possesses. As has so often been noted by critics, Eliot's poetry seems by nature dramatic. Had *Murder in the Cathedral* been a beginning instead of an end of his full use of verse, Eliot might not have the box-office success he now enjoys, but his contribution to religious drama and dramatic literature might have resulted in works comparable to *The Waste Land* and *Four Quartets* in dramatic form. He might have given us a spiritual work in the tradition of Dante (on whom Eliot is an authority) and produced an English *Soulier de Satin*. We seem to have waited in vain for the time he would feel able to make "more liberal use of poetry". For this writer would forego twenty *Confidential Clerk's* for one *Murder in the Cathedral*, and would sacrifice the whole of Eliot's drama for his poetry.

So many critics have had their say on Eliot's career (not to mention Eliot himself) that the ground has already been well trodden; yet some attempt must be made to comment on the development of Eliot's career as a dramatist in order to argue that *Murder in the Cathedral* surpasses anything he has since written for the theatre, and that though Eliot himself believed that it only had a "negative merit" and was a "dead end", this in fact need not have been the case. It will further be suggested that remoulding the poetical drama in the naturalistic furnace and shaping the verse into contemporary idiom is not the solution for poetical drama. Somehow an audience must be found that is willing to treat the theatre seriously, an audience like the one Shaw gathered in the old Court Theatre, where his plays were followed because they were different from the conventional, and where the audience was held as a collective congregation. While Eliot wishes his plays to appeal at all levels, there is a danger that naturalism is driving poetry and poetic vision right out of his plays; it is naturalism, not poetical drama, triumphant. It threatens no longer to be a case of poetry and prose being indistinguishable; it may be that no poet will ever dare to risk any flow of imagination not in conformity with naturalistic canons. This critique does not seek to belittle Eliot's position as one of the leading dramatists in the theatre to-day; it is because he is capable of greatness in certain directions that we judge here his long ascetic discipline in theatrical forms severely in view of the results so far. He may prove himself justified in the long run — we sincerely hope so — but Eliot took ten years to produce a play after *The Family Reunion* and, as Lord Keynes once said, in the long run we are all dead.

*

Born in St. Louis, Missouri, U.S.A., in 1888, Thomas Stearns Eliot came to Europe in 1910, after his education at Harvard. He read literature and philosophy at the Sorbonne and subsequently studied at Merton College, Oxford, and in Germany. In 1915 he settled in England, worked first as a schoolmaster and then as a banker in Lloyd's Bank, London. After eight years there, he joined the firm of publishers which later became Faber and Faber. Already during the war years his work had started to appear in magazines, and then in small volumes, his first being *Prufrock and Other Observations* (1917). *The Waste Land,* his most famous poem, was published in 1922. During this time he began his editorship of *The Criterion,* a literary review which had great influence in the inter-war years.

In 1927 Eliot became a British subject. He defined himself as a Royalist, a Classicist and an Anglo-Catholic. In 1948 he was awarded the Nobel Prize for literature and he received the Order of Merit from King George VI. Few writers have been more highly respected or more widely translated on the Continent, a return in itself for someone who believes whole-heartedly in the consolidation of Western literary traditions and movements.

For many years before his first experiment in dramatic form Eliot had shown interest in the drama, writing essays on "Rhetoric and Poetic Drama", "Four Elizabethan Dramatists" and "Dialogue on Dramatic Poetry". His first experiment in drama was *Sweeny Agonistes,* a fragment which could hardy have been made into a full-length play, though it is of considerable interest from the language viewpoint. A pageant play, *The Rock,* followed, written explicitly for the building fund of a London diocese. The invitation to write the words for the spectacle came, Eliot tells us, "at a moment when I seemed to myself to have exhausted my meagre poetic gifts, and to have nothing more to say". He learnt in *The Rock* to experiment with a choir or chorus, finding that the more voices there were, "the simpler and more direct the vocabulary, the syntax, and the content of your lines must be". But there is no need to linger over *The Rock.*

Preliminaries and tentatives over, Eliot was ready to give the theatre a major work, though it was only through the initiative of Dr. Bell, then Dean of Canterbury, that he was approached and commissioned to write a play for the Canterbury Festival. The result was the production of *Murder in the Cathedral* in the Chapter House of Canterbury Cathedral in 1935, an occasion which will be remembered in theatrical history. "He has reanimated a literary form which in England has been dead or dormant for nearly 300 years . . ." rejoiced *The Spectator*. Eliot had made full use of the opportunity, for he was in the unique position of being certain that his play would be attended by an audience sharing the same religious outlook and moral conventions. His religious play would be followed by a congregation, willing almost, as he puts it, "to be patiently bored". He therefore felt himself justified in the use of verse, and the only problem was the type to use. He wished to avoid any echo of Shakespearian blank verse and decided to keep in mind a variation on the *Everyman* type of verse. One cannot help remarking on Eliot's modesty, for the play has been widely performed and an outstanding success in the commercial theatre where there is no hint of the audience ever being "patiently bored", and only the 'sermon' has perhaps not been theatrically effective — but it, in any case, is not written in verse. It is the admirable concentration and the unity of the dramatic construction that interests the spectator, together with the ritual character of the setting. The introduction of the Chorus in the Greek fashion, but in the guise of the common women of Canterbury, adds both to the sense of foreboding and tension, and to the celebration of the Christian Faith as a link between Becket and congregation. For the subject of the death and martyrdom of Becket is not treated as a chronicle play, but as a kind of Mass in memory of an event which took place in the same cathedral 800 years earlier. Hear the urgency of the voices:

O Thomas, return, Archbishop; return to France.
Return. Quickly. Quietly. Leave us to perish in quiet.
You come with applause, you come with rejoicing,
    but you come bringing death into Canterbury:
A doom on the house, a doom on yourself, a doom
    on the world.
We do not wish anything to happen.
Seven years we have lived quietly
Succeeded in avoiding notice,
Living and partly living.

r the Chorus can turn into a liturgical chant:

> We acknowledge our trespass, our weakness, our
>   fault; we acknowledge
> That the sin of the world is upon our heads; that the
>   blood of the martyrs and the agony of the saints
> Is upon our heads.
> Lord, have mercy upon us.
> Christ, have mercy upon us.
> Lord, have mercy upon us.
> Blessed Thomas, pray for us.

hus does the Chorus provide the link as well as acting as narrator.
ut attention is centred on Becket himself in his isolation, his hour of
risis when he is tempted by the four tempters, who balance the later
ppearance of the four knights. We listen to the Christmas Day
ermon, in which the implications of the ritual are elaborated. After
ae murder the four knights then come forward in a Shavian fashion to
istify themselves, the intention being, as Eliot explains, "to shock the
idience out of their complacency". It may have been a trick, but it is
neatrically effective.

Great though the achievement was, *Murder in the Cathedral* did not
atisfy Eliot, who in any case does not believe that success can ever be
epeated, and "therefore one must always try to find something new".
lis aim in *The Family Reunion* was to explore the possibilities of a
erse-play when applied to every-day life, and to find a "rhythm close
o contemporary speech". He therefore decided to curtail his verse, to
abordinate it to the exigencies of the ordinary business of life, a task
vhich Eliot could not be expected to have accomplished in one experi-
tent and which was, in fact, to lead him to *The Confidential Clerk*.
The Family Reunion is a subtle and complex play, still ritualistic in
pirit, though this aspect, like the poetry, is more hidden. It is a transi-
on play, thought provoking, difficult, ambiguous, unresolved, and
nsatisfactory — yet it occupies a central position in Eliot's dramatic
evelopment and cannot be lightly dismissed as a failure.

The Family Reunion is, one feels, a vehicle for personal experience,
nd perhaps it is because Eliot wanted to say too many things that the
lay is better read than seen performed. It makes too many demands on
ae audience. There are long scenes dangerously undramatic, and the
xperiment of using as Chorus four minor characters, whose sudden

;

ritualistic chant seems quite out of harmony with their previous rôl
can only be described as embarrassing. For plot Eliot returns to t
favourite Orestes pursued by the Furies theme, and transfers this to
upper-class country house called Wishwood in the wind- and rain-swe
countryside of the north of England. The season is winter. Amy, t
Dowager Lady Monchensey, is expecting her son Harry for h
family reunion — the first time he will have attended for eight yea
She has placed all her hopes on Harry's return so that he will take ov
the family seat and fortunes from her. Amy has, as it were, lived for tl
day when she can see Harry taking over his responsibilities, and sl
hopes that he will marry his cousin Mary, whom she has kept beside h
these years with this ultimate intention. Even when Harry made ;
unfortunate marriage Amy never doubted but that he would return
the family, and now that he has lost his wife — she was drowned at s
in mysterious circumstances — Amy is prepared for the last fami
reunion and then to die in peace. This bourgeois plot gives way
quite another level at which the play asks to be judged; it is not only
conflict between the older and younger generations.

The arrival of Harry introduces the spiritual side of the play. H
rushes to pull the curtains before he even speaks to his mother. W
know he is a man sick in mind, pursued by the Furies, as in the Gree
legend. They have followed him to Wishwood, yet no one else can s
them. He is alone, apart, cut off from understanding:

> But how can I explain, how can I explain to *you?*
> And you will understand less after I have explained it.
> All that I could hope to make you understand
> Is only events: not what has happened.

The uncles and aunts who make up the reunion (but not Agatha) tr
to solve Harry's *angoisse* — he believes he pushed his wife overboard i
mid-Atlantic — by the only practical methods known to then
questioning his butler and seeking the family doctor. But Mary, h
cousin, and Agatha, his mother's sister, realise that it is only throug
spiritual discovery that Harry can be helped. Harry says himself tha
his illness is "deeper than what people call their conscience", it
neither his conscience nor his mind that is diseased, but "the world
have to live in".

Mary evokes for him the past, until he almost believes he could sta
at Wishwood, but with the appearance again of the Furies he know

at that is impossible. Nevertheless, it is at Wishwood that he discovers
here his redemption lies, the choice that he must make if he is to follow
is salvation. By learning more of the past, he learns through Aunt
gatha that his father fell in love with her and wished to murder his
other while she was bearing him in her womb. Through this revela-
on Harry is able to be delivered from his conscience; the knowledge of
ansmission of the sin from father to son, his own desire to kill his
ife, enables him to find redemption. For when he tells Agatha that it
as possible that only in his imagination did he push his wife over-
oard, she replies:

> So I had supposed. What of it?
> What we have written is not a story of detection,
> Of crime and punishment, but of sin and expiation.
> It is possible that you have not known what sin
> You shall expiate, or whose, or why. It is certain
> That the knowledge of it must precede the expiation.
> It is possible that sin may strain and struggle
> In its dark instinctive birth, to come to consciousness
> And so find expurgation. It is possible
> You are the consciousness of your unhappy family,
> Its bird sent flying through the purgatorial flame.

Harry realises that the vengeance of the Furies is over and that
nstead of their pursuing him he must pursue them. The unknown way
s the only way for his salvation and the realisation of his destiny. His
hoice must be between the tragedy of his mother or his own recon-
iliation with God and the rediscovery of his soul after eight years of
espair and loneliness in the wilderness. His departure brings about
he death of his mother, and with the symbolic "the clock has stopped
n the night", what has been done or thought is over for ever. He has
toned, and will follow his calling wherever it may lie, leaving the
thers behind in a state of bewilderment (except Agatha) not under-
tanding "a single thing that's happened".

This moment of choice is present in all of Eliot's plays, from
Murder in the Cathedral to *The Elder Statesman*. The road to salvation
s also the theme of *The Cocktail Party* (1949), written after a lapse of
en years after *The Family Reunion*. In the ten years we find a major
change in Eliot's dramatic style; gone is the need for any Chorus, and
the evocation of the supernatural has also been disposed of; rejected is

any poetry "which could not stand the test of strict dramatic utility" and in *The Cocktail Party* there is only one runic chant which remind one of *The Family Reunion*. Eliot himself believes "that it is perhaps a open question whether there is any poetry in the play at all". *Th Cocktail Party* may be said to have broken almost completely wit ritual and poetry, though not with Eliot's theology, which it attemp to interpret in the most secular and sophisticated circumstances po sible. It is a spiritual investigation into the malaise of society and pos war futility, as depicted by the set who are to be seen at the right parti — the type Noël Coward has mirrored in his early comedies.

Described as 'a comedy', we must assume there is an ironic inter pretation of the word for this most depressing play, concerned as it i with the breakdown of a sick society and an individual's inability t seek a way out of the super-civilised maze without calling on th assistance of the nearest psychiatrist. Our need for guidance "to wor out your salvation with diligence" is examined by the divine investi gator who indicates the cure and who gives his patients their momen of obligatory choice. The play opens with a cocktail party which is failure from the start because Edward must do his best to carry on an hide the fact that Lavinia, his wife, has just left him. There is in th party an unidentified guest who in the second act turns out to be Si Henry Harcourt Reilly, the doctor Edward has gone to consult abou the nervous breakdown which is threatening him. Edward is suddenl confronted with his wife and they are examined together, for as Si Henry explains:

> And now you begin to see, I hope,
> How much you have in common. The same isolation.
> A man who finds himself incapable of loving
> And a woman who finds that no man can love her.

After which advice it remains for Edward to say "Lavinia, we mus make the best of a bad job".

No special treatment is prescribed apart from reconciliation, an their case is passed over in order to consider that of the next patient Miss Celia Coplestone, whom we met at the party as Edward's mistress Hers is a very different case, and the most unexpected, in view of ou introduction to her at Edward's party. She wishes to atone, to seek t be cured of the emptiness and failure for something outside of her Sir Henry offers her the choice of living a normal life, marrying, th life of two people who do not understand each other, and breeding

ildren they do not understand and "who will never understand
em", or alternatively that of choosing faith, the faith which "issues
om despair". This second choice has no destination, and the journey
blind and terrifying. Celia chooses this way of absolute sacrifice,
hich is her vocation.

In the third act we are introduced into an almost Pirandellian world
here the masks are torn off. Edward and Lavinia now understand the
neliness of one another and are reconciled; their lot in life is to con-
nue giving and going to cocktail parties. Celia, on the other hand,
as reached the end of her terrible destiny, which was none other than
rucifixion. Joining a religious order she was sent to a far land where
ere was a native rebellion and she was crucified and her body eaten
y ants. Such was her martyrdom.

The idea of atonement as presented by Celia's sacrifice is in the
radition of certain Catholic conceptions, such as Claudel presented in
is plays (i.e. the midnight reunion of *Partage de Midi*, or Violaine
mitten with leprosy in *The Tidings Brought to Mary*), but its accept-
nce on aesthetic grounds is here open to grave doubts; it is not a
uestion of what Sartre might contemptuously call "Dieu n'est pas
rtiste" (as he applied the phrase to Mauriac), for Claudel has shown
hat the most cruel atonement need not offend an audience but lead it
o genuine compassion. Claudel's plays, however, are far nearer the
itualistic interpretation of Catholic dogmas (which are largely under-
tood by his audience) than are Eliot's cocktail-drinking characters
vho, apart from the divine inquisitor, have nothing spiritual about
hem. Violaine, almost from the start of Claudel's play, is removed from
his world and we can accept — as we cannot with Celia — her rôle
s a holy recluse. Whatever the reason, Eliot's characters have too
nuch the action of automatic robots responding to the strings of the
igh priest in a 1984 atmosphere; the play has an inhumanity which
loes little to recommend it to religious bodies. While there is no
lenying that it is a work of major importance, must a modern secular
nterpretation of a religious theme itself fall victim to the atmosphere
of the disease it sets out to analyse and cure? *Partage de Midi* has made
nany converts; one wonders whether *The Cocktail Party* does not
ccentuate the inhumanity of despair.

In *The Confidential Clerk* (1953) one has the feeling that Eliot has
attempted to make his characters of flesh and blood, and yet has failed
o make us identify ourselves with these characters who remain
strangely aloof. The last traces of poetry disappear, and Eliot has

carried "the machine he set in motion" with *The Family Reunion* —
when he wished to bring poetry to terms with a contemporary them
— to its logical conclusion. Eliot, it is true, preserves in his pent
metres a persuasive sense of rhythm, but can this "frothy, superfici
humour", this narrowness of mental outlook and hollowness of phile
sophy, really for one minute make an audience believe that "they to
could speak poetry"? The play can be judged, like *The Cocktail Part*
at different levels, but its most serious level seems to be a debate on th
proposition: "If you haven't the strength to impose your own term
upon life, you must accept the terms it offers you." No longer are w
dealing with matters relating to life and death, but merely to our choie
of what we want to do in this world. Sir Claude Mulhammer wante
to be a potter, but rather than be a second-rate potter he chose to be
come a power in the city, where no one could deny his competenc
Colby, whom he imagines to be his son and whom he has appointe
his confidential clerk, decides in favour of being a church organist (an
probably a second-rate musician) and (as an after-thought) the poss
bility of considering, later on, ordination. But his choice is a fairly safe
realistic, unadventurous one, and bears little resemblance to th
suffering of Celia on her road to salvation.

The plot, again taken from Greek classics (the *Ion* of Euripides), is
far-fetched confusion of offspring and foundlings, where the need fo
self-knowledge seems to be the key to the solution of the cryptogram
The play does not gain significantly on second reading, and tends t
close instead of open up mental horizons. For this reason it may be tha
this play, for all its supposed light-heartedness, is even more depressin
than *The Cocktail Party*. The people are those with whom you woul
certainly not want to waste an evening, even those cocktail parties o
Lavinia and Edward might be less dull. And the clash between th
mundane and the wildly improbable situations makes the whole pla
seem out of focus. Something has gone wrong somewhere.

Nor is *The Elder Statesman* (1958) a very much happier play
though it is simpler in conception and more human in treatment
It again falls into the vein of ironic comedy, but the characters lack th
delineation of light and shade to made them interesting as individuals
Lord Claverton — the statesman in question — might have suffered
the anguish and torment of, for example, Ingar Bergman's professo
in the Swedish film *Wild Strawberries*, but in Eliot's study his rôl
seems monotonous. The theme, however, is an ambitious one. Her
we have a man, retired from the political scene in glory and with a

eerage, who as he comes face to face with death sees for the first time
the reflection of his true self, of a life spent avoiding reality and the
sense of guilt which comes from moral cowardice.

The illusion of success must be kept for the sake of his loving
daughter, Monica. At the rest-home he is confronted with two shadows
from his past. There is Gomez, once a poor fellow student at Oxford,
and who has served a sentence in England for corruption, whereas in
South America corruption has enabled him to become a respected
citizen. Then there is an ex-musical comedy actress Maisie Mountjoy,
now Mrs Carghill, who once had tried to sue Claverton for a breach
of promise. There is also his son Michael, in debt like Gomez had been,
and wishing to break all ties with his family. It is Gomez who will give
him a chance to succeed, under another name, in South America. For
Claverton the only way out is confession to the one he loves, Monica.
And Monica makes this easy by accepting at once her father as he is,
with all his failings. Through her he achieves the serenity of perfect
understanding.

The Edinburgh Festival Production, subsequently seen in London,
was less satisfactory than the two previous Eliot premieres, although
Martin Browne was again at the helm. For some reason miscasting
made the characters appear at odds with the text, but it is doubtful if
even perfect casting would have succeeding in making them cross the
frontier from Eliot's own mythical world to appear as more than wishy-
washy creations in our own world. Can it be that in bringing them
down to humanity and the ordinary business of life Eliot has made
them people without faces?

This culmination of Eliot's later dramatic vein must come as a
great disappointment to those who had hoped that *The Cocktail Party*
was the beginning of an experiment towards a new dramatic system.
His real failing must be, as Mr. Lionel Abel has observed in *Partisan
Review*, that he has not succeeded in this main task. Strindberg, Shaw,
Pirandello or Giraudoux, yes, but "Eliot did not, though he did create
a poetic system before turning to plays". Be this as it may, Eliot has
brought to the contemporary English theatre lucidity of style and the
sensibility of his intellect which have not gone unrewarded.

SIX

FORWARD TO BRECHT
—FROM EXPRESSIONISM TO
EPIC THEATRE

"If you want the audience to profit from the reality of
the play, that is, to learn something from it, the theatre
must evolve a style of performance which prevents the
audience from identifying itself with the principal character (the heroine)."

BERTHOLT BRECHT

"The hero of this play is petrol."

LEO LANIA

CLAUDEL and Giraudoux both led the French reaction against
naturalism towards impressionism, each in his own way, but
both were reasonable ways, without compulsion, regimentation
or the sacrifice of aesthetic values. The individual is respected, an
appeal is made to his sensibilities, there is faith in man as there has been
throughout the tradition of French civilisation. The extreme reaction
against naturalism, as perhaps was to be expected, came from Germany,
where from the time of the first world war until about 1927 the Expressionist movement held sway — an example of the blind leading the
blind through the chaos of destruction and taking almost sadistic
pleasure in doing so. Expressionism was an all-out onslaught against
any sense of values which had survived the disaster, as topsy-turvy
in its thought, as perverted in its results, as the backcloth of the Germany it reflected. It is not our purpose here to examine the works of any
of its individual members (it produced no dramatist of equal stature
to Pirandello, Giraudoux or Claudel, or even the German naturalistic

dramatist Hauptmann), but rather its subsequent influence which was to make confusion reign in the German theatre long before Hitler became its master *metteur en scène*, and from which the German theatre has not to this day recovered.

Expressionism, it may be claimed, became an international movement, spreading as it did to Czechoslovakia, Poland, England and Ireland (it by-passed France), and America. This is true, but the ferocity and impact of its mood and influence were felt only in Germany, for expressionism belonged so much to the German spirit of the times that abroad its associations were missing. In the plays of Auden and Isherwood, for example, or Priestley's *Johnson Over Jordan*, Elmer Rice or O'Neill, we only heard a subdued echo of the expressionist howl. It was as if the German nation had kept its emotions repressed under rigid conformity and Prussian discipline for too long, and in the sudden explosion logic and reason had given way to primitive emotions and declamation. Expressionism has been described as an exigency of the mind, a mixture of ecstasy and obscurity, both facets being peculiar to the German temperament, and, let us admit it, language. No wonder and thank goodness it has never been assimilated neat by others.

These plays are depersonalised. In Germany, it seems, it was not considered right that the individual should be allowed to use his imagination; indeed, to the expressionists as to the Nazis, the very word individual is suspect. Who, then, were these expressionist writers and what exactly were their theories? Here we run right into the confusion, for expressionism in Germany is not a coherent movement with a developed style, but a group of writers varying greatly in style and even politics, and often abandoning so-called expressionism after their first attempt, choosing instead their own *mélange* somewhere between crude realism and expressionism. Frank Wedekind (1864–1945), Karl Sternheim (1878–1943), and Georg Kaiser (1878–1945) are generally regarded as the initiators, but their successors, Ernst Toller, Fritz von Unruh, Bertholt Brecht, and Walter Hasenclever were at one time included in the list. It has also been suggested that the later dream plays of Strindberg were the original inspiration.

The consequences of expressionism were as devastating as confusing, and it is extremely difficult to trace any pattern between, say 1927, when Toller's *Hoppla! Wir leben!* ("Hurrah! We are Living!"), one of the last of the expressionist plays, was produced, and the burning of the Reichstag in 1933. After the expressionists with their contempt for reality came those who wanted to return to reality, though not necessarily the naturalism of Zola. Erwin Piscator, introducing what he described as a "knock-about style", attempted to replace both naturalism and expressionism by epic theatre (*episches Theater*), and his theories were closely followed by Brecht, who gradually saw the scene set for his "narrative realism". This was a period, however, when almost every known style was being tried out in the German theatre, and notably play after play appeared based on German history (the Napoleonic war period seemed the favourite choice) — strong patriotic dramas and generally exceedingly bad plays. But these were the writers who were later to respond so readily to official demand and guidance, once the political battle had been won.

In short, if any style characterised the German theatre in the inter-war years, it was a style suitable for political drama. The theatre was used as a battle-ground for political warfare, and there was no possibility of its seeking refuge in some ivory tower. Even in the golden age of German literature, Goethe may at times be said to be political, as can Schiller in his historical political dramas, and certainly as can Kleist and Büchner. Hauptmann was not political, but the expressionists with their revolt against convention could not help entering the political arena, and with Kaiser they become more overtly social-political in their approach. With the Communists Piscator and Brecht, the forces of Bolshevism fighting Nazism, the theatre came to represent the political and spiritual faith of the nation. It must be regretted that in the extremes there was no room for moderation; liberalism was squeezed out in the struggle between revolutionary Marxism and national chauvinism. When Piscator wrote: "The drama is only important in the degree to which it relies on the testament of document", little did he realise that in the German drama of that decade, and especially his own theatre, we can see a clear reflection of the appalling mental state and depravity of a Germany ripe for Hitler's plucking, an all-too-true mirror of the decay of society and indeed a "testament of document".

Expressionism, then, ensured that the stage was set for political offspring, and until they had to flee before Nazi persecution, many of the expressionists became militant in politics. Piscator was the first to enter the political theatre, opening the "proletarisches Theater" in a working-class district of Berlin. "The style of our actors," he declared, "as well as that of the author and producer, should be of a complete and concrete nature (like the manifesto by Lenin . . .)". There was to be "no expressionism" any more. Piscator stressed the collective nature of production which had to be transmitted to the audience so that they too should be inspired by the spirit of their work.

After working for a time as producer to the Volksbühne he founded the Theater Piscator. His first play was Toller's *Hoppla! Wir leben!*, which is to-day regarded as a culmination of the expressionist technique. Toller's social satire (hardly brilliant) and methods were not radical enough for Piscator, who introduced in his *mise-en-scène* fresh material in film (which occupied about half the production time) to give the punch he felt the play lacked. Episodes in the film develop the idea of war, inflation, boxing, dancing girls, and other scissors-and-paste effects from newsreels, etc. We have already seen that Claudel experimented in *Christophe Colomb* with the idea of using the screen as a 'magic mirror' to complete, as it were, the atmosphere of the text. The idea can be used in moderation with great effect (Piscator's methods were a sensation), but beyond a certain point the method becomes a trick as precious as a toy-like 'Cinerama'. It is no substitute for good drama, and the temptations it offers for crude sensationalism are only too apparent.

Any separation of politics and the art of the theatre was quite out of the question for Piscator, for "the destiny of the masses" was the "heroic factor in the new drama". The task of revolutionary theatre was "to take reality as a point of departure and underline the discord of society so as to introduce the elements of accusation, revolution, and the new order". And thanks to the film this lofty theory could be put into practice by showing sequences of the Russian Revolution, flashing statistics one minute and showing the horrors of war the next, drumming blatant propaganda the whole time into the thick heads of his audience.

*

Brecht has taken up these ideas and applied them as a challenge to the whole fabric of Western drama. It was during the period of the Weimar Republic that Brecht found roots, where in his experiments with mask and shadow plays his own cynicism corresponded to the mood of the times. It was in reaction to the unhealthy nihilism of so many of the expressionist works that made him of a sudden turn to Marxism as a way back to certainty, an established order, stability and a grammatical explanation of history and war. The time had come to make a clear sweep of what was still left, the dramatist's duty as Brecht saw it was to change nature, humanity and the world. There must be no more of the "let's pretend" aesthetic of naturalism, nor was there any question of trying to strive for the ecstasy and magical elements which were responsible for the *hara-kiri* of the expressionist movement. On the contrary, what was required was the theory of 'alienation'. It was wrong for the audience to participate when they should judge, for an actor to play when he should report, and for a stage to be a stage when it should be what it is, a platform. So Brecht devised the alienation of emotion to prevent the audience from identifying itself with an actor, or from losing itself in the supreme moments of theatre, only to be brought down to earth with a bump when it was over There were to be no supreme moments and consequently no fall. Emotional straight-jackets were once again in fashion.

Of course some illusion had to remain, if the audience was itself to remain in the theatre. The question was one of selection. There was never an attempt at complete illusion but one of selected illusion; a room may be depicted showing only part of it, such as one wall, a table and some chairs. In *Mutter Courage* for example there is the fastidious detail of her provision wagon, ageng throughout the play more markedly than Mother Courage herself. It is all a questiton of omission and inclusion and those items finally selected are given very special consideration. The idea is not without momentary excitement — what are we to make of it?

First Epic Theatre has borrowed very many of the oldest stock properties known in the theatre. There is nothing new in bringing the audience into the argument, improvisation (pretended), song, commentary, montage sequences. Brecht has merely experimented in these tricks further than other writers, he has more need of them. For something must be offered by way of spectacle and stylised production to make up for the loss of emotion and self. It is the cold abstract, the iron soullessness of Communism which attracts him and the frigidity of his approach has a terrifying inhumanity. Facts and figures do not make up for dramatic intensity and concentration, absence from emotion does not make the heart grow fonder. Brecht's political insistence defeats its own ends; the Communists were the first to realise that he would not win converts, however much intellectuals in the West might point to Brecht as representing truth, socialism and the promised land.

Brecht is undoubtedly gifted, "unfortunately gifted" as Thomas Mann once stated. His dogmatic certainties reflect the uncertainties of his own life. Even his Christian name changes from Berthold in his unorthodox period to Bert in his creative period and Bertolt at the end of his life. Born in 1898 in Ausburg in Southern Germany, Brecht first studied medicine and science. During the First World War he worked in a hospital where he sang his first songs inspired by Rimbaud and Villon (in his plays song of course is introduced not to heighten conflict, but to alienate it). In 1923 he became assistant to Max Reinhardt, and it was Reinhardt who first presented a Brecht play to the public, *Trommeln in der Nacht*. This sharp satire on military heroism, mocking a soldier's return to his defeated fatherland and unfaithful bride — bearing the child of an armament's manufacturer — won the Kleist-Preis. Piscator produced Brecht's version of Hasek's *Brave Soldat Schweik*, but it was the adaptation of John Gray's eighteenth-century Beggar's Opera, *Dreigroschenoper* that made Brecht famous overnight. This supposedly merry romp of beggars, vagabonds and thieves served as a pretext for an assault on "bourgeois bad taste". But as Mr. Herbert Luthy has observed in *Encounter*, the public misunderstood Brecht's intentions, taking them as a pretext for the enjoyment of the pathos, romance and sentimentality of the original. This was not the only occasion the public have applauded Brecht for the wrong reasons. When *Mother Courage* had its premiere at Zurich the bourgeois audience took the play to be a testament of the indestructibility of people like Mother Courage, and no doubt identified themselves with her small trader's attitude to war and profiteering.

When the Nazis came to power, Brecht fled to Denmark, where he lived for the next six years, but on the outbreak of war he went to Sweden and from Finland took a ship to America, although one might have expected him to make for Russia. After two rather superficial propaganda pieces of no importance Brecht's creative period begins, including his best known work *Mutter Courage* (1938), *The Life of Galileo* (1938) and the *Good Man of Szechuan* (1939). In Galileo we have a reflection of Brecht's own dilemma, and as Luthy has commented, compromise. Galileo is prepared to recant before the Inquisition so that he can continue his work in secret and undisturbed. Rather than accept privation and freedom he accepts the riches of the Florentine court of the Medicis, with the proviso that he submits to the jurisdiction of the Church. Brecht himself was a crafty opportunist, and perhaps neither side could ever really trust him. In 1949 when Brecht returned to East Berlin to run his own experimental theatre he kept his links with the West, including a bank account in Switzerland, open.

Between 1949 and his death in 1956 Brecht's contribution as a playwright ceases. Even in *The Caucasian Circle of Chalk* (1945) we have a difficult and faulty work, due to two plots alternating. The result sadly lacks harmony. But as Brecht the dramatist declines we have Brecht the producer, as if he had finally realised where his true genius lay. "Epic" experiments are best conducted at the switchboard of the controls which banish all risk of passion according to the master plan, like a pilot feeling the air brakes. The visits of the Berliner Ensemble to Paris and London have made a deep impression from the point of view of *mise-en-scene*, but if the style offers memorable moments, any theatre that depends on techniques rather than the actual play is merely taking us up a cul-de-sac. An interesting experiment, but a substitute for pure theatre, and in lesser hands, *ersatz* theatre.

As a writer of truth Brecht was muzzled by his East German masters. We now know that the message of solidarity he sent to Ulbricht after the workers revolted in East Berlin in June 1953 was merely a sentence taken out of context from a long letter. In the memorial volume of the East German literary review *Sinn und Form* there are a group of significant poems, dated 1953, in one of which Brecht refers to his feeling of guilt, and another where we gather Brecht is merely sticking it out; he remains convinced of an eventual thaw, but forsees that this will not come in his life.

In *Mutter Courage*, to take Epic Theatre's most successful work, we have not a play, but a chronicle of the Thirty Years War, an endless trek far removed from the Western theatre's concept of dramatic unities. The miseries of war are as interminable as the miseries of life, yet it must be admitted that the production carries with it even a hostile spectator. There is here what one critic has called "a certain feeling for the animal spirit in human nature" which holds the 'epic' together, while the very simplicity of its socialist and narrative realism, its single-purpose theme, its silhouetted characters, the absence of sentiment and sympathy, ensure that the conscience rather than the imagination is sounded. *Mutter Courage* opens with the mother and her dumb daughter sitting in their provision wagon while her two sons pull it (the stage revolves as they do so) in the wake of the Swedish army. They are singing the song of Mother Courage. The stage is bare, suggesting the desolation of war, the war from which Mother Courage derives her existence, which she will follow to the bitter end, losing her two sons and eventually her daughter to its cause. She never realises the disaster, she never learns her lesson, she sees no urther than the money that the war brings her. War is her destiny.

Epic Theatre will probably not in itself continue indefinitely without Brecht, because Brecht was Epic Theatre. But undoubtedly many modern dramatists have been considerably influenced by some of its production techniques and possibilities. In Britain Osborne was clearly under Brecht's influence when he wrote *The Entertainer*, and Theatre Workshop productions have also Brechtian overtones, even though one suspects that Joan Littlewood is not a consistent admirer of Brecht. Just as Brecht borrowed to suit his style, so modern playwrights and more especially producers will borrow from Epic Theatre. Critics in Britain have talked of the Brechtian type of production given to Brendan Behan's plays, but this is Brecht without politics, or Brecht with tears. From the cul-de-sac we are back in the traditional stream of dramatic history, with the dramatist serving art and not a dogma. Meanwhile in Germany and elsewhere producers will continue to assimulate Brecht's theories of production and the Berliner Ensemble will always be worth a visit. But creatively the East German theatre will find itself in another straight-jacket, one imposed not by Brecht but by the inquisition of commissars.

★

If such is the outlook for drama in Eastern Germany, what has Western Germany and West Berlin to offer? The answer is not very much. Gone are the days of Max Reinhardt, who in the inter-war years made Berlin the centre for all those interested in creative theatre and experimental production, whether the mass spectacles which embraced the audience as part of the play, or intimate performances which he gave to the élite in art theatres. Hitler drove Reinhardt out of the Deutsches Theater, and he died in exile in America in 1943. In the decade following the end of the war it is almost unbelievable that the German theatre has not found one promising new playwright, and virtually nothing from the old pre-Hitler playwrights. Instead of renewing contact with the point where the German theatre left off in 1933, apparently (apart from Brecht) the political battle is over, or the Germans prefer to try and forget the past, and the present dissensions. It is less controversial to catch up with what has been happening abroad during these years, and the present refusal to face facts and the desire to escape instead is underlined by the vogue that the French existential writers have had recently. We shall consider this attitude at greater length in a later chapter.

The Germans have not even returned to producing the expression ists, and the only pre-war writer who has known success in post-war Germany is Carl Zuckmayer, whose *Des Teufels General* ("The Devil' General") has been an outstanding commercial success in Western Germany and a moderate one in London. This play has a somewhat naïve falsity whatever its sincere intentions, and neither it nor his other great success, *Der Gesang im Feuerofen* ("The Song in the Furnace"), comes near the standard of his pre-war *Captain of the Köpenick* (1930). The general unwillingness to accept responsibilities has closed the theatres to plays of ideas. Only two Swiss Germans, Max Frisch and Friedrich Dürrenmatt, seem to have had some success. The Austrian dramatist Fritz Hochwälder found very little enthusiasm in German for his remarkable play *Das Heilige Experiment*, although under the title *Sur la Terre comme au Ciel* it ran for two years in Paris and has since been produced in London under the title "The Strong are Lonely". We shall discuss this together with his "modern miracle play" *Donnestag* (produced Salzburg Festival 1959) in a later chapter.

From expressionism to epic theatre covers over forty years. Where the future will lie in German drama, whether its eventual awakening will produce a return to the horror and morbidity of the 'twenties, or produce a healthy desire for sanity and abolition of mysification and obscurity, is anybody's guess. It may even be that material prosperity will shut out culture, for when all's well there is no time to think of politics (so dangerous from past experience), or worry about problems until you are faced with them. Making Germany a go-ahead country economically requires the attention of the whole Western part of the nation. But when the time does come for a return to serious theatre one wonders whether Herbert Ihering's words, written before the war about a French play, will prove right or wrong: "A Frenchman will judge this play on the perfection of dialogue and aesthetic charm. A German will not judge it because of its perfect technique, since that is out of the circle where problems and judgments have importance". From the aesthetic point of view — and does Ihering forget Reinhardt? — or from the point of view of epic theatre? Or will West Germany turn to the one, and East Germany continue with the other? In this case the theatrical styles of East and West will never meet, as insolvable as are the problems of a United Germany.

LORCA — COCTEAU — O'NEILL

THE extreme reaction of the expressionists against naturalism was itself over before the more important modern dramatists had appeared, but its influence had shown them glimpses of a broader horizon and had disturbed their ambitions. The search for expression, the need for writers to experiment in new forms, was a serious challenge. Our next three dramatists, García Lorca, Jean Cocteau and Eugene O'Neill, each attempted to find in diverse artistic media their individual aims, but of the three, only Lorca may be said to have found his strength. Lorca, the only important dramatist to be killed in the war (and right at the beginning of the Spanish Civil War, an innocent victim of political vengeance) was as great a loss for world drama as for Spanish literature — the more so as he only finished his experiment in the pure folk tragedy of his last work; undoubtedly he would have given the theatre his full genius had he lived. With Jean Cocteau we have an artist who throughout his life has striven to find new means of expression, but whenever he has caused a mild stir he has suddenly turned away in pursuit of a yet newer idea. Eugene O'Neill was perhaps the only really professional playwright of the three, an early follower of expressionism who in his erratic trials and errors has covered the whole artistic field up to existentialism, displaying promising competence and talent. He has bequeathed his epic to us to read in a quarter of a century's time.

And meanwhile, the search for expression continues with a younger generation of writers, must continue, if the theatre is to remain alive . . .

SEVEN

A SPANISH TRAGEDY:
FEDERICO GARCIA LORCA

Le ganó con la verdad de la muerte a la razón de la vida.
("He was won for the cause of life by the truth of death.")
MIGUEL DE UNAMUNO

THERE is a word in Spanish which defies translation: *duende* (literally it means 'elf' or 'hobgoblin'). It signifies that incantatory force which distinguishes the artist from all others; it is a quality of greatness which cannot be acquired. But it is more than that. It requires a living interpreter at an 'exact present'. All the arts are capable of it, but in Spain they are inspired by it. We witness it when a dancer, for example Antonio, holds an audience by his *zapateado,* so that they feel and shake to the very tempo of his movements; unless a bull-fight is alive with it the ceremony becomes meaningless. For *duende* is something which can make even a modern sophisticated audience aware of primitive emotion. "One only knows that it burns in the blood" is how Federico García Lorca once described it in a lecture on "The Theory and Art of the Duende".

Lorca's own plays depend absolutely on the creation of this strange power. Since his drama is merely a natural extension of his ballads in terms of the theatre, the most important element is always the audience and their ability to identify themselves with his leading characters. From his very first theatre piece, *The Witchery of the Butterfly,* written with the delicate fantasy of a boy poet, to the grim realism of his last completed work, *The House of Bernarda Alba,* everything depends on their ability to come across to the audience, who will be not so much entertained as animated and haunted by an apprehension unrelated to reason. An audience on Broadway or Shaftesbury Avenue which does not know that it is already in Granada, which does not fear the wild mountain-sides of the Sierra Nevada, which remains indifferent to the strange lyricism, unaware of the mystifying bond between romance and death, unafraid of the tyranny of Bernarda Alba, can never hope to enter the spirit of his plays by any intellectual process. They will only see in such a performance what Wolcott Gibbs described in an American production of *Bernarda Alba* as "apt to seem more comic than really dramatic".

In an interesting article on "Lorca's Audience" by Mary Otis (*Theatre Arts*, May, 1951), this failure of Lorca to establish himself with American audiences is discussed, and Miss Otis suggests that his inability to do so is not because the productions have been too Spanish for American understanding, but "not Spanish enough". "In Spanish dancing", as Miss Otis emphasises, "the genuine thing is always unconsciously recognised". On the other hand, we have the comment of Rafael Nadal, who, writing on the New York failure of *Blood Wedding* (produced under the ridiculous title, "Bitter Oleander"), believes that "whether we like it or not, Spain is from many points of view a world apart, and an attempt to transfer, in Lorca's most Spanish poetry, Spanish values of men and things met with an almost unsurmountable barrier." This barrier is not only confined to the English-speaking public, for *Blood Wedding* also failed in its Paris production in 1938, in spite of an excellent translation, praise from Left-wing critics and the politically favourable atmosphere of the time. Arturo Barea, writing of this production, explains that it had to fail "because foreign spectators only understood it through a laboured intellectual process, not through the swift, piercing associations and sensations it produced in a Spanish public. Indeed, in any Spanish public — for in Hispano America it was as great and lasting a success as in Spain itself." It would seem that there is danger of Lorca's plays losing their *duende* more or less completely without an audience which, if not Spanish-speaking, has a knowledge of, and sympathy for things Spanish.

To understand Lorca, then, we have to understand Spain, the hopes and sufferings of Spain, the rules of conduct and honour in Spain, the pride of the people, life and death in Spain. "I am a Spaniard and it would be impossible for me to live outside my geographical boundaries", Lorca once told a journalist. Throughout his entire work Lorca is excessively a Spaniard, both in thought and action. Spain has always presented life in a sharper perspective than that of other European countries; it is at once exaggerated in its simplicity and passion

he strident colours are brighter and darker; a merciless sun hides
.othing. In this nation with such a tremendous zest for living the
longated shadow of death is everywhere present. If in other nations
leath is kept in the subconscious mind, in Spain it is for ever in the
onscious. The capacity for living is made one with a capacity for
lying; death should be triumphant, not an euphemism which is to be
politely whispered. With this vision of death, it is understandable that
religion in Spain should be so vastly important, rigid and extreme. In
religion, as in politics, as in honour, the Spaniard imposes the severest
liscipline.

It is not without consequence that Spain has remained throughout
history isolated, outside the European sphere of influence and culture.
Spanish writers have written directly for the Spanish people, and an
attempt during the eighteenth century to impose a pseudo-classicism
on the Spanish stage as in France was to kill the Spanish drama until a
eturn to its own tradition was made in the nineteenth century. Spanish
art and music are equally distinguished in their perception of national
emperament. Indeed, the arts in Spain have not and never have had
he civilising pattern of European arts, for as Lope de Vega wrote in
The New Art of Writing Plays in this Age (1609): "But since we are
o far away from art and in Spain do it a thousand wrongs, let the
earned this once close their lips". Spanish individualism can swim
against the spirit of an age and bring its own rewards.

Lorca was less successful when he tried to expand his horizon; he
was never the poet of burning intensity away from his Andalusia. His
visit to America did not result in any broad understanding of the
American scene or interest in their way of life. His *Poet in New York*
is a testament of his failure there. His voyage, however, terminated a
vitally important stage in his career, for he was able to realise that he
was not to be the poetical opposite number of his artist friend Salvador
Dali, who seemed in his painting to possess a universality that made
him as much at home in America as elsewhere. It was a very different
Lorca that was to return to Spain, for he had decided to abandon his
gipsy romances and devote himself more and more to playwriting. But
t was still Andalusia that attracted him for his themes.

Not only was he regional in writing about Andalusia, but he chose
his own Granada, with its ancient towers nestling beside the bleak
mountain-sides, or Cordoba, "remote and lonely", rather than Seville
with its softer colours and more inviting calm. Lorca was an Anda-
usian minstrel who selected his themes from the diversity of life around

him, from the people he met, to be recited preferably to the people he knew.

Lorca immediately reminds us of Burns in our own literature. Both are poets of international renown, yet both are essentially regional poets who, writing about their own locality, become the national poets of their respective countries. Lorca in New York was no more at home than Burns would have been in Oxford; the very thought of an Anglicised Burns, a Burns with a 'B.B.C. accent', is beyond the wildest probabilities of farce. But in spite of the distance between Scotland and Spain, the poet of Tam O'Shanter might well have chosen the subject matter of *Preciosa and the Wind*, though their interpretation of ideas would reveal the fundamental differences between Ayrshire and Andalusia. These differences are, of course, national differences, not a different vision of poetry and its uses. Both Burns and Lorca were master of the ballad, and the *duende* that comes from good story-telling.

Because Lorca was never so happy as in his Andalusia, he disregarded the advice of his friends not to go south to Granada in July, 1936. His tragic murder, which has been dramatically investigated by Mr. Gerald Brenan in his book *The Face of Spain*, was to turn Lorca for a time into a Republican martyr, thus unfortunately identifying him with a political cause. His politics had never been more pronounced than wishing to be friends with everyone in all countries, and not sacrificing the latter for narrow nationalism. If anything, at any rate on the surface, Lorca was more conservative than progressive, and plays such as *Mariana Pineda* (1929), as Arturo Barea has pointed out, might well at another time have been taken up by the Right, instead of being championed as an attack on the decaying dictatorship and monarchy of the era.

The truth is that Lorca could not help becoming identified as a poet of the democratic movement, for it was the progressives who were the intellectuals and who had supported and encouraged him. Moreover, the emotional onslaught against the conventional rigidity of the middle class such as his folk tragedies ventilated, ensured powerful enemies. His plays portrayed much that was wrong in the state of Spain, and while some believed his satires an occasion for a political demonstration (much to Lorca's disgust), others took exception to the 'realism' they saw in the mirror. These were the years when Spain seemed on the road to freedom of thought and social justice; a new renaissance had arrived for Spanish literature. It was the Republican government who appointed Lorca director of La Barraca, a national theatre company which toured Spain with a repertory of classical plays by such authors as Lope de Vega, Cervantes and Calderón. This work stimulated Lorca and encouraged him also to write and produce his own plays for his company.

For the last six years of his life Lorca was a professional playwright working within his company; his earlier failures were a closed chapter, for now he had made contact with his public and gathered confidence in each play he wrote. His poetical evolution led him, ironically enough in his last play *The House of Bernarda Alba,* to reducing the lyrical element so drastically that he could go no further in this direction; he had written a play which had been pruned bare, consisting only of bones and the impact of Spanish realism. But even though Lorca re-joiced that there was not 'one jot' of poetry in this play, its whole con-ception is that of a poetic vision, a drama, with the economy and precision of a well-made ballad.

Those who only know Lorca through this severely disciplined work can have little idea of the gradual evolution of Lorca's arrival there; those, on the other hand, who know him only by his other plays would find it difficult to believe that a mind so unusually sensitive to the qualities of lyricism should have deprived itself so completely of its opportunities.

It is true that the struggle between poetry and prose in his plays does not always lead to satisfaction, but it is a conflict which all poets have to solve for themselves in the theatre. Their fusion can only be arrived at by experiment. In these experiments Lorca was tempted by other methods, such as surrealism, which he finally discarded, and rightly so, in order to concentrate on his pure folk tragedies. For it is by these that Lorca is remembered. In them he endeavoured to introduce into the Spanish theatre the folk speech, lyricism and poetic imagination while at the same time to reduce life to an outline or skeleton of bare essen-tials. He wished to replace the bourgeois realism of the commercial theatre of his day, which was not specifically Spanish, with a return to the beauty of the Spanish language as spoken by peasants who retained its purity. Lorca wished to ally this with a return to the traditional Spanish theatre, the models set by Lope de Vega and Calderón, which had been discarded. For though Jacinto Benavente had for so many years been acknowledged as Spain's leading dramatist (he was a Nobel Prize winner in 1922) he had surprisingly neglected much of the tradi-tion of the Golden Age (in fact he shares with Lope de Vega only the

distinction of having had a long life in which to write a superabundance
of plays). Lorca delighted in the lyrical and emotional elements in
Lope de Vega's plays, specially in his own productions of them. But
possibly he revered more the austerity and spiritual exploration found
in the plays of Pedro Calderón de la Barca, and especially his concept
of honour which figures in many of his works. We must, however,
remember that Lorca was only in the tradition of these Spanish
classical writers, they were only the forefathers of a common heritage.

★

The world of Federico García Lorca (1898–1936) was from his
early childhood an imaginary world of the theatre, and the whole of
life was to him a mysterious drama in which he was an actor. In a
preface to *Three Tragedies* his brother Francisco tells us how the first
toy that Federico ever bought was a model theatre. Since there were no
plays provided he had to make them up for himself. We are also told
that one of his favourite games was to play as priest and deliver a
sermon to his sisters, the servants, and any others who would willingly
participate; the only condition was that everyone had to weep. Life
was to Lorca an occasion for tears and laughter, and that was what he
wanted of his audience.

It is not perhaps surprising that Lorca failed to establish a *duende*
with his Madrid audience in his early career. Its urbanity was far removed from the childhood simplicity needed to give way to a flood of
tears. *El Maleficio de la Mariposa* ("The Witchery of the Butterfly"),
presented during the 1919–1920 theatrical season by Martinez Sierra,
ran for one performance and was vigorously booed. Written before he
was twenty, the subject matter of this piece was related closely to
Lorca's verse written about the same time. He tells us of the longing of
a sordid cockroach to know the world of a wounded butterfly. Eventually the butterfly is able to use its wings again and flies away to the
world the cockroach will never know. For the cockroach life becomes
unbearable because of the witchery of the butterfly.

In 1927 Lorca, with the aid of Salvador Dali, who designed the sets,
had his first full-length play, *Mariana Pineda*, produced. The play, an
historical romance, takes for its heroine a woman from Granada who
embroiders a Republican flag in preparation for a revolution in the
1830's. When the police discover the plot the cowardly revolutionaries
flee abroad and she is arrested; unwilling to betray the names of the

onspirators, although they have deserted her, she dies on the scaffold. Mariana, however, is not made to die for a political cause; like Lorca himself, she is not interested in politics, but is an innocent victim caught in their web. It must be remembered that the place of a Spanish woman is at home; she would evoke little sympathy in dying for a political cause. It is, on the other hand, very much in the Spanish tradition for a woman to sacrifice herself for love. Mariana Pineda is in love with a liberal conspirator. How can she show this more fittingly than to embroider a flag for him with his party's emblems on it? It is through her love that she must die, and die alone, for all the revolutionaries are shown up as pitiable funks.

Lorca calls this play a 'popular ballad'. To the obvious dramatic opportunities in the theme he has introduced many lyrical passages of distinction, but it is not altogether a satisfying play. His greatest difficulty is to make his characters appear to live instead of remaining merely figures in a plot. Perhaps this is an inevitable danger for a writer of ballads, where so much less importance is attached to characterisation than in a play.

After *Mariana Pineda* Lorca started writing a series of plays which experimented with the folk idiom on the stage, and which were to clear the ground for his more important folk tragedies. *Amor de Don Perlimplín con Belisa en su Jardín* ("The Love of Don Perlimplin for Belisa in his Garden"); *La Zapatera Prodigiosa* ("The Marvellous Shoemaker's Wife"); and *Retabillo de Don Cristobal* ("In the Frame of Don Cristobal") form the three plays of this group. Perlimplin is a dear old rich bachelor who, urged on by his housekeeper Marcolfa, rashly asks for the hand in marriage of Belisa, a voluptuous beauty who lives next door. She accepts readily, but it is not long after their wedding night that Perlimplin learns that she has a lover. He tells her he will be content to love her as a father does a daughter. In the last scene Perlimplin approaches Belisa while she is waiting for her lover. He tells her that if she really loves her lover, he does not want him ever to abandon her, and "so that he may be yours completely, it has occurred to me that the best thing is to stick this dagger into his gallant heart." Perlimplin runs after a figure and after a while returns, wrapped in a red cape. He is wounded, and before falling dead in Belisa's arms rejoices that Belisa is now able to have a soul as well as a body. Through his own suicide he has given Belisa a soul. It is indeed a play for tears and laughter.

The Marvellous Shoemaker's Wife, the most successful of this series, may be described as a poetic farce, with song and dance interwoven in its theatrical structure. The young sensual shoemaker's wife is, like Belisa, married to a nonentity of a husband, far older than herself, and no match for her insatiable desires. In fact, for the poor shoemaker life is made a hell, and he is eventually forced to flee from his home. The marvellous wife turns his workshop into an inn which all her lovers frequent. The shoemaker returns in disguise and finds that with all the temptations available to his wife, she has nevertheless remained faithful to him. Everything would seem ready for a happy ending, but no . . . when the disguise is discarded we are back where we were, and the merry-go-round begins again.

In the Frame of Don Cristobal is a puppet farce, a highly spirited piece which opens with the poet addressing the audience about the meaning of his play, and having an argument with the producer about what he is allowed to say (the producer of course wins). Again it is a story of a faithless wife, Rosita, who having been bought in marriage by Cristobal, offers herself to any man, and when she gives birth to quadruplets pleads that they are Cristobal's children. He beats her to death for it.

There are two plays belonging to Lorca's surrealist period *Así que Pasen Cinco Años* ("If Five Years Pass") and *El Público* ("The Audience"). *If Five Years Pass* is a highly complex play, which has as many incidents, characters appearing and disappearing, as one might expect to pass through the mind when contemplating a span of five years. It is certainly too meandering for any adequate synopsis of contents, and the title itself tells us all we need to know about the plot. On the stage its violently surrealist approach must either conquer the audience or dumbfound them. A list of the characters: Young Man, Old Man, Stenographer, Manikin, Valet, the Friends, the Betrothed, the Rugby Football Player, Cat and Boy, three Gamblers, a Harlequin, a Clown . . . requires a fertile imagination to envisage them all as complementary characters in the framework of a play. There is no doubt that Lorca was attempting to rid himself of all the restrictions of dramatic conventions and achieve in the theatre the complete freedom of a poet. His other surrealist experiment, *The Audience*, may be considered as an attack on the commercial theatre, in which the audience itself is on trial.

After these *ballons d'essai* Lorca finally turned to his folk tragedies, where his genius was best fitted to assert itself. *Bodas de Sangre* ("Blood Wedding"); *Yerma; Doña Rosita la Soltera* ("Doña Rosita the Spinster") and finally *La Casa de Bernarda Alba* ("The House of Bernarda Alba") complete Lorca's drama. The heroines of these plays compel our admiration, for their portraiture of Spanish womenfolk is Lorca's superb achievement. In his plays the women accept the stern code of honour which is more important to them and their families than life, and should they fail, should they be driven by sexual passion to forfeit their virginity or honour they are aware of their punishment. An honest woman commits suicide to protect her purity.

In *Blood Wedding* (1933) the emphasis is on the word blood; blood is associated with the blood of old family feuds which have never healed. The characters in this play are nameless, except the one who causes the bloodshed, for this is a study not of characters so much as of attitudes and ethics. The only living son of a mother who has seen her husband and other sons killed in a feud murder, is planning to marry a girl who was previously engaged to Leonardo, a member of the family who took part in the murder. Leonardo has since married the girl's cousin, but it is not a happy marriage and Leonardo still loves the girl he was to marry. The wedding takes place between the son and the girl, but after the ceremony the bride suddenly elopes with her old lover.

When her father hears the news, he pleads: "It can't be she. Perhaps she's thrown herself into the cistern."

To which the mother curtly replies: "The pure and honourable throw themselves into the water. Not that one, no! But now, she's the wife of my son! Two clans. Here there are two clans."

They all join in the hunt to avenge the crime, and the mother knows that in doing so her only son is going to his death. "The hour of blood has come again."

So the young lovers are pursued through the woods, and in the beginning of the third act, set in the dark, supernatural atmosphere of the weeping forest, Lorca brings a sombre lyrical imagination to bear on the mounting tension of the human hunt. Symbolism is also present; three woodcutters represent a mournful Greek chorus; then the moon, the messenger of death, rises, lighting the stage with "an intense blue radiance". The moon gives way to the beggar woman, who personifies Death. In the final scene the bride returns leaving behind the bodies of both husband and lover, and submits herself to her mother-in-law's fury; the mother strikes her and she falls to the ground:

BRIDE   Leave her: I came to let her kill me so that I would be taken away with them. (*To the Mother*) But not with your hands:

with hooks of wire, with a sickle, and with a force that will break my bones. Leave her. I want her to know that I am clean, that I shall go mad, but that they will bury me without a single man's ever having seen the whiteness of my breasts.

MOTHER Be quiet: be quiet: What does that matter to me?

BRIDE But I went away with the other, I went. (*In anguish*) You would have gone. I was a burnt-up woman, full of wounds within and without, and your son was a spring of water from which I expected sons, land and health: but the other was a dark river full of branches which rushed towards me with the song of its reeds and its stifled song. I ran with your son who was like a little boy made of cold water, but the other sent me hundreds of birds which impeded my course, and left frost in my wounds of a poor pining woman, a girl caressed by the fire. Your son was my aim and I never deceived him, but the arm of the other swept me away like a great sea-wave, like the butting of a mule, and he would have swept me away even had I been old and all the children of your son had been clutching my hair . . . Revenge yourself on me. Here I am. See how soft my throat is. It would be less trouble to cut a dahlia in your garden. But not that! I am chaste, chaste as a newly born child. And strong enough to prove it. Light the fire. We'll put our hands in it — you for your son, I for my body. You'll pull yours out first.

MOTHER But what does your honour matter to me? What does your death matter to me? What does anything matter to me? Blessed be the corn because my sons lie under it, and it wets the faces of the dead. Blessed be God who lays us out together to rest.[1]

Blood Wedding was the first play of major importance which Lorca wrote, the first play where his maturity had developed to a point where he was as much a dramatist as a poet.

The following year Lorca was determined to move along the road towards dramatic realism, while still retaining important lyrical scenes. *Yerma* is still described as a 'tragic poem'. Like *Blood Wedding* it is a tragedy which underlines the Spanish acceptance of sex as borne by women and the torment suffered by the soul of a woman who ad-

[1] Translation by Mr. Roy Campbell.

eres to the conventions and must reject all compromise. The word 'Yerma' means 'unsown' or 'uncultivated' and in this particular play it efers to a woman who is sterile, through no fault of her own. She only married to have children, but she fears her husband is impotent. She becomes obsessed with the desire for a child, and she is attracted by Victor, a strong shepherd whom she knows would be able to consummate her love. Clearly they were made for each other. But Yerma is a Spanish woman first. Although she is driven to hate her husband for his rigidity she has her code of honour. Although her body feels the need for children, her soul thirsts for children, better to remain barren than give herself to a man who is not her husband. In vain she consults other women, but they cannot comfort her. The behaviour of her husband drives her near frustration. He tells her that "life is sweeter without children. I am happy not having them." Yerma must resign herself to this fact, but this she will not do. Instead, in an embrace, she siezes her husband by the throat and in a mad frenzy of passion strangles him. Her tortured being could no longer accept, there was no other outlet for her emotions; what she did was instinctive. Now she can find peace, knowing for certain she will be barren for the rest of her life.

> Withered! Withered, now I know it for certain, and alone. I am going to sleep without ever waking in a start to see if my blood feels another new blood. Barren forever . . . what are you all looking at? What do you want to know? Don't come near, for I've killed my son. I myself have killed my son!

Doña Rosita the Spinster (1935) restrains the passions and there is little action or drama in its study of spinsterhood and old age in nineteenth-century Granada. But whether intentionally or not, the play makes a more open attack on the narrowness of middle-class life which was to be interpreted politically. Rosita waits in vain for the return of her fiancé, who many years before went abroad and who has actually married somebody else. The deception, however, is kept up by Rosita, who remains always faithful to him.

The House of Bernarda Alba completes the journey to dramatic — or should one rather say Spanish — realism. Everything is subjected to realism, right down to the names of the characters. In an article by Claude Couffon in *Le Figaro Littéraire* (26 December, 1953) Lorca's cousin Doña María told M. Couffon that "Bernarda Alba and her daughters really existed. They lived in a little village in the open country, where the parents of Federico owned property: Valderrubio. The two houses were adjoining. The actual well was mid-way. It was one summer, when he was staying at Valderrubio, that Federico discovered this strange family of girls over whom their mother, widowed for many years, exercised a tyrannical guard. Intrigued by this, he decided to overhear the intimate life of the Albas. Using the well as an observation-post, he spied, studied, took notes. Two months later the play had taken shape." And we learn from Doña María that even the mysterious character of Pepe el Romano, who is behind the action in the play but never actually appears, played the same rôle in real life and had the name Pepe el Romilla.

There are no male characters in *Bernarda Alba*. The female studies of his previous plays had been so important — whereas one soon forgets his male characters — that it seems as if Lorca was determined to consecrate a play entirely to them. So we have Bernarda Alba, the domineering head of five daughters (aged thirty-nine to twenty), only the youngest of them attractive and not yet resigned to being a spinster. The daughters know nothing about what goes on outside their windows; they are barred, and the stifling atmosphere of repression, suppressed desires, results in a clash of wills. A marriage has been arranged between Pepe de Romano and the eldest daughter Angustia, but Pepe has already seen the attractive youngest daughter Adela and meets her in the stables. Their meetings are betrayed one night by another jealous sister who is also in love with Pepe, and Bernarda rushes out of the room with intent to shoot Pepe. Adela is given the false news that he has been killed, whereas in fact Bernarda missed. Believing him dead, Adela goes and hangs herself in her room. Bernarda orders them to:

> Cut her down! My daughter died a virgin. Take her to another room and dress her as though she were a virgin. No one will say anything about this! She died a virgin. Tell them, so that at dawn, the bells will ring twice.

For the others the house remains a prison, of jealousy, bigotry, unhappiness, ruled by the rod of iron of Bernarda.

In *The House of Bernarda Alba* Lorca reached the end of an experiment in playwriting, and it resulted in his most successful play. Throughout his life Lorca had never been content with doing things the same way twice, and whether he had at last found where he really wanted to go, or would, had he lived, have started new experiments, we shall never know.

That Lorca died in his prime of life is one of the greatest tragedies that could have happened, not only for Spanish literature, but for world theatre. Of all the dramatists of his era, he was the one who was capable of achieving the calibre of greatness. Many atrocities were committed on both sides in the Civil War; what is done is done. Lorca was a victim of the forces of violent death he himself described so vividly, for it was by always living in face of death that he lived so fully, with every moment precious to him. Death continually lurked by his side, haunted his imagination, and he lived forever under the presentiment of its shadow. Lorca found no consolation in the Catholic conception of death, and nowhere in his writing does he show any reference to a belief in any life beyond. For him, death was an eternal sleep which deprived one of the senses. So be it. Lorca has survived death, and lives every time his work creates that *duende* of which he was master. His name lives on as do his plays. As an epitaph we can quote his *Cásida de la Huída:*

> I want to sleep for a while,
> For a while, a minute, a century,
> But all shall know that I have not died,
> That there is a stable of gold on my lips,
> That I am the little friend of the West wind,
> That I am the giant shadow of my tears ...

EIGHT

THE COCTEAU LEGEND

"It is not the business of the dramatist to bring life into
the theatre but to bring the theatre to life."

JEAN COCTEAU

COCTEAU is no longer a name — he has become a legend.
A legend of the 'twenties, who (alone of his generation) has
continued the race for new means of artistic expression through
the twilight of the 'thirties, the havoc and despair of the 'forties, and
right into the 'fifties. "You're a wicked playboy", the great Colette
once told him, "because you don't know how to relax without doing
anything." That is as true of Cocteau's career as it is of his life; he can
never be accused of resting on his laurels. If in his life he has sampled
everything from opium to religion (to his credit he has never attempted
the Marxist equation of the two) so in art he has tried everything. From
poetry to painting, criticism to novel writing, and, of course, as *homme
de théâtre*, there is no literary peak or band-wagon of fashion that
Cocteau has not attempted to climb. But he refuses to admit victory as
he refuses to consider defeat, for no sooner is he half-way up one peak
than he is immediately more interested in what the view from the next
one will be like. He is never satisfied with his own achievement; he no
more believes in trying the same thing twice than loving at second sight.
"Respecter les mouvements, fuir les écoles" (Pay respect to literary
movements, flee from literary schools) is his conviction, his
strength, and his weakness. So we have his *poésie graphique*, his
poésie de roman, his *poésie de théâtre*, and his subsequent *poésie ciné-
matographique*. His definitions are exact. He is not a poet attempting to
bring poetry into the theatre; he wishes instead to seek a poetry of the
theatre, in whatever style it can be realised. It is a vastly more dangerous height to reach and one which only the greatest poets attempt —

unless, like Cocteau, they have the balance of a tight-rope walker with the precision of a magician's sleight-of-hand.

The precision of a magician — the very French word *prestidigitateur* suggests euphoniously the lightness of touch that is required — is Cocteau's secret. But it is not the old professional magician who produces rabbits from top hats as if from slot machines, it is rather like an earnest young magician who is producing the rabbit for the first time in his professional career: since Cocteau is only interested in performing the trick once he does it creatively. With the irresponsible ambition of youth he has ransacked the history of the theatre, and given his version to the major periods; the ancient Greek legends, the folklore of the Middle Ages, Elizabethan passion, classical tragedy and romantic drama are not forgotten in his own *théâtre*. And to complete the history he proves that he can take a boulevard success and make his model that will hold its own with the box-office. You may perhaps question the word 'creative' when Cocteau so follows the footsteps of others rather than creates a new style of his own; yet Cocteau's signature is clearly evident in all his works, however diverse. Whatever the form of expression we are sure that only Cocteau could have been the artist.

Cocteau replies to such critics that he is a poet, bound by no school. He does not want, like his Orpheus, to suffer at the hands of the Saint-Germain-des-Prés mob, but he knows, like Orpheus, that one is never forgiven for not being faithful to a school, if one has once 'flirted' with it. It is not easy to-day, as he complained in a talk given on the B.B.C. Third Programme, to refuse lifts on the autostrade, to remain simply 'the cat who walked by himself'. Cocteau's freedom is the absolute freedom of an artist; freedom to exploit the full resources of poetic vision in its immensity. His talent demands that he should 'reflect further', and since he never tires of life, he never tires of his seeking after the beauty of life. And in all his experiments Cocteau preserves the inquisitiveness of youth; his characters epitomise the expression of a youthful mind.

Youth is never satisfied; it fears nothing, for though it can be haunted by death, death remains an abstraction or some theatrical character who has not yet become a present reality. The young man can reflect in the mirror, the same mirror as in the *teatro dello specchio* of Pirandello, where he will see "death working like bees in a beehive". But for Cocteau mirrors are the means of passing from one plane of existence to another, the real to the unknown. Cocteau surveys the possibilities of the unknown with the limitations of the known. "Man

is a cripple", he writes in *Journal d'un Inconnu*, "I mean that he i
limited by the dimensions which surround him and prevent him from
understanding the infinite where dimensions do not exist." It is the
meeting of the real and the imaginary, the natural and the supernatural,
that inspires Cocteau's poetry. He can only conceive the latter in terms
of the former, for "reality alone, even when well concealed, has power
to arouse emotion". Or, as the surrealist André Breton expresses it
"what is admirable in the fantastic is that there is nothing fantastic,
it is only the real". Cocteau, even in his most surrealistic adventures,
always describes his poetry in terms of the world we know and understand.

Cocteau is insatiable for the secrets of the great mystery; we feel he
is not afraid of death, but regards her rather as an artistic partner. In
Orphée he introduces her to us not as a weird and midnight hag, such
as we assume her to be in popular mythology, but as a glamorous,
dark-haired beauty dressed for a ball, apparently because no one would
recognise her in such an attire. And the ever-youthful spirit of Cocteau
waltzes with her in order that she should lead him behind the scenes,
through the magic mirror, but with the promise of a return ticket from
the underworld.

Such are the methods of Jean Cocteau, where the mystery of life
remains a mystery under the magician's wand, where we are always
fascinated to go further, to know more, where we believe that the
impossible is always possible, but where we must keep silence and not
ask questions, lest we disturb the actors, who are playing very high and
without safety nets, and cause them to fall from their great heights.
We all know what happened to humpty-dumpty.

*

Jean Cocteau has been called "the spoilt child of the century".
Certainly everything about his childhood had a touch of the 'silver
spoon in his mouth'; born in 1892 and brought up in bourgeois
luxury in the Rue d'Anjou in the centre of Paris, he was already a
genius at the age of ten. Cocteau has continued his precocity throughout his life, and those who refuse to accept his behaviour as becoming a
poet, willingly forgive him for being a publicity agent for the latest
snobisme. The infant prodigy grew into a somewhat precious young
man, who would be sure to 'dear' you in the manner of theatrical people
on first meeting, and offer you some opium. Nevertheless his friends

and acquaintances have included nearly all the outstanding figures in the French literary scene during this century: Proust, Claudel, Gide, Apollinaire, Mauriac, Giraudoux, Picasso. . . . But no wonder Gide despaired of him, when writing in his *Journal* on 20 August, 1914, he noted: "I have not had the pleasure of seeing him again in spite of his extreme kindness. But he is incapable of seriousness and all his thoughts, expressions, sensations, all this extraordinary dash of his ordinary speech shocks you as an article of dazzling luxury does at a time of famine and mourning." But how was Gide to know then what sort of 'brave new world' the armistice was to bring, or that 'articles of dazzling luxury' were to be the fashion! And by no means all the fashions that Cocteau wedded were as vulgar as posterity has decreed. The fashions went out with the 'twenties, but Cocteau's work survives. Somehow we have the feeling that Cocteau would survive in any age through his charm, so long as a place can be found for a poet.

Although we sense he is a lonely man, his life has been surrounded by friends, who have so testified their friendship that there have been times when they held Cocteau's judgment sacred, his tastes impeccable, when one word from him on a controversial topic was final. His early friends who met him every Saturday included Radiguet (his personal discovery), Picasso, Cendrars, Tristan Bernard, Rubinstein, and many others. Then suddenly in 1923 Radiguet died of typhoid fever and Cocteau was struck down with grief. Neither Monte Carlo, nor opium nor religion was sufficient, alone work offered an escape, a possibility to explore the mysteries through artistic expression. In the years that have followed, Cocteau has lost many of his friends (the Gestapo assassinated several) but his search goes on, giving him little time for reflection or memories.

And so we come to Cocteau's work, and in this respect we shall concentrate on his work for the theatre, which is fully as important as the rôle he has played in the other arts. Each of his plays has brought a new horizon to the modern theatre, whether it be a return to the purity of Greek legend in *La Machine infernale*, the legends of medieval Europe in *Les Chevaliers de la Table Ronde*, the classical tragedy *Renaud et Armide*, or the brilliant monologue *La Voix humaine* where a wife holds a last and unavailing telephone conversation with the man who has left her for good. His theatre has caused famous scandals, notably *Les Parents terribles* which the Paris municipality condemned for its 'incest', and *Bacchus*, said to be anti-religious, and by which a friendship of youth, with François Mauriac, was broken in an evening.

Yet in all these plays there is the common element of, shall we call it, poetry, and in spite of the pre-war Paris municipality, taste.

Since his first work in the theatre, *Parade*, written in 1917 for the Diaghilev dancers (music by Satie, décor by Picasso), Cocteau has given us some seventeen plays, from which we shall select for consideration his admirable *Les Parents terribles*, his controversial *Bacchus*, his romantic *L'Aigle à deux Têtes*, his treatment of classical legend in *La Machine infernale* and also in his *Orphée*. Though outside the province of this book, Cocteau's career in the cinema has been an extension of his theatrical activity, and in the film version of *Orphée* Cocteau is justified in his claim to have realised his supreme ambition.

*

All Cocteau's plays have a great sense of the dramatic. No one knows better than he how to treat an old and worn legend, or for that matter a conventional boulevard situation, in terms of the theatre of to-day. In his first major work *Orphée* (1925), for example, we see how he turns to a familiar old Greek plot and makes it acceptable for a modern audience, giving it not only dramatic unity but contemporary interpretation as well. The legend becomes a means of expressing Cocteau's own preoccupations with the dividing line between the conscious and the unconscious, the real and the fantasy, humdrum life and the adventure of death. Orpheus becomes a poet whose inspiration is death, and his poetry responds to mysterious force instead of the poet's self.

All sense of time in the play is indefinite; we are neither in the past, present nor future. Orpheus has married Eurydice. Orpheus is the national poet of his country; Eurydice has left her secret cult and the Bacchantes (commanded by Aglaonice) to get married, and has consequently kindled their hatred against her. One day Orpheus is intrigued by a horse in a street and takes it home. The horse communicates to him, through an alphabetical system, mysterious phrases such as "Madame Eurydice will come back from hell", and gradually Orpheus is bewitched by the invisible power of this horse, much to the distress of Eurydice. She confides in Heurtebise, a glazier, who passes each day. Heurtebise in fact turns out to be an angel who watches over the destinies of Orpheus and Eurydice. While Orpheus is absent entering for a poetry competition Aglaonice succeeds in poisoning Eurydice, and Death arrives to carry her away. Orpheus learns what has happened and decides, with the help of the angel to go and bring her back from the underworld. As in the legend, he is allowed to do this provided he does not look at her on the journey, and of course the inevitable happens. On his return Orpheus is warned that the Bacchantes are coming to kill him, since they believe that he is a mystifier, having read his poem "Madame Eurydice will return from hell". Instead of saving himself Orpheus gives himself to the fury of the Bacchantes and to Death.

Cocteau adds, as it were, an amusing postscript where the Bacchantes declare to the police that they found Orpheus dead. The police arrest the angel Heurtebise, who, when asked his name replies: Jean Cocteau. The angel disappears to join Orpheus and Eurydice now united forever.

The little episode is an excellent *jeu d'esprit* on the lack of imagination which humans possess, and what could be more human than the prosaic plodding of police methods? The play is described as a 'tragedy in one act and one interval'. The description emphasises the timeless element of the play; we witness a scene in the middle of the play twice, as if in rehearsal. There are numerous such tricks throughout the play, some less effective, as when a member of the audience is asked for the loan of his watch, but on the whole the comedy and tragedy are carefully interposed, and the play has coherence. The two themes, poetry and death, become one whole, just as Orpheus and Eurydice are united in death. The premium then is on death, but death, as we have seen in Cocteau, leads to the revelation of the artistic unknown. The fusion of poetry with death is an adventure story.

Orphée was the first love of Cocteau. His return to the theme for his film deserves mention, if only to understand his development a quarter of a century later, and to see how his ideas had had an opportunity of spreading their wings in the greater freedom of the cinema, in ways in which the proscenium arch could never compete with 'the magic box'. The film *Orphée* is set in the contemporary world (the period is defined) and the realism is intensified. Orpheus becomes a modern poet who wishes to avoid the Saint-Germain vogue and consequently makes himself unpopular among them. Death is a Princess who drives about in a Rolls Royce; Heurtebise is her chauffeur. Eurydice used to work at a club called The Bacchantes. The whole accent is thus different from that of the play. The film sweeps through the mirror to the shades and desolation of 'no-man's land', the journey through the underworld. We make the grand tour. Then there is a most important variation in the theme: the Princess Death kills Eurydice for jealousy because she is in love with Orpheus. This is why Eurydice is allowed to go back with Orpheus, but this time it is Eurydice who forces him to see her. Orpheus is shot in a riot on his return, but the Princess returns them both while she must go another way, to face trial for her crimes.

The film is an adventure story derived from the play. Although the play never drags, it does not succeed in carrying the audience with it as does the film. Both the film and the play deal with the same unknown, an exploration of death through dream, a mysterious journey into the hinterland of the imagination. There is no need to struggle against death, for acceptance is so very much more exciting.

Cocteau turned again to Greek mythology in *La Machine infernale* (1932, produced by Jouvet in 1934), this time the old (not to say worn) legend of Oedipus. Once again he transforms it into something vital, alive and coherent. The inevitability of events is shown from the start, again in a manner acceptable to a modern audience. The horror of a son who murders his father and marries his mother is made real and convincing. Oedipus is a young man, full of conceit and certainties. How easy it is to disprove the oracle's prophecy that he would commit such crimes; all he has to do is flee from the land where he was brought up, Corinth, and go to Thebes (not knowing that this was in fact the country of his birth). As for killing his father, he has only killed one man in his whole life, and that was a stranger by accident (not knowing it was his own father). In Thebes there is a monster ravaging the country, and he is determined to kill it and claim the hand of the Queen (his mother). The monster is called the Sphinx, but when the Sphinx sees Oedipus she falls in love with him (to tell the truth she had already grown tired of killing). She saves his life by whispering the answer to the riddle that all must be asked when they challenge her. Oedipus in his conceit thinks he has beaten her, and not looking at her goes off to claim the Queen. The Sphinx in fury decides to let him go, for his punishment is a crime worse than death.

La Machine infernale is full of theatrical situations, where the audience already knows what Oedipus does not know. He understands nothing until it is too late. Each act is a decisive step towards the inevitable, but the final tragedy clears the crime of incest, for Jocasta reappears from the dead no longer as his wife, but as his mother, leading away the blind Oedipus.

Les Parents terribles (1938) must be considered on its own, for it has no comparison with any of Cocteau's other works. It is a realistic tragedy, bare in outline, devoid of those flamboyant frills which

Cocteau so often delights in; it is pure melodrama and admirable in its intensity. Nowhere else does Cocteau succeed so clearly as a man of the theatre, nor does he display in his other work the depth of character study that he has here created. The play is a biting social comedy concerning a mother's neurotic infatuation for her son, who has fallen in love with a girl who turns out to be his father's mistress. However triangular and contrived the plot may seem in outline, there is nothing artificial when reading the play or seeing it in performance. Yvonne, the mother, an invalid, neglects her husband and saves all her passionate affection for her son, Michel. Then there is Léonie, Yvonne's sister, who has always been in love with Georges, the man her sister married. She lives in the same household and as she suffers her own unfulfilled love, she is the witness and the figure of destiny. Emotions explode when Michel announces he wants to marry Madeleine. Yvonne refuses to share her son with someone else, while Georges forbids the marriage for other reasons. It is Léonie who helps Michel marry Madeleine in the end, a sacrifice more than Yvonne can bear, choosing suicide rather than acceptance.

Few plays in the modern theatre have the economy, the telling efficiency of *Les Parents terribles;* we have here a social satire more biting than anything of Becque's, the lies, petty jealousies pile up for the earth to open. Then in a Pirandellian fashion the masks are torn away from the characters and they see the truth for the first time. Cocteau concentrates on writing what he calls parts for 'great actors'. With no distractions, bound within the confines of the French bourgeois stuffiness, the claustrophobic atmosphere of *Les Parents terribles* is the backcloth for a genuine tragedy.

We shall not consider the boulevard 'portrait' *Les Monstres sacrés* written in 1940 and produced with success, but we shall mention more briefly Cocteau's two most recent plays, *L'Aigle à deux Têtes* (1946) and *Bacchus* (1951), neither of which adds to his status as a dramatist, though they both have considerable interest.

In *L'Aigle à deux Têtes* ("The two-headed Eagle") Cocteau turns to romanticism. We are in Ruritania (more exactly, "an imaginary castle in Germany"); it is the tenth anniversary of the assassination of the King on the day of his marriage. For ten years the Queen has been living in solitude, with the memory of her lover. The anniversary comes round and, as usual, she will dine alone in her bridal chamber. We hear the thunder of a storm, and then the sharp clatter of revolver shots. A young man jumps through the window. The Queen's bodyguard knock at the door and the Queen hides her intruder (who closely resembles the portrait of the King). They have come to warn her that an assassin is at large with intentions of killing her. The Queen does not give him up, but left alone with him they find themselves mutually attracted. But in a Cocteau play (as in contemporary French drama) there is no easy solution. Death alone can unite the two, which is melodramatically realised at the end by the assassin taking poison and the Queen, frantic, lying to make him kill her.

Like all Cocteau's work it is delicate. In Paris Edwige Feuillère turned the play into a triumph, as did Eileen Herlie, although in a very inexact translation, in London. But what a premium one has to pay for happiness!

The scandal of *Bacchus* seems completely unjustified. Only in its period and setting does the play have any similarity to Sartre's *Le Diable et le bon Dieu,* and even if Cocteau was attempting to outshine Sartre he has at any rate written a very different type of play. There is no character in *Bacchus* who represents the Devil. Criticism of *Bacchus* is justified not on the Mauriac line, but for the far simpler reason that it is not a very good play. Mauriac, as M. Stanislas Fumet explains in a debate on "Atheism in the Contemporary Theatre" (organised by the Centre Catholique des Intellectuels and printed in *Le Théâtre contemporain*) sees the Church as a mother, while Cocteau sees it as a theatrical partner. It is the clothes of the Renaissance, the ring of the bishop, the purple of the cardinal, that catch Cocteau's eye. The theme deals with the election in a little German village of Bacchus, who for five days will speak as master. The period is that of the Reformation and the Peasants' Revolt. The villagers choose the village idiot Hans for this task, a man who wishes neither to become a new Luther not to assume the powers of the Pope, but rather to free the people from the oppression of the nobles and the Church. He hates tyrants in any form, he wishes to preach only the love of God and the freedom of the individual. But his ideals only make him hated by all. The people are going to burn him, and to save him it is suggested that he enters Holy Orders. But Hans prefers to remain free. He shows himself to the mob and is hit by an arrow. The Cardinal, however, is determined to cheat him, and announces that before his death Hans had entered the priesthood.

It is easy to understand why the play suggested affinities with the atheistic *Le Diable et le bon Dieu,* but Cocteau has merely taken a Sartrian subject and treated it in his own way, as he had done with Greek legends and romantic dramas in the past. Cocteau protests his

eedom from 'isms', but may we suggest that this freedom is also
ae failure of Cocteau to give his undoubted artistry any sense of
irection. He has squandered in tremendous diffusion his poetical
nergy, but he has never held this energy in check to assure an
verwhelming victory. Even poets, after all, cannot be jacks of all
aedia, and while all poets must experiment by trial and error towards
ae realisation of their creative genius, the truth must be faced that
aroughout his career Cocteau has only experimented. His is a genius
·hich has only shown itself here and there in unexpected places, and he
as ended up in the most unexpected place of all, with a seat among the
mmortals' of the Académie Française. Had he talent only he would
oubtless have gone farther and secured a more important, though
erhaps less controversial place, in the arts. But it seems somewhat
iggardly to complain that a genius never showed more than promise
a his works; would we exchange him on this account for a hard-
·orking apprentice who believes that poetry and any of the arts can
e taught in 10,000 difficult lessons?

NINE

A DRAMATIST IN THE WILDERNESS: EUGENE O'NEILL

"IF our life were endless and painless it would probably occur t[...] no one why the world exists", says Schopenhauer. "Do not tak[...] pain away from us! It is our truth. Without pain there is noth[...]ing . . ." comes the O'Neill echo. "I do not know what eternal life is[...] but this one here is merely a wicked joke", says Voltaire. "The lie o[...] a pipe dream is what gives life to the whole misbegotten mad lot of us[...] drunk or sober", is the philosophy of O'Neill's last-produced pla[...] *The Iceman Cometh*. Out of thirty-seven of O'Neill's plays it has bee[...] observed[1] that there are only five free from murder, death, suicide o[...] insanity. In the others the score is eight suicides and one unsuccessfu[...] attempt, twelve important murders (not counting incidental episodes)[...] twenty-six deaths, nearly all due to violence, and eight cases of insanity[...] Since this count was taken the victims have increased, but thes[...] figures will suffice.

It was not the way of Eugene O'Neill (1888–1953) to show restrain[...] His theatrical career was as restless as his early life (from gold pros[...]pector, seaman, to down-and-out) had been reckless. He was foreve[...] blazing trails in his writing to explore 'beyond the horizon', but some[...]how his imagination fails him; on the edge of the unknown he react[...] like a flat-earther about to fall into infinity. His undaunted courag[...] forever leads him into labyrinths from which he cannot extricate him[...]self. It was because O'Neill never knew what he wanted out of lif[...] that he never knew where he was going, or what were the things fo[...] which he felt instinctively he should be searching.

As a thinker O'Neill's aspirations were too roaming, adventurous[...] romantic, to allow for profundity. He let others do the thinking fo[...] him, as in the two examples already given. Yet his indebtedness t[...]

[1] Barrett H. Clark in *Eugene O'Neill*.

German philosophers, from Nietzsche and Schopenhauer to Freud, did not replace his Catholic upbringing and discarded faith with something positive; in his later work pessimism becomes an obsession and we feel the absence of any set of values as much as O'Neill does himself.

It has often been remarked that O'Neill's greatest failing was one of language; in setting out to write a great epic he seldom took into account his own limitations. The subjects of his tragedies demand a language approaching poetry, whereas they are clothed (except for one or two isolated lines) with a facile dialogue conforming to the pedestrian standards of modern inadequacy. Even the most important scenes of *Mourning Becomes Electra* could have been written by any good Hollywood scriptwriter. The exigencies, not of prose but of conversational expression may be severe in the English-speaking theatre, but no dramatist can do himself justice until he has freed himself of its petty dictatorship and found a style. It is style rather than poetry that the contemporary drama so sadly lacks. Without being able to distinguish his plays with either style or poetry, O'Neill was never able to translate adequately his chosen canvas in terms of the drama. Nor was he adept with a sense of humour; his satires such as *Marco Millions* require a pungent, fiery wit that is the blessing and the curse of so many Irish writers — O'Neill never inherited this gift from his Irish stock.

Yet when all this has been said and taken into consideration (and they are serious faults to find with any important dramatist) O'Neill's reputation does not collapse like playing-cards. His achievements should no more be underrated than they should, as in the past among certain American intellectuals, be worshipped with superlatives. In the first place, O'Neill undoubtedly occupies the seat of honour among American dramatists. He has, so far, no challengers. Sidney Howard, Robert Emmet Sherwood, Elmer Rice, Maxwell Anderson, Philip Barry, Lillian Hellman or Marc Connelly — such candidates from O'Neill's generation look small in comparison. For O'Neill is the grand old man of the American theatre, he was the first dramatist to endow his theatre with a critical status. He was the first American playwright to achieve an international reputation, with his works performed the whole world over, from Russia to France, Scandinavia to South America.

If the speed of O'Neill's rise to fame is true to the pattern of a typical American success story, he was also to suffer the fate of old soldiers, not dying, simply fading away. It is a strange paradox that O'Neill was always as ahead of his times in the American theatre as he

was behind them in the European. He stormed the barricades of Broad
way without getting hurt and without even a publicity agency, a tasl
which one might imagine would be much more difficult to-day. Afte
he had found a small experimental group, the Princeton Playhouse
who were willing to produce any play O'Neill wrote for them, wor
soon got round. A professional production followed, and with thi
came a Pulitzer Prize. Nothing was to stem the O'Neill tide. Critic
such as George Jean Nathan and Barrett H. Clark pressed his claims
The censors did their best to silence the rebel by providing him witl
the wrong sort of audiences. But literary awards brought their merits
and O'Neill's prestige culminated in 1934 with the award of the Nobe
Prize for Literature. At the height of his fame he retired, and for th
next twelve years no new play from O'Neill was published or pro
duced. There were a few revivals, without great success, and his books
tucked away on library shelves, continued to be read by the faithful few
But O'Neill's name was no longer bracketed with those of Shaw an
Ibsen.

During the years between 1934 and 1943 O'Neill was hard at work
In 1939 he completed *The Iceman Cometh*, in 1940-41 his autobiogra
phical *Long Day's Journey Into Night*, and in 1943 *A Moon for th
Misbegotten* and *A Touch of the Poet*. It was during the same perio
that O'Neill had ambitiously envisaged two cycles of plays. He com
pleted first drafts of three double-length plays, *The Greed of the Meek
And Give Me Death* and *More Stately Mansions*, which he groupe
in a cycle called *A Tale of Possessors Self-Dispossessed*. The first tw
he destroyed, and he intended to do the same with *More Statel
Mansions*, of which a handwritten manuscript survived, because h
was dissatisfied with them as they stood and, already ill with Parkin
son's disease, he was unable to undertake revision. *More Statel
Mansions* is now in the hands of the Stockholm Royal Dramatic Theatr
— to which O'Neill had left *Long Day's Journey Into Night* as
"deathbed legacy" to a nation whom he felt had been more loyal t
him than his own. Of the second cycle of plays, to be called *By Wa
of Obit* O'Neill completed only one one-act play, *Hughie*.

According to O'Neill's will all copies of *Long Day's Journey Int
Night* were to have been locked in his publishers' vault for twenty-fiv
years and the play was never to be staged in the United States. Copie
were stored in the vaults of Random House and it looked as thoug
we would have to wait until 1978 in order to see the *magnum opu
which O'Neill had once described in outlines to Barrett H. Clark:

All the dramatic episodes of my life I have so far kept out of my plays, and the majority of the things I have seen happen to other people. I've hardly begun to work up all this material, but I'm saving it up for one thing in particular, a cycle of plays, to be acted on nine successive nights; together they will form a sort of dramatic autobiography, something in the style of *War and Peace* or *Jean Cristophe*.

Three years after O'Neill's death, in February 1956, *Long Day's Journey Into Night* was published with Mrs. Carlotta O'Neill's consent though Random House preferred to cancel the contract rather than break the terms of the will. Meanwhile in Stockholm the play was received with enthusiasm. Subsequent productions followed in New York (7 November 1956) and in London two years later. *A Moon for the Misbegotten* was produced in New York in 1957 and *A Touch of the Poet* opened the 1958-1959 Broadway season. Although the majority of the critics highly praised these plays they have made far less impact than one would have expected from the major works of the leading American dramatist. Perhaps it is that for a man who had striven throughout his life at experiment in new forms, this retreat to the traditional naturalism seemed almost a surrender of his imagination. In these plays O'Neill returns to many of his earlier themes, but the fog thickens, the pessimism deepens, the characters become ghosts, and the dramatic conflict and power is submerged. We can feel the disease gaining hold. Written "in tears and blood", O'Neill was too close to his old and his new sorrows and it is only human in the circumstances for him occasionally to put life before creative art.

It is almost impossible to forecast O'Neill's position in the future, for even his present reputation is insecure. There are so many items which cancel out on the balance sheet. O'Neill is an 'all but' dramatist; he moved from realism to expressionism, Greek tragedy with modern psychology to studies of miscegenation and philosphical symbolism; yet he never 'quite' found himself in any of these experiments. The characters in his plays are seldom remarkable, his female portraits tend to be devoid of sympathy and human only through sexual thirst. Yet his sense of the dramatic in life and its realisation in the theatre is ever present, and certainly nothing can cancel out his innate ability to tell a story.

There is no shortage of plays to write about; fortunately it is not our purpose here to give a history of O'Neill's theatrical career, or a list

of his works in chronological order, the majority of which are alread
forgotten and are unlikely to be seen again. Some critics have suggeste
that O'Neill has never equalled, even in his most far-reaching exper
ments, the stark realism and humanity of his four early sea-play
Bound East for Cardiff (1916), *In the Zone* (1917), *The Long Voya*
Home (1917) and *The Moon of the Caribbees* (1918) — plays which a
generally linked together under the title *S.S. Glencairn* and which we
filmed in 1940 as *The Long Voyage Home*. This is perhaps true, for nc
only did O'Neill know the characters he was writing about, but he ha
also the ability to visualise certain dramatic situations which give shap
form and purpose to his playlets. But while with the realistic sea-play
he proved himself a promising young dramatist, he could never hav
achieved distinction and fame as America's leading playwright withou
his ambitious experiments and many-sided assaults on the convention;
drama of the day. He brought to the stage a breadth of vision, showin
the means whereby the theatre could reveal for its audience life, wit
its infinite possibilities, at once real and fantastic. No matter if O'Nei
failed in his own plays, he influenced the American dramatists to thin
big, and to continue the attack. And even in his own plays, the surpris
is not so much what O'Neill failed to do, but how much he did in fac
achieve.

Which are the plays that have lasted? Undoubtedly his expression
istic *The Emperor Jones* (1920), a psychological study of how fea
seizes a Negro's soul and sends him terror-stricken into the jungle
has lost none of its power. Here is a play which O'Neill might hav
written for broadcasting, for the effect on the nerves of the rhythmic;
beating of the drums is oppressively exciting and outstanding radi
material. *The Hairy Ape* (1922) is half expressionist, half realist, an
had not only novelty but dramatic intensity. In *Desire under the Elm*
(1924) O'Neill gives us his first important work with a tragic visio
where he reaches near the heights of his theatrical achievements. Set in
New England farm in the 1850's, *Desire under the Elms* explores th
'desire' to possess, in its different forms. Abbie, the young wife of th
old puritanical farmer Ephraim Cabot, desires security; Ephraim, th
love of his wife and sons which is denied him; Ephraim's thirty-two
year-old son Eben desires to possess what he believes is his birthrigh
the farm. Abbie gives herself to Eben, and the passions of desire unfol
a misfortune which races towards a tragic disaster; life is presente
naked and without hope, reciprocated love or comfort, indeed withou
meaning.

The Great God Brown is not likely to survive, in spite of — or perhaps because of — the use of symbolism and masks, but in one speech in it, O'Neill projects what may well be his own character and unhappy philosophy. It is also one of the passages where his language displays latent power.

> Why am I afraid to dance, I who love music and rhythm and grace and song and laughter? Why am I afraid to live, I who love life and the beauty of flesh and the living colours of earth and sky and sea? Why am I afraid to love? Why am I afraid, I who am not afraid? Why must I pretend to scorn in order to pity? Why must I hide myself in self-contempt in order to understand? Why must I be ashamed of my strength, so proud of my weakness? Why must I live in a cage like a criminal, defying and hating, I who love peace and friendship? *(clasping his hands above in supplication)* Why was I born without a skin, O God, that I must wear armour in order to touch or to be touched? . . . Or rather, Old Graybeard, why the devil was I born at all?

Neither *Lazarus Laughed* (1926), nor *Marco Millions* (1928) nor *Strange Interlude* (1928) has weathered the years. There remain for examination O'Neill's most famous play *Mourning Becomes Electra* (1931) his much discussed *The Iceman Cometh* (1946) about which critics have divided into the 'Ayes' and the 'Noes' camps, with an apparently unbridgeable gap between them and *Long Day's Journey into Night*. Neither *A Touch of the Poet* nor *A Moon for the Misbegotten* have the same scope or staying power. There is good reason for selecting these plays for discussion; *Mourning Becomes Electra* is not only the best known and most widely acclaimed of O'Neill's works, but in it he set out to achieve definite aims, which he explains in an article contributed to *European Theories of the Drama*.[1] In *The Iceman Cometh* we have a vastly different type of play, which harks back to his early career for its characters and setting, although all resemblances to the sea-plays end there. It is a play of allegorical content, of waterfront types who are caught up in their own 'pipe dreams' and suddenly made aware that they must face up to their responsibilities and seek redemption. It has a signification which makes one of O'Neill's most profound studies; one need hardly add that it is an intensely depressing play. *Long Day's Journey Into Night* reveals

Edited by Barrett H. Clark, revised 1947, New York.

the secrets of O'Neill's own family — secrets which had already been hinted at or guessed from his earlier work. He has attempted to write his own tragedy "with deep pity and understanding and forgiveness for *all* the four haunted Tyrones."

*

In the spring of 1926 O'Neill made the following note in his diary "Modern psychological drama using one of the old legend plots of Greek tragedy for its basic theme — the Electra story — the Medea Is it possible to get modern psychological approximation of Greek sense of fate into such a play, which an intelligent audience of to-day possessed of no belief in gods or supernatural retribution, could accept and be moved by?" Two and a half years later when *en route* for China the idea persisted. By April, 1929, he had visualised the period and some of the departures from the story, coming to the conclusion "no matter in what period of American history play is laid, must remain a modern psychological drama — nothing to do with period except to use it as a mask — what war? . . . Civil War is only possibility — fits into picture — Civil War as background for drama of murderous family love and hate."

O'Neill tells how he decided to follow the Greek practice and make a trilogy of the Electra plot, the first play introducing Agamemnon's homing and murder, the second following Electra's revenge on mother and lover, using Orestes to help her, and the third play: "retribution Orestes and Electra". By August, 1929, O'Neill had completed his scenario of the three plays. The task of writing them occupied two years, and in August, 1931, he was able to write: "has power and drive and the strange quality of unreal reality I wanted — main purpose seems to be soundly achieved — there is a feeling of fate in it, or I am a fool — a psychological approximation of the fate in the Greek tragedies on this theme attained without benefit of the supernatural."

So we have the trilogy realised. In *The Homecoming* we witness the return of Ezra Mannon and his son Orin from the war, and the murder of Ezra Mannon by his wife Christine, because of her affair with Captain Brant. In *The Hunted* Lavinia, who loved her father and despises her mother Christine, is aware of her mother's crime. She urges her brother Orin, who despised his father and loves his mother, to avenge the murder. Orin surprises Captain Brant and shoots him in front of Christine, who as a result commits suicide. Orin believes that he is growing like his father and is driven to suicide. Lavinia, left alone, tormented in her soul, accepts her punishment worse than death by living in the ill-fated Mannon house. The modern approximation of being haunted by the Eumenides is as devastating as any torment known in Greek drama.

The trilogy moves with melodramatic suspense, the Freudian under-currents are subtly conceived, the mask-like face of Lavinia dominates the stage, a symbolic portrait to match the portraits of her Mannon ancestors on the wall. The tragedy remains strangely cold; we are in an ice-box of repressed emotions. In the end we realise that in spite of the tension, admirably built up, the mask-like figures are merely instru-mental to the theme; they are not characters of flesh and blood nor are masks a substitute for language. Whatever our admiration, the trilogy lacks the essential substance to turn it into human tragedy.

★

Whereas *Mourning Becomes Electra* keeps emotion subdued and sheltered from the harsh winds of conviction, *The Iceman Cometh* smothers our emotions with a stifling atmosphere of booze, smoke, and 'pipe dream' credulity. *Mourning Becomes Electra* is a tragedy without tears; in *The Iceman Cometh* the time for tears is past. The curtain rises on a group of drunks who spend their days in Harry Hope's saloon, a cheap ginmill of the five cent whisky variety; the year is 1912. One of the drunks aptly describes the dive as:

> No chance saloon. It's Bedrock Bar, the End of the Line Café, the Bottom of the Sea Rathskeller! Don't you notice the beauti-ful calm in the atmosphere? That's because it's the last harbour. No one here has to worry about where they're going next, be-cause there is no further they can go. It's a great comfort to them. Although even here they can keep up appearances of life with a few harmless pipe dreams about their yesterdays and to-morrows, as you'll see for yourself if you're here long.

Each of the drunks has his life behind him, either dodging the 'dicks' or merely as a down-and-out; each finds consolation in an alcoholic stupor. There is Larry Slade, a sixty-year-old Irish ex-anarchist turned philosopher who declares that all his pipe dreams are dead and buried. 'What's before me is the comforting fact that death is a fine long sleep,

K

and I'm damned tired, and it can't come too soon for me." Then Hickey arrives. Hickey is "a hardware drummer. An old friend of Harry Hope's and all the gang. He's a grand guy. He comes here twice a year regularly on a periodical drunk and blows in all his money." But this time when Hickey arrives he is a reformed and therefore unwelcome intruder. He is on the water wagon. He has finally had the guts to face life, throw overboard all the "damned lying pipe dreams" and find peace. Furthermore he means to save them all from their pipe dreams. "Just stop lying about yourself and kidding yourself about to-morrows" he tells them.

The results are the opposite of what he expected. The salvation cure just does not work with the others; instead the atmosphere becomes one of gloom and depression. Then Hickey confides in them that his wife, whom they used to joke about being left in bed "with the iceman" is dead. Later on he tells them the whole truth. He has murdered her because she loved him too much and he loved her too much. He has killed her to save her from the continual sufferings he caused her. He started hating himself for his weakness, and in hating himself he came to hating her. He knew that he could not control his cravings, and he had not the courage to rely on his wife's infinite forgiveness. It would eventually have broken her heart. He could not tell her he was leaving her, it seemed so much kinder not to allow her to wake up, to leave her in her dreams.

Suddenly in making this confession he sees that he must have been crazy to do such a thing, it had merely been a 'pipe dream' for himself. The others, who have listened in awe to his confession, breathe a sigh of relief and accept his solution as a return to the good old days before Hickey made them start thinking about redemption. Hickey gives himself up to the police, one of the drunks commits suicide and Larry, left alone, the philosophic commentator, remarks "Be God, I'm the only real convert to death Hickey made here. From the bottom of my coward's heart I mean that now." We are back where we were, the wheels have turned full circle.

Like all O'Neill's plays, *The Iceman Cometh* has its faults. Rich though the play is, one regrets that it was not abbreviated to a more economical length (the first night on Broadway started at 4.30 in the afternoon and continued until 10 p.m.) There is room for considerable pruning of dialogue among the secondary characters who add little to the body of the play, but O'Neill was never able to condense his thoughts. He has certainly managed to convey an atmosphere which is not easy to forget. It is a play of the day before yesterday, the days of O'Neill's youth which he spent on the waterfront, but it could not have been written in his youth. O'Neill is not here attempting any autobiographical situations such as, say, George Orwell did in *Down and Out in London and Paris*. He has attempted to show us his 'have beens' in a dramatic situation as he has done with his sea-play characters, only this time he is a wiser and a less contented man. For this is his most depressing play. But to deny its theatrical effectiveness, however distasteful its subject matter may be, we would ourselves have to indulge in some pipe dreaming hara-kiri . . .

*

"Pipe dreams" were not only in Harry Hopes bar in 1912, but also in the living-room where the four "haunted Tyrones" set out for their solitary *Long Day's Journey Into Night*. James Tyrone, the father, is sixty-five, "but looks ten years younger"; he was once a popular actor and the stamp of his profession is still unmistakenly upon him. His wife Mary is a drug addict, though wishful thinking on the part of the family imagines she has been cured. The black sheep of the family is the elder son Jamie, a ne'er-do-well actor, with the signs of "premature disintegration" on his face. Edmund, the younger son is sensitive and has intellectual leanings. He is ill with "a bad summer cold" which like O'Neill in 1912, turns out to be consumption. He faces the possibility of death with a mixture of longing, fear — and anger. It is the anger which sparks off a series of recriminations on the part of each of the family. The father is a miser and thinks he can economise by sending Edmund to an inferior and cheap sanatorium. In the end he agrees to a better home — the one in fact which O'Neill went to and was cured. Gradually the fog seeps through your veins, the impersonal moaning of the fog horn resounding like the voice of fate on these tortured characters, veiling the truth of life and obscuring man's tragic ability to understand, either himself or others.

It has been remarked that it is the misfortune of the American drama that O'Neill should be its number one exhibit. In fairness it is an equal misfortune that O'Neill should have been elevated to the ranks of the exceptional when he was only the head of the youngest drama of the world. He had an outstanding sense of theatre and could write a good play; but he was not a genius and never wrote a masterpiece. He was the tallest figure among little men. He was a disciple of Strindberg and other European figures, but he remained a disciple, he never became a master. It was not in his generation that his nation was to reach artistic maturity. Through his work, however, the American theatre caught up with the European theatre. It started exporting as well as importing. The balance of cultural payments seems already equal, and it may well be that in another generation America will be repaying a cultural debt. Then the teacher can watch his pupils 'do'.

THE APPROACHES OF DESPAIR

WITH *The Iceman Cometh* of O'Neill we have already reached the gates over which is written the grim warning "lasciate ogni speranza voi ch'entrate". Our characters, this time in the respectable company of their authors, hesitate, except for two disreputable tramps of Irish extraction, discovered on the Paris Left Bank where they were waiting for a benevolent old man with a long flowing beard called Monsieur Godot, and who are now prepared to sit down and go on waiting for him in this no-man's land. From anti-social to *anti-theatre*. Sartre of course is there, his characters enclosed *huis clos* in this dark corner, committed to a freedom which absolves them from moral laws. For them man is nothing other than the totality of his acts. The characters of Salacrou are far less certain; they have no grammatical interpretation of the universe to explain life—they simply do not understand. Lucie Blondel for example tells us that she is a woman like any other woman; she has the freedom Nora sought in Ibsen's day, but alas, this does not lead to happiness. If only, she is convinced, she knew what life was about then one day she could be happy. The characters of Salacrou speak and behave like children; they want to be happy. Those of Anouilh — and there are many eccentrics among his characters — are obsessed with a nostalgic longing for a lost innocence, the childhood when they were so happy, and which they will never find again. And the Americans? It is economic and political despair which Arthur Miller portrays, both in the tragedy of a salesman who at the end of his life realises that it has been a pipe dream, that he is a victim of a certain way of life which he failed to "lick". Just as others of his characters have been victims of political events such as the Salem witch hunts in 1692. The characters of Tennessee Williams suffer physically for the maladjustments of an age; the image of a "cat on a hot tin roof" may be applied to their own rendezvous with life.

These playwrights hold very different positions in the theatre world of to-day, as they do at the approaches of despair. But they do, all of them, tend to present a partial view of our times which falls far short of the complete vision which is that of all great writers. We are, of course, too close to the scene ourselves, we can merely be the defendants, not the judges. But as we shall see in the following chapter, there is a hope that the deliberate cult of pessimism might give way to broader horizons.

TEN

SCHOOL FOR PESSIMISM: SAMUEL BECKETT AND EUGÈNE IONESCO

"Pessimism, when you get used to it, is just as agreeable as optimism. Indeed, I think it must be more agreeable, must have a more real savour, than optimism — from the way in which pessimists abandon themselves to it."

ARNOLD BENNETT

THE great pessimists in literature are great revealers, their vision is personal, creative and for all time; they are not to be confused with what may be called the modern school for pessimism, with its accent on neutral observation, abstract or specialised interpretation, and the *mal de siècle,* which is the stimulant of their despair, their orgy of sensationalism and the hotchpotch of their so-called 'authenticity'. They are impersonal because freedom has become a meaningless symbol; whereas the aim of all art is to illuminate life, their aim is to reflect in the fashion of the deceptive headlines of tabloid newspapers 'the nightmare of the civilisation' into which we have been born. If we examine the world created by sincere pessimists, such as Thomas Hardy or Pirandello, to take two examples, there is an innate difference between their contemplation and horizon and that of so many new pessimists who evolve their style and attitude in harmony with the prevailing romanticism of despair. As a mirror to the topsy-turvydom of the times it is understandable — it is also fashionable. And it is the fashion of despondency which keeps up not only the existential bonfire, but also drives out the humanist element in literature without which the life force of art cannot survive, whether pessimistic in its inspiration or not.

Our modern pessimists prefer to criticise rather than create, and their criticism, based on false assumptions and demoniacal gods, completes the destruction — in a frenzy of despair — of a suffering world. Their whole impulse is negative and infective. For modern pessimism is neither the gift nor the sole possession of the existentialists, even though they are responsible for the shockers while the others have merely delivered the goods. In one way or another there are almost no important 'rising' playwrights on the Continent or even in the United States who have escaped the pessimistic scourge, and only in Britain (if we exclude Graham Greene) has this mood found no roots in the theatre (presumably because the theatre is regarded as a diversion). But the cheerful optimism which we find on Shaftesbury Avenue, such as the smug complacency of J. B. Priestley's wartime tub-thumping of *They Came to a City*, to say nothing of the post-war banality of *The Linden Tree*, makes one wonder whether this injection against pessimism is not as bad as the disease itself.

It was of course natural that the years of crisis, defeat, the overthrow of Christian principles and conduct, the humility of a conquered Europe followed by the hollowness of a cold peace, should provoke downright pessimism, as it had done in the dejected Germany after the first world war. What was not forseen was the excess to which certain French existentialist writers would drive the sordid and perverted outlook, which had hitherto only found expression in the instability and obscurity of the German mind. To be fair to the school for pessimism, however, this manifestation was confined to a few members who were too morally sick to come up for air after the liberation. The majority of the school had not the genius of eccentricity; many of them doubtless believed that pessimism was the only approach valid for their times; others with greater cynicism took to pessimism instead of to whisky, a new French *snobisme*.

Pessimism had arrived, it had been proved true when all the refugees, fleeing from Hitler or Franco or Stalin, arrived. Who could deny the foreboding of doom prophesied by Kafka, or the nihilist revolution of Koestler, or Gide's return from the U.S.S.R., or Orwell's return in his *Homage to Catalonia?* Everything was a confirmation and the reaction was to turn pessimism into a reality. The roots lay also in another source, the need for religion, which was to culminate in the failure of religion to prevent a war which threatened the annihilation of man. Was this the punishment on a grandiose scale for the intoxication of sin which man had individually tasted and which novelists such as François Mauriac had described?

The consequences of the peace completed the triumph of pessimism, but if we consider it as a school, it should be emphasised that the mood varied in conception and allowed for different manifestations. The three main sources which determined its growth can be traced, first of all, to the philosophies of Martin Heidegger, dating from the Germany of the 'twenties, which the existential writers took up; secondly, the spiritual dilemma as posed by certain Catholic novelists; and thirdly, the nightmare literature of political refugees (which is very different from the testament of human courage in face of bestiality which has been handed down to us — often posthumously — from the victims of the concentration or elimination camps). So our school ranges from atheistic existentialism, which is responsible for the works of Sartre, Camus, Simone de Beauvoir, on the one hand, to the bitter farces such as those by Marcel Aymé (notably *La Tête des Autres*) and the Jean Anouilh of *Ardèle,* on the other. In between may be placed numerous writers, grouped in two's and three's. François Mauriac and Graham Greene have both transferred the atmosphere of their novels to the stage, and it remains to be seen whether the religious portrayal of evil will find its place in the theatre as it has done in the modern novel. Removed from belief but in desperate need of belief in God, we find writers like Armand Salacrou. It is no longer the happy-go-lucky melody to banish the blues of the 'twenties, "I want to be happy", but "how to be happy?" which becomes the melancholic chant of the Continental playwrights as well as of American playwrights such as Arthur Miller and Tennessee Williams. Yet all these moods, from the existentialist refusal, the search for and despair of religious salvation which becomes the futile pilgrimage of so many, to the blinding and merciless accusation of farce — all these aspects are united in a mighty dedication to the decline and fall of man in Samuel Beckett's play *En attendant Godot.* Together with its sequel *Fin de Partie* (Endgame) a flood of misery is let loose which is both inspired by and epitomises the logical conclusion of the school for pessimism. Better even than Sartre, Beckett may be said to have incorporated all the features of the void which confronts man in his present compromise with the world. For just as man cannot live by bread alone, he now realises that he cannot continue to live by mere thinking or hanging on in vain for a salvation which does not exist. *En attendant Godot* becomes, for those in need of uncertainty, a bible of pessimism, We have had many plays where a mysterious Stranger, always spelt with a capital 'S', arrives, leaving no doubt as to the implications of his rôle; *En attendant Godot* is about the Stranger, the mysterious "Monsieur

Godot" who never arrives and who never will arrive because nothing happens in the play at all; no one comes or goes; all is just nothing.

It seems high time to rebel against the savage exploitation of pessimism, for in France (as in Germany) critics seem to have accepted the mood as normal, and — to judge from the exaggeration of the notices — the play as a *chef-d'oeuvre* "equal in importance" (to quote the words of Jean Anouilh) "to the first Pirandello mounted at Paris by Pitoëff in 1923". More surprising is the success the play has had among certain intellectuals following its London production, for this is a play which is "despairing to men in general and dramatists in particular". Even at the risk of sounding like a second Clement Scott writing on a new *Ghosts*, it seems to this writer that this play is more akin to a cesspool of the degradations of human souls than a tragedy of misfortune. Is there no limit to the depths to which man may descend, and is there so little faith left in man that he must lie there forgotten? Will he never be given a resurrection, will we never again have new horizons opened to us through the nobility of man, and be able to enter a world not altogether unlike our own where there is no exploitation of facile optimism or morbid despair?

En attendant Godot combines many styles into a single mood; it has elements of circus and pantomime, philosophical musings and attempts at existentialist suicides (which unfortunately never succeed). We meet on some strange no-man's land two down and outs, Vladimir and Estragon. Their conversation leads them nowhere, nothing happens, their minds and their bodies remain numb as they wait, every night, for the Stranger. Here is a typical excerpt from the dialogue:

ESTRAGON   Let's go.
VLADIMIR   We can't.
ESTRAGON   Why?
VLADIMIR   We're waiting for Godot.
ESTRAGON   Ah! (*a moment's reflection*). You're sure it was here?
VLADIMIR   What?
ESTRAGON   That we were to wait.
VLADIMIR   He said by the tree (*he looks at the tree*). Do you see any others?
ESTRAGON   What is it?
VLADIMIR   I don't know. A willow.
ESTRAGON   Where are the leaves?
VLADIMIR   It must be dead.

And so on, and so on, page after page, until we meet two further characters, two strangers as mysterious as the mythical M. Godot himself. The following stage directions explain their appearance:

Enter Pozzo and Lucky. The former directs the latter with the help of a cord fastened round his neck, so that we only see Lucky first trailing a cord long enough for him to reach the centre of the stage before Pozzo emerges from the wings. Lucky carries a heavy suitcase, a folding chair, a basket full of food and an over-coat (on his arm); Pozzo carries a whip.

Pozzo (in the wings): Quicker! (crack of his whip. Pozzo appears. They cross the stage. Lucky passes in front of Vladimir and Estragon and goes away. Pozzo, on seeing Vladimir and Estragon, stops. The cord tightens. Pozzo draws it in violently). Back! (noise of falling. It's Lucky who falls with all his load. Vladimir and Estragon look at him, torn between the desire to go to his rescue and the fear to get involved with something which doesn't concern them. Vladimir makes a step towards Lucky, but Estragon draws him back by the arm.)

We have here plenty of symbolistic food for thought, and more is to come. Clearly Pozzo is not Godot, and on learning their mistake Vladimir and Estragon deny even knowing Monsieur Godot.

The play cannot be described satisfactorily or even read; its impact can only be felt in the theatre. Lucky, with his long hair flowing over a ghostly white face, his elongated figure, his thin chop-sticks of legs, stands burdened under his load without ever placing his suitcase and other objects to rest. He merely stands dumb and shakes rhythmically while Pozzo cracks his whip or eats a chicken. He is completely the slave, responding to orders from Pozzo to dance and think. This is his chance, words flow out of his mouth in a non-stop jabber; three and a half pages are filled without a punctuation or even half a dozen words of continuous meaning; doubtless the unrelated words and phrases are meant to convey deep meaning, but it overwhelms an audience as it does eventually the characters, who throw themselves on Lucky to put an end to his thinking.

The only other character in the play is a young boy who arrives with a message from Godot saying that Godot will not come that evening, but to-morrow "for certain". There is, however, something strange about this boy, who makes two appearances and yet denies, on the

second, that he had ever been to see Vladimir and Estragon before
The play ends as it began, with the two beggars waiting in vain fo
Godot. The dialogue continues on its doleful repetitive course, th
'nothingness' of everything becomes nauseating. There is nothing lef
for them but to try and hang themselves — but alas, we know that the
cannot even succeed in doing that:

ESTRAGON   You haven't got a bit of rope?
VLADIMIR   No.
ESTRAGON   Then we can't.
VLADIMIR   Let's go.
ESTRAGON   Wait, here's my belt.
VLADIMIR   It's too short.

They finally make one last attempt at hanging themselves with the cord
from Estragon's trousers, but it breaks. Eventually Estragon says:

ESTRAGON   I can't go on like this.
VLADIMIR   That's what you think.
ESTRAGON   If we parted that might be better for us.
VLADIMIR   We'll hang ourselves to-morrow (*pause*). Unless Godot
           comes.
ESTRAGON   And if he comes?
VLADIMIR   We'll be saved.

VLADIMIR   Well? Shall we go?
ESTRAGON   Yes, let's go. (*They don't move*).

CURTAIN

What further in the way of comment is required? One should add in
fairness that *En attendant Godot* comes across to an audience in its full
pessimism, and whatever the subject matter, it offers remarkable scope
for actors and an imaginative *mise en scène*. Both in London and Paris
the script was treated as a tragi-comedy, but in the American productions the same lines were played for comedy. The first American
production, on its opening in Miami, went as far as to bill the play
"the laugh hit of four continents". One wonders who had the last
laugh there.

En attendant Godot was written in 1947-48 and produced on the
narrow stage of the Left-Bank Theatre Babylone, Paris, on January 5th,

953. In 1956 by way of a post-script Beckett wrote *Fin de Partie*,
first produced in French at the Royal Court Theatre, London on
April 1st, 1957. In this one-act moan of uncompromising gloom we
are immersed in a pessimism beyond all limits of suffering, life and
certainly art. We are like flat-earthers falling into space. We cannot
save ourselves, and no one else will. We share the Beat philosopher's
credo that "the existentialist cat dug like that the positive answer of
nothingness, in the face of nothingness, is positivism — we dig that the
positive answer of nothingness, to nothingness, is nothingness — Man,
isn't that father out?" The four characters are like outcasts, untouch-
ables, in a dying world. Already as if in a coma they are beyond
hypnotizing us with their misery. They are all cripples, Hamm cannot
rise from his chair, Clov cannot sit down, while the other two, Nag
and Nell, cannot rise out of the dustbins that imprison them. Here is the
cruel imagery of suffering humanity, as one French critic observed,
like in the nightmare world of Bosch and Breughel. Listen to their
dialogue:

HAMM: Nature's forgotten us.
CLOV: There is no more nature.
HAMM: . . . But we breath, we age, we lose our hair, our teeth, our
          youth and ideals.
CLOV: Then she's not forgotten us.

or, as Nell says from her dustbin, "Why this play-acting every day?"
Time has lost all meaning, it is the time it usually is. Hamm takes a
tranquilizer in the evening and a stimulant in the morning, other
characters are living by tears. "What's Nagg doing?" — answer: "He's
crying." "Then he's alive." No more words, no more pity.

    We are far beyond the frontiers of theatre, of what can hold an
audience by its dramatic intensity, as Godot did. Perhaps Beckett may
indulge in his pessimistic orgies better in the novel where he can
address a reader individually rather than in the theatre where all
depends on collectivity. *Krapp's Last Tape*, a monologue written in
English, proved the more bearable part of the English production of
Fin de Partie (Endgame). Here Krapp, racked with disease, almost
blind, grey tousled hair sweeping over a ghostlike face, his beard badly
shaven, recalls on his tape recorder the moment of intimacy he had, or
believes he had, over thirty years ago, with another individual. The
idiosyncratic Beckettian moan has also a tape-like resonance in his

Third Programme play *Embers* (1959), where an old man on a sea shore relives his tormented past.

Beckett's characters are isolated from life, terrified in their isolation His language is also one of isolation, and in his choice of French Beckett finds the language of his own separation from his native Ireland. In a short radio play, *All that Fall*, one of Beckett's characters says: "I use none but the simplest words, I hope, and yet I sometimes find my way of speaking very — bizarre." The language of Beckett has a purity, a simplicity, a style which is a dimension away. The language we hear is like our own echoes, but echoes resounding from the abyss of the infinite. In this theatre of style and language Beckett approaches another dramatist who has chosen to express himself in French, Eugène Ionesco. As the American dramatist William Saroyan although an enthusiast of their work has remarked, "I certainly took tired Europe to make them, an Irishman and a Roumanian in Paris." Ionesco is entirely unlike Bekett, but together they may be said to be the exponents of antitheatre.

EUGÈNE IONESCO

Ionesco has in ten years created a theatre full of adventure, paradox, parables, burlesque, surrealism, monodrame and scenic naturalism All things are possible, reality is ourselves home in the evening, alone in our room, with the same dreams and nightmares as others, the same fear of death. "Like a naked body on a beach" Ionesco has written "astonished at being there, astonished at his astonishment, beside an infinite ocean, alone under the penetrating sun, inconceivably and irrefutably there." So Ionesco marvels at his own journey through life, from his birth in Roumania in 1912, a childhood in Paris, an adolescence in Bucharest and a return to France where he has lived since 1938. His greatest surprise in life must have been to find himself a playwright, with, in 1959, three plays running simultaneously in Paris

For many years Ionesco remained a convinced enemy of the theatre He could not reconcile its so-called tricks, its exaggerated world and the one in which he lived. In 1949 he wrote his first anti-play, *The Bald Prima Donna* (La Cantatrice chauve), a parody making fun of other plays. Originally entitled *English Without Tears* he found the material for the first scene out of a French-English phrase book. It was not until the production of *La Cantatrice chauve* that Ionesco saw the theatre in a new light and recognised his mistake: the weakness of exaggeration became the theatre's strength, it was in fact essential to 'exaggerate still further, stress and accentuate as far as possible, to push the theatre beyond the intermediate zone which is neither theatre nor literature, to its natural limits." From his discovery he was able to turn to the problems of technique with a fresh mind, free from the usual worries whether he should write in a naturalistic or anti-naturalistic style. He would write for the theatre, pure theatre, he would try and communicate "an incommunicable reality", but nevertheless a reality which can now and again — and that's its paradox, be communicated. For him the theatre becomes a confession of his inner mind. He writes with no axe to grind. "I try to say how the world appears to me" Ionesco affirms "as sincerely as possible . . . I try to be the objective witness of my subjectivity. When writing for the theatre I am only concerned with personifying, in a tragic and at the same time comic sense, reality. That shouldn't prove a difficult problem . . . trying to be *avant-garde* before writing, not wanting to be, or refusing or choosing which kind of *avant-garde* it is to be, is, for someone creative, going about things the wrong way."

In the same way it is not the duty of a playwright to give any kind of message (like Sam Goldwyn he would remind us to try Western Union) or to offer to save the world in any form. A playwright must content himself with being a witness, reflecting from his own sufferings, and from those of others, or perhaps — which is rare — his or their happiness. This statement on the rôle of a dramatist was made by Ionesco in reply to the famous *Observer* controversy of 1958, when Kenneth Tynan, who had been one of the most ardent critics to introduce Ionesco into Britain, suddenly had his doubts. Tynan feared that Ionesco had wandered off "the main road", and while his theatre was interesting and exciting it remained a marginal *divertissement*. His world was one of "solitary robots", an escapism, whereas a playwright is inevitably committed to reality, in his view social reality. Social reality, Ionesco retorted, was the most superficial kind, which had made Sartre (for political melodramas), Osborne, Miller and Brecht merely the "new authors of the boulevard" conforming to prescribed left-wing doctrines as sorry as any of those on the right. This reply, like his remark that Brecht was merely a "theatre of boy scouts" created enemies among those who might have been his friends. But as a playwright Ionesco is determined not to encourage any cult or faction, but to be judged on his own merits.

How far do the plays come up to Ionesco's intentions? Much has been said about their hovering between the sublime and the ridiculous, and no doubt there are complaints that *The Bald Prima Donna* is no about an opera singer. In fact no prima donnas enter at all to share th long English evening with the Smiths, and their guests, the Martins, o to listen to the irregular and nervous chimes of the clock with its expres sion of unutterable boredom. Everything is a reality turned upsid down, even the discovery of the Martins that they are after all husban and wife "comme c'est curieux et quelle coincidence!" It is true tha many of the mannerisms are French rather than English, Englis people seldom complain about draughts in the way the French do even if it is for something to say. The final summing up on Ionesco' first play is that it is an amusing enough joke at the expense of th theatre, but hardly to be taken seriously. And yet out of this *reducti ad absurdum* a style emerges which sets the framework for his futur plays.

Tynan's *divertissement* certainly applies to *La Cantatrice chauv* as to his next play *The Lesson*, where a professor proceeds to th murder of his fortieth pupil, a young girl who looses her enthusiasn and falls back on such excuses (real or invented) as toothache, whil the professor changes from a mood of false gentleness to intolerance

In *The Chairs* Ionesco first attracted more serious attention. It wa produced in 1952, a few months before Beckett's *En Attendant Godo* (produced January 5th, 1953), yet already Ionesco has surpasse Beckett in imagination, though close to him in the expression o "nihilism". An old couple in their eighties live in a tower surrounde by water. Before his death the old man wishes to leave his legacy t posterity, and he and his wife invite a large number of friends an important personalities to hear his lecture. The guests arrive, invisibl to us, but made real by the conversation of the elderly couple, wh pile up more and more chairs in the tower. Everybody has arrived generals, the emperor himself, and finally the orator whom the ol man, fearing emotion might overcome him, has asked to deliver hi message for him. But as the old man and his wife disappear out of th window to their tragedy, the orator turns out to be deaf and dumb and can only speak gibberish.

Six years later in 1958 Ionesco wrote another theological nightmare *Tueur sans gages*, his first full length play. Like Kafka's *The Castle* th play opens with the arrival of the hero, Béranger, at a strange place without knowing how he has arrived. Béranger is an ordinary citize anxious to help others; he finds himself in a model *cité radieuse* magnificently designed with fine buildings, broad avenues lined with trees and gardens full of flowers. It is the lost paradise, and the architect is obviously meant to represent the almighty architect of the world. The city, however, is almost deserted, because a mysterious killer is roaming the streets at large. Béranger cannot accept the fatal indifference of the authorities, the architect is taken up with the problems of creation, the police with regulating the traffic; so he takes it upon himself to rid the city of this menace. In the second act he discovers documentary proof as to the identity of the killer, but on the way to the authorities, the architect, the chief of police, he finds himself alone on the broad highway, he has lost the evidence and is face to face with the killer. His only hope is to argue the case of humanity, but neither flattery, promises, concessions, or threats are of any avail. The killer is unmoved by pity, vanity, words. To each he replies with a cynical chuckle. Giraudoux would have won his argument for life, Ionesco looses it. After a glimpse of a spoilt paradise we are again in despair.

Rhinocéros (1958) presents another leap in the imagination, to a world where the inhabitants change from being human to become rhinoceroses. Again Béranger, who is himself suffering from the symptoms which have turned others into rhinoceroses, pleads the case for humanity. From the logical beginning of "how can human beings change their form into that of a rhinoceroses" we are shown how easy it is, once a thing has been proved possible, for others to follow the crowd. The leader of the faction who believes it is scientifically impossible, himself becomes one, and even the hero's girl friend joins the others. The individual is like a specimen in the zoo, gazed at by a world run and inhabited by rhinoceroses. *Rhinocéros* was produced by Jean-Louis Barrault in his first season at the *Théâtre de France*.

From a study of these plays, or his earlier works such as *Comment s'en débarrasser*, *L'avenir est dans les oeufs*, *La jeune fille à marier* it is clear the Ionesco has already produced a style which is a very personal interpretation of life seen in terms of the drama. His weakness is that his plays are peopled by abstract characters rather than individuals, Even in Béranger there is little that is subtle or deep. Ionesco gives proof again and again of his ability to write dialogue — like the park bench conversation between the lady and the gentleman in *Jeune fille à marier*, but until he is able to draw the delineation of individual characters he will remain marking time as a dramatist. Some will see him only as a writer of charades, unable to keep the frivolous element at bay, others, believing he is a writer of more than *tours de force*, will see him as a serious dramatist *manquée*. If Cocteau is a cat who walks by himself along the "main road", there is more than an element of truth in Tynan's quip that Ionesco is a "solitary robot". There is a flash of space travel in Ionesco's vision, but in our world humanity is earthbound.

There are other names which are generally included in the lists of antitheatre, but it will suffice here to mention two in passing. Georges Schéhadé belongs to the poetical antitheatre. His best known play *Histoire de Vasco,* which Jean-Louis Barrault presented in 1957, provoked a lively controversy. Vasco wanders across life, like Mother Courage without Brecht's genius, until he is shot by soldiers of our world run riot. 'Histoire de Fiasco' was a personal comment after seeing Barrault's meandering production. Arthur Adamov, a well-known name in *avant-garde* circles, may be placed in the metaphysical antitheatre. Adamov owes much to the German expressionists; his theatre is scant and arid, a theatre of solitude where its solitude is recognised *a priori* and not therefore pronounced. In his plays, such as *La Parodie, l'Invasion, le Professeur Taranne, Tous contre tous* and *Paolo Paoli,* everything is made bare, including the human soul. Understanding between individuals is from the start impossible. In *La Grande et la Petite Manoeuvre* physical mutilation proceeds scene by scene with moral mutilation. In *l'Invasion* (produced 1950) the discord of the mind is reflected in the chaos of the room in which his characters live. But does this, to use Antonin Artaud's own maxim, "festival of destruction" offer us more than a morbid divertissement?

Another writer whose work leads direct to antitheatre is Jean Genêt, yet does the sordidness of subjects he chooses in *les Bonnes* and *le Balcon,* lead us any further than a writer like Becque, who would have merely used them to delight his bourgeois public? With all this looking through the wrong end of the telescope we seem a far cry from the mainstream of drama.

Agreed, we should not expect the living traditions of the drama to affect the contemporary scene. Only great writers are capable of rising above the immediate present and the immediate past. The others are crushed with the materialistic victory of nineteenth-century capitalism and the reaction against the sprawling ugliness of shoddy suburbia, while many have become religious exiles since Darwin threw so much of the teaching of the Church into confusion. The two world wars have not damaged society half so much as they have the human mind of the twentieth-century man. Yet there have always been wars, and life has a continuity which is often forgotten. The power to survive also depends on the will to survive, and this will is the most powerful force in life and is present in all genuine pessimists. It is a will to survive against an omnipotent fate which must defeat them; it is never a self-willed defeat of their own choice. Our modern pessimists, on the other hand, are those who live only from day to day; the importance they seem to attach to the present uncertainty has something reminiscent of the exaggeration of a movie-trailer — there is no continuity to the sequences they present, to say nothing of complete distortion of the whole. By all means close the shutters and put on the light if there is darkness at noon, but why our school for pessimists should deliberately abandon themselves to the passing storm is surely the twilight of common sense.

ELEVEN

EXISTENCE IN THEORY:
JEAN-PAUL SARTRE

"L'homme est condamné à être libre . . . l'homme est liberté."

SARTRE, *L'Existentialisme est un Humanisme*

"O liberté! Que de crimes on commet en ton nom."

MADAME ROLAND ON THE SCAFFOLD

AFTER the first world war came the heyday of the Dadas and the surrealists; after the second war it was the turn of the existentialists. No doubt there had to be something to correspond to the frustrated mood of a war-ravaged continent. In France the occupation had paralysed the community more completely than any plague could have done, while its stench lingered long after the liberation. Was man really responsible for this orgy of evil which had consumed nations? Were you, for example, to blame for the gas chambers of Buchenwald, the massacre of the innocents by bombing, the torture of patriots, the lynching of collaborators, the ravishing of women, the ignominy of starvation, the collapse of morals and morale? If many believed that man could only find hope in a return to religion and the realisation of human inadequacies when God is excluded, the pessimism of the age was to bring about an equally marked atheistic reaction: that man is nothing except his life and that consequently he is fully responsible for his actions. Man can save himself only through himself. He must choose for himself his course of action, and in doing so, he automatically chooses for everyone. He is not given the choice of inaction. In an existentialist world man is committed, whether he wants to be or not.

Just as the movement Dada had set itself the task of seeking a new order from anarchy, just as the surrealists had sought in Dali's words "the conquest of the irrational", so the existentialist writers condemn man to his liberty. It is, whatever Sartre may say to the contrary, a doctrine impregnated with pessimism and cannot in any way justify the claim to be a 'humanism'. It is not true that repeating a phrase like 'black is white' often enough makes people believe in the phrase — not at any rate where existentialism is concerned. In wishing to supress God Sartre has so excelled himself that he has supressed humanity. In sweeping away Christian ethics he has emptied out the baby with the bathwater. For Sartre's approach to man, living in a state of 'solitude in common', is not to bring him any message of hope to show his confidence in man; it is merely the introduction of a new vocabulary of Orwellian 'doublethink' to act as a key to his grammatical dialectics. Condemned to be free, our Sartrian superman finds freedom does not offer greater interpretation than would be the definition given by Radio Moscow, while descriptions such as 'lache' (coward) and 'salaud' (skunk) are applied indiscriminately to those situations and standards which are respected in any Christian — indeed in any self-respecting — society.

Though both the surrealists and existentialists have philosophic leanings, it is through their literary offspring that they have become known to the general public; recently existentialism might be said to have become almost entirely a literary movement — not without French philosophers breathing a sigh of relief. For existentialism as elaborated by Sartre from the theories of Martin Heidegger (who worked in defeated Germany after the 1918 war) is not of overwhelming interest to-day to a professional philosopher, and is in fact much less regarded in France than, for example, Emmanuel Mounier's *Le Personnalisme*. Nevertheless, the principles of existentialism are to be found in a massive volume of 724 pages, *L'Etre et le Néant*, which few people have attempted to read — and fewer still have been successful. But, like Karl Marx, realising that bulk counts more for prestige than popularity, Sartre has reduced his theories into a short existentialist manifesto, *L'Existentialisme est un Humanisme*, where the A–Z of his system is expounded in an ABC language.

It is in his literary works, and in the theatre in particular, that Sartre has reached his public and indeed achieved fame. If his success in politics and philosophy has not been decisive, he has known a blaze of glory in the French theatre. His name is as well known outside

France as within, though in London and New York his plays have never scored more than a *succès d'estime*. Certainly Sartre is a highly gifted melodramatic writer, a fact which makes the theatre a more natural home for him than the novel.

His attempt, however, to bring philosophy into the theatre to reach a wide public is both his strength and weakness. From it all his limitations spring. It is responsible for his characters, who remain far too often merely abstract figures, never people of flesh and blood and human warmth. They are seldom complex beings but are created as theoretical types. It is true that in the better plays (not necessarily the most interesting) they do assume lives of their own; but the more Sartre's play is a *pièce à thèse* the less his characters reveal themselves to us. For propaganda is not the true purpose of theatre.

Yet this is precisely what Sartre holds to be the purpose of theatre. He is only interested in presenting a practical application of his philosophic theories, and one could write a complete exposition (and criticism) of existentialism from his plays alone. That he is not interested in character is admitted by him in an article on "Forgers of Myths" which appeared in *Theatre Arts* in June, 1946. "As a successor to the theatre of characters we want to have a theatre of situation", he writes. "The people in our plays will be distinct from one another — not as a coward is from a miser or a miser from a brave man, but rather as actions are divergent or clashing, as right may conflict with right." Situations are, it is true, vitally important (more important than most Broadway or West-End managements would care to admit) but the characters, whether they be mythical figures or not, are no less important. In the plays of Giraudoux or Claudel, even of Anouilh, the characters belong to life, not philosophy. It is worth stressing here a point which we will discuss further in the next chapter, that in linking himself with Anouilh, Camus and Simone de Beauvoir (the young playwrights of France) Sartre gave rise to the widely held but mistaken belief that Anouilh is an existentialist playwright.

Though Sartre goes on to claim that the theatre he is writing about is not inspired by any preconceived idea, his own theatre most certainly is. It is the very essence of being committed. He writes his plays with the partiality of a system which must both be defended and rigorously applied at the expense of everything else, including, if need be, the artistic criterion (as in *Le Diable et le bon Dieu*). A critic who is old fashioned enough to judge a play first from artistic standards must decide whether he is to remain faithful to what he believes are permanent dramatic values, or whether he should, like ancient Romans watching Christians being thrown to the lions, 'get to know his times'. At all events we shall judge the plays of Sartre first as plays. But we cannot ignore the philosophy, since it is so much the *raison d'être* of the play. It is as if, in dialectical justice, Sartre forces a critic to criticise him (and nearly all critics have) whether they want to or not. At least he condemns a critic to condemn. But although condemned to suffer and criticise existentialism, there is an escape for the critic through the great literature of the past and even the present which is not *engagée*, even at the risk of becoming quite contentedly what Sartre contemptuously calls a "vieux critique". As Sartre would have it, the die has been cast.

*

There is nothing particularly revealing about the early life of Jean-Paul Sartre to suggest that he would one day become the celebrated demolisher of bourgeois morality — except that his own upbringing had all the middle-class respectability and conformity that any would-be revolutionary (theoretical or practical) could wish for. Born in Paris on 21 June, 1905, Sartre belonged to a Liberal and Catholic family; his father, a naval officer, died of fever in Indo-China when Sartre was still young; his mother remarried, but life under his stepfather seems to have been uneventful. He was, however, a delicate child, tormented with nightmares which made him seek reading and writing as an alternative to sleep at an early age. At six Sartre was writing alexandrines in the manner of the fables of La Fontaine, and he was soon absorbed by the scientific adventures of Jules Verne. At school he was a bright pupil in all subjects except mathematics. From a Baccalauréat in philosophy he proceeded to take his Licence in philosophy, and then, after his military service, to a post as teacher of philosophy at Le Havre. So far, a very ordinary career.

But during this time he had started his literary activities. At eighteen he had already founded a review with a Communist journalist, Nizan, called *Revue sans Titre*, in which he achieved print for the first time. Publishers, however, rejected his manuscripts, and his first success came in 1936 with an essay on "L'Imagination" contributed to *La Nouvelle Encyclopédie Philosophique*. In 1938 an essay called "La Nausée" was accepted, and the publishers, in order to promote its sales, described it as 'a novel'. This trick turned a philosophical essay into best-selling fiction, and had not its contents been so defamatory to traditional values, it would certainly have gained one of the literary prizes that are to French publishers what Oscars are to Hollywood.

Then came the war. During the winter 1940–1941 Sartre was a prisoner of war, but was repatriated for health reasons. During his captivity, however, he staged and acted a Christmas play which, in his own words, "while pulling wool over the eyes of the German censor by means of simple symbols, was addressed to my fellow-prisoners. . . . As I addressed my comrades across the footlights, speaking to them of their state as prisoners, when I suddenly saw them so remarkably silent and attentive, I realised what the theatre ought to be — a great collective, religious phenomenon." Such was the premise of Sartre, the playwright.

Sartre was henceforth to combine playwriting and philosophy as his two dominant interests; in 1943 he established himself in both these fields. Drawing on his Christmas play experiment, he wrote *Les Mouches* where, through symbolism and the use of classical legend, he was able to portray the sufferings of a France humiliated under the Vichy policy of repentance and collaboration. His classical parallel, which suggests on first sight (only) affinities with, say, Giraudoux, pulled the wool over the eyes of the German censors, and it was permitted to be staged by Charles Dullin at the Théâtre de la Cité (the Sarah Bernhardt Theatre renamed to appease Nazi racial policies). Along with Claudel's *Le Soulier de Satin* and Anouilh's *Antigone* it proved the outstanding success of the occupation years.

It was in 1943 also that Sartre's philosophical treatise *L'Etre et le Néant* was published. During the war years one can but wonder at Sartre's remarkable industry, writing secretly for *Les Lettres Françaises*, making valuable contacts with the Resistance and belonging to the Comité National des Ecrivains, an underground organisation for French writers. Officially he was lecturing on Greek drama. In May, 1944, Sartre's second play *Huis Clos* (produced in London under the title "Vicious Circle") was staged at the Vieux-Colombier, and continued triumphantly after the liberation.

Thus, whereas Sartre had before the war been little known to the public, he had by the end of the war established himself, if not as their leading writer, at any rate as their leading exponent of the school of 'Littérature engagée', which has been without doubt the most controversial and acclaimed development in post-war literature — an influence not confined to the frontiers of France. Truly in 1945 Sartre became the most talked about of men.

During that year we saw the rise to fame of Saint-Germain-des-Prés with its cafés where the *nouveaux-existentialistes* were soon replaced by the *nouveaux-riches*; more important, the year saw the birth of Sartre's review *Les Temps Modernes*, which still plays a leading rôle in French intellectual life. 1945 also saw the publication of the first two volumes of *Chemins de la Liberté*, and in addition to all this Sartre visited the United States as reporter for *Le Figaro* and *Combat*.

A decade later Sartre had consolidated his position; only in the last few years has he turned to long-term projects. He has even survived the last existentionalist. It is wrong, however, to accuse Sartre of ever having been a publicist — the wild and irresponsible youths who siezed the existentialist banner were none of his doing. It was not publicity for himself that Sartre sought, but for his ideas. Not content with the theatre and novels, he turned to the cinema and to politics. A competent film has been made from his novel *Les Jeux sont faits*, and he has taken his place among the French illustrious in Nicole Vèdres's *La Vie commence demain*, where in an interview he states once again the case for existentialism. Whether Sartre will one day look to television remains to be seen; unfortunately he lacks personality in the flesh, and appears to talk down in a somewhat disconcerting manner to an audience. Perhaps it has been this failing, as much as anything else, that has prevented Sartre from realising political ambitions.

The politics of Sartre, like his philosophy, are negative and destructive. Having destroyed the *status quo* he leaves the ruins to take care of themselves. Sartre is removed by more than class from the proletarians he wishes to embrace, and the political applications of his theories do not have the attractions offered by the Communist Party, to which they are so akin in spirit. Sartre is a man who has lost both God and the Communist Party. He does not believe in the Stalinist blend of Communism, but the outcome of literature for him is nevertheless "bound to that of the working class". Until the Hungarian rising all attacks on Russia were for him absolutions given to the capitalist world. He even went so far as to declare: "To have the right to criticise a movement as important as the Communist movement one has to work with it". He has not followed the path of those for whom the Party became "the God that failed". Sartre's "Return from the U.S.S.R." was a much happier one than his return from the U.S.A. The French Left, he believes should return to the *Front Populaire*, with all that alliance with the Communist Party implies.

Perhaps this is the place to explain briefly some of the philosophical

ideas of Sartre which are essential to any understanding of his plays
Here, then, are the golden rules of existentialism, which I summarise
from *L'Existentialisme est un Humanisme:*

(1) Existence precedes essence. If God does not exist, there is a
least a being with whom existence precedes essence, and this being i
man, or, as Heidegger puts it, human reality.

(2) Man is nothing other than he makes himself, he is nothing excep
his life. He exists only to the extent he projects himself towards the
future, he is nothing except the totality of his acts.

(3) Man is thus responsible for what he does, and is also responsible
for mankind. In choosing for himself, man chooses for mankind.

(4) When we choose, we of course choose the good, and not evil
Nothing can be good for us without being good for others. Thus our
responsibility is much greater than we imagine, for upon our choice
depends humanity.

(5) The only judgment which can be made of this choice is not one
of value, but of authenticity. For if God does not exist, everything is
permitted. Man is bound neither by laws nor orders, nor the necessity
to receive them from others. Man is free, we are in fact:

(6) Condemned to freedom. Condemned because man has been
thrown into this world — he had no say in the matter — and being free
he is responsible for his acts.

Thus we find that in existentialism man is committed, and he
commits in his actions the totality of mankind. Man, since God does
not exist, is the legislator for himself. In short, Sartre claims that
existentialism presents a coherent system of atheism. In this world
which Sartre creates, a world without law or moral values, without
help, without explanation, a world of violence which Sartre exploits
to the full in his literary works, we must ask ourselves whether in
condemning man to be free, M. Sartre does not at the same time
condemn man without choice to a living hell. It is the logical conclusion of his dialectics.

*

Unlike Claudel, Sartre did not have to wait for his audience. While
in *la belle époque* no audience would have tolerated a play which set
out not to entertain but to unfold philosophical situations, the public
in recent years has been willing to accept both Claudel and Sartre, and
other playwrights treating religious and philosophical subjects within

ae framework of the drama. In the eighteenth century Voltaire had
sed the stage for his philosophic reflections, as had Diderot, but not in
he way Sartre uses the theatre unsparingly to communicate his ideas,
owever abstract or complex. He sets out deliberately to attack the
udience's mind collectively, to throw its prejudices into confusion, to
eave it, if necessary, with a headache. His are plays which trouble our
onscience, discover our anxieties, uproot our belief. Other writers
ave followed, such as Camus with *Le Malentendu*, and Simone de
Beauvoir with *Les Bouches inutiles*, while there is the Christian existen-
ialist Gabriel Marcel who has also had his very philosophical plays
vell received in Paris. But Sartre succeeds where others only partially
o so because he has an unfailing dramatic sense, and whatever else he
may be, he is never dull. Like the Ancient Mariner, his plays hold even
reluctant audience; there is no escape from his spell.

It is difficult to find a unity of inspiration in the works of Sartre.
His plays may be divided into two types, first of all the symbolic, as
epresented by *Huis Clos* and *Les Mouches*, secondly the realistic, such
s *Morts sans Sépulture* ("Men Without Shadows" in London produc-
ion) and *La Putain respectueuse*. "Our plays are brief and violent",
vrote Sartre in *Theatre Arts* in June, 1946, as if defining his aims in the
heatre, "centred around one single event; there are few players and the
tory is compressed within a short space of time, sometimes only a few
ours. As a result they obey a kind of 'rule of the three unities' which
as been only a little rejuvenated and modified. A single set, a few
entrances, a few exits, intense arguments among the characters who
defend their individual rights with passion . . . ." In following these
ules in his early plays, Sartre soon found their limitations tedious and
estricting. It is evident that he wished to write a drama of unmeasured
limensions and wildly ambitious, a play which would rank not only
with Claudel's *Soulier de Satin*, but with *Faust* or one of the Elizabethan classics. In its original form *Le Diable et le bon Dieu* (published
n Britain under the title "Lucifer and the Lord") would have taken six
ours to perform, and even with the cuts that Jouvet insisted on being
made it still ran for four hours. As for its scene changes and number of
he cast, both would be beyond the resources of any type of production
in a British or American theatre other than a musical. More recently
Sartre has adapted the *Kean* of Dumas, a melodramatic 'pot-boiler'
which, to say the very least, seems to cater more than enlighten,
while his political farce *Nekrassov* has more in common with the work
of a *chansonnier* than that of a serious playwright. The public had to

wait till the production of *Les Séquestrés d'Atona* (1959) for a play t
match his earlier intellectual brilliance.

In the meantime let us return to the first play of Sartre, *Les Mouches*
which, though it is not so ambitious as *Le Diable et le bon Dieu*, s
nerve-racking as *Morts sans Sépulture*, so despairing as *Huis Clos*, s
melodramatic as either *Les Mains sales* ("Crime Passionnel" in Lon
don, "Red Gloves" in New York) or *La Putain respectueuse*, yet ha
a depth which is in harmony with its subject and treatment, while it ha
a language which Sartre has never attained in his other plays. It ma
not be a perfectly constructed play, and perhaps the reasons for it
topicality would not be so strong to-day, but it certainly deserves
place if not among the important plays in theatrical literature, at an
rate in the halls of Liberty for its denunciation of tyranny. The short
coming of *Les Mouches* is not, as some critics have suggested, th
dramatic failings, but a far more damning weakness — the failure t
treat the enemy with any sympathy or respect. Anouilh did not mak
this mistake in *Antigone* where Creon presents his viewpoint so force
fully that for a time rumours went around Paris that *Antigone* was i
fact a Nazi play. In *Les Mouches* we mind less that Sartre has not spared
his opponents, for we know the enemy for what it is worth. But in
play like *Le Diable et le bon Dieu* we are not sure that we are any
longer on the same side. We cannot forgive Sartre for presenting only
the atheistic side of the picture. In *Les Mouches*, however, we are stil
in the days of the united front against the enemy. We are not ye
divided into political factions.

For *Les Mouches* Sartre has taken the Orestes-Electra legend, and
adapted it to suit his purpose. From the moment the curtain rises or
the square in Argos, with its walls stained with blood, with the stench
of carnage permeating the city, the swarms of flies infesting the air, the
wailing women dressed in mourning, we know that the city is being
punished and is repenting. Orestes returns unannounced to Argos with
his tutor. He meets Jupiter at the gates, but does not disclose his
identity. Jupiter (God of flies and death) tells him that the plague of
flies has been attracted to Argos since the death of Agamemnon
fifteen years ago. Jupiter goes on to describe the events that have
happened since the seizure of the throne by Aegisthus after the murder
of Agamemnon.

"Does Aegisthus repent?" Orestes asks Jupiter.

"Aegisthus? I should be very surprised if he did. But why worry?
A whole city is repenting for him", is the reply.

Piercing screams are heard coming from the direction of the palace.
Jupiter tells Orestes that these cries mark the beginning of the Ceremony of the Dead. Discussing the events of the murder, Jupiter raises
the name of Orestes, saying that he does not know whether he is really
dead or alive, but hopes for his sake that he is dead. "Why?" demands
Orestes.

JUPITER   Imagine him turning up one day at the city gates ... I'd say
to him: "Be off, young man! What do you expect to get
here? You think to establish your rights, eh? You're strong
and keen, you'd make a grand captain in a battle-thirsty army,
you have better things to do than reign over a town half dead,
a decaying, fly-infested carcase of a town. The folks here
about are great fishermen as a rule, yet here they are now on
the road to redemption. Let them, young man, leave them
alone, do them credit for their painful endeavour, but tip-toe
very far away ... Pleasant journey, young man, pleasant
journey. Order in a city, like order in men's souls, is a fickle
thing. Touch it, and you bring about catastrophe. (*Looking
him straight in the eye*) A terrible catastrophe which will fall
on your own head.[1]

But despite these dire warnings Orestes stays and meets Electra, who
has just been banished from the city by Aegisthus for ridiculing the
Ceremony of the Dead by discarding mourning and in fact being happy
and dancing before the crowd. Electra tells him she will stay in Argos,
and seek shelter in the temple of Apollo. She must stay, for she is
waiting for her brother Orestes, who she knows is not dead and will
one day return. Orestes then discloses his identity, but Electra refuses
to believe him. She is suddenly afraid of him, for he is no longer the
innocent Corinthian youth she had taken him to be. Aegisthus and
Clytemnestra are killed by Orestes. Electra approaches Orestes with a
candle after the crime:

ELECTRA   I must light up your face, for night thickens and I can no
longer see you very well. I need to see you. When I no
longer see you, I am afraid of you. I must not take my eyes off
you. I love you. I've got to think I love you. How strange
you look.

See original on p. 295.

ORESTES I am free, Electra; freedom has flashed upon me like a thunder
        bolt.[1]

Together they seek refuge in the sanctuary of Apollo, the shelter c
men — and flies.

    In the last act Sartre expounds some of the essential ideas of the pla
when Orestes meets Jupiter and renounces him at the same time as h
renounces repentance for his crime. Electra, however, is tormented b
the thought of what has happened, and is willing to accept Jupiter'
offer, paying the price of "a little repentance". With Orestes, howeve
compromise or obedience is no longer possible:

ORESTES Yes, you are king Jupiter, king of the Gods themselves, kin
        of the rocks and the stars, king of the waves of the sea. But –
        you are not the king of men.
JUPITER Not your king, of course, cheeky grub. But who created you
ORESTES You did. But was there any need to create me free?
JUPITER Your freedom I gave you to serve me.
ORESTES I, Jupiter, am neither master nor slave. What I *am* is m
        freedom. You had hardly created me when I no longer belonged t
        you.

Learning from Orestes that the people of Argos are his own men whor
he must enlighten and deliver from their feeling that they must repen
Jupiter has his own reactions:

JUPITER Poor people! The present you are going to give them i
        loneliness and shame; the coverings I kept over them you ar
        going to snatch away; and what they got for nothing, thei
        mere existence, their drab obscene existence you will suddenl
        drag into the light of day.
ORESTES And if the despair in me is their lot too, what right have I t
        conceal it from them?
JUPITER What will they do with it?
ORESTES Whatever they like. Aren't they free? And human lif
        begins the other side of despair.

See original on p. 295.

upiter takes his leave, warning that his reign — though drawing to an
nd — is not yet over, and that he is not abandoning the struggle.
lectra chooses repentance. Orestes decides to leave Argos, and takes
n his shoulders the responsibility for all its crimes. He compares him-
elf to the piper of Hamelin, who with his flute attracts all the rats and
:ads them out of the city. So when he leaves Argos he takes with him
he Furies and the flies; he rescues the city from repentance. Argos is
ree.

How in 1943 the very thought of freedom must have stirred the
magination! To-day we can be more dispassionate, and realise that
he freedom offered by Sartre did not offer much scope to the imagin-
tion. Freedom to recognise one's despair, one's existence which had
10 significance anyway. In this play there are the seeds of an inhumanity
vhich was to grow in each successive work of Sartre.

Let us now imagine a situation where three people, each guilty of a
rime, are shut up in a monstrously ugly and uncomfortable room
vithout escape, not for life, but for eternity. That is a fair approxima-
ion to the concept of hell given by Jean-Paul Sartre. "Hell is other
•eople" ("L'enfer c'est les autres") is the theme of *Huis Clos*. The
etting, with its barren walls, its bricked up windows excluding day-
ght so that night and day are alike, the space where a mirror once hung
for in eternity one must look at others, not oneself any more), is all
•art of a masochistic nightmare where continuity becomes an endless
ymphony of torture worse than any physical torture. There is no
onger any hope, passion or human dignity. Love is as useless as
atred. There is no escape or intermission, neither sleep, silence, privacy
1or death exists any more.

There are only four characters in the play, and the porter who shows
he newly-dead to their room in the first place makes but a brief
ppearance. It is a drama of three, a sadist, a lesbian, and a child
murderess. One man, two women. No love is possible in the presence
of the third, no end is possible since the three must be together for
:ternity, "neither the knife, poison, rope" can enable them to escape
his fact. The play presents an endless repetition, a study in monotony
which, far from being monotonous, is in fact intensely dramatic and
most seducing.

Sartre's next two plays do not sustain this level. *Morts sans Sépulture*
"Men Without Shadows" in London production) and *La Putain*
espectueuse were presented in a double programme at the Theatre
Antoine in Paris in 1946, and in London the following year. Of the

two, *Morts sans Sépulture* is undoubtedly the better play, and shoul
not be considered merely on the level of stimulating macabre sensatio
alism. It is a study of mental disintegration undergone in face of physic
torture by a group of captured Resistance members in occupied Franc
It is a dialogue between torturer and victim. The prisoners seek courag
to enable them to keep their secret, one of them is raped, another leap
to death outside a window. But the secret they know becomes fals
They can give it and save themselves. But one of the guards shoo
them all the same. "They're just animals", is the justification for th
torture.

La Putain respectueuse is an example of the supreme dangers
Sartrian theatre, the dangers of trying to over-simplify by cruc
melodrama and surface logic a problem which defies simplification. I
dramatising the colour bar problem in the southern States, Sart
stumbles into all the pitfalls that a blatant propagandist in the name
Soviet realism might deliberately choose; the result is so outrageous
false that this treatment is only one stage removed from mock-melc
drama.

The play introduces us to Lizzie, a prostitute newly arrived in
southern town from New York, where she is in trouble. On the trai
she witnessed an assault on two innocent Negroes by a group
drunken white youths. One of the Negroes is shot, the other on
escapes. The youths, in order to defend their crime, have spread th
rumour that the Negroes attempted to rape Lizzie. Everything depend
on what Lizzie tells the court. The play opens with the Negro furtivel
knocking at Lizzie's door and asking her to tell the truth at the tria
Lizzie promises this, and slams the door in his face; for she is enter
taining her first client in the town, Fred, who turns out to be
cousin of the youth who shot the Negro. He tries to blackmail Lizzi
to give evidence in his cousin's favour; Lizzie insists that should sh
be forced to go to court, she will tell the truth. The idea horrifies Fred
who warns her that she'll be testifying for a black man against a white

LIZZIE   But it's the white man who's guilty.
FRED   He isn't guilty.
LIZZIE   Since he killed the guy, he's guilty.
FRED   Guilty of what?
LIZZIE   Of having killed.
FRED   But it's a nigger he's killed.
LIZZIE   Well . . .

Jean Cocteau

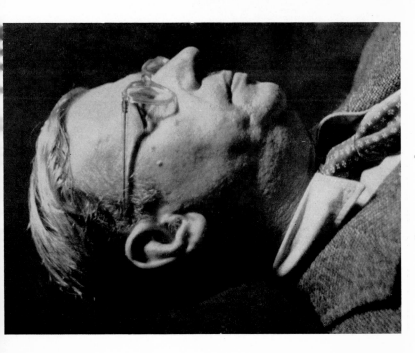

Jean-Paul Sartre

And so it goes on, until the point is well rubbed home. Two inspectors start giving Lizzie the third degree when the Senator, Fred's father, enters and kills Lizzie's conception of kindness, not through violence — but through kindness and an appeal to sentiment. Of course, he tells her, she must tell the truth since she knows the Negro is innocent, and he must go and tell his poor sister, the mother of the murderer, Lizzie's decision. Lizzie asks the Senator to help her. Then think, volunteers the Senator, how my sister might see the problem.

SENATOR Just figure Uncle Sam stepping up to you suddenly . . .
What would be his angle . . . He'd sure have a lot to say to you. Such as "Lizzie, you have to choose between two of my sons. One or the other must go. What do you figure you do in such a case? You keep the better one. Let's try? . . . Lizzie, this negro you are shielding, what good is he? Born by accident, heaven knows where. I've fed him and what does he do in return? Nothing . . . I wouldn't even notice his death . . . On the other hand, our Thomas has killed a black, which is very wicked. But I need him. He's a hundred per cent American, descended from one of our oldest families, studied at Harvard, an officer — we must have officers — and employs two thousand workers in his factory. Two thousand unemployed if he dies. He is a born leader, a solid bulwark against communists, the unions and Jews. He has a duty to live and it is your duty to save his life. That is the picture. Go ahead and choose.

Lizzie gives way under the stress of emotion, and signs the fatal document incriminating the Negro. The hunt is on.

The second scene of this short melodrama concerns the girl's efforts to hide the Negro. Already an innocent Negro has been torn to pieces through mob violence. The Senator and Fred pay Lizzie separate calls. Lizzie, too late, realises the Senator's trick, but she cannot bring herself to shoot Fred, for, as he tells her, "A wench like you cannot kill a gentleman". Lizzie accepts the compromise, with Fred's promise to install her in a large house. The Negro escapes until the next time; Lizzie prepares to give her body. As in *Huis Clos* there is no end to the cycle. The problem will end with the lynching of the last Negro.

It is surprising that French critics of repute have commended this play so highly, even to declaring it Sartre's *chef-d'oeuvre*, whereas outside France it has been attacked not only by critics but by any one who has a knowledge of the colour bar in the south, as well as by American Negroes. As a Negro from the south told this writer, "our problem is summed up in the words of the play by James Gow and Arnaud d'Usseau — *Deep are the Roots*". The problem is vast and complex. Lynching does not win much sympathy these days, and therefore Sartre is on safe ground for winning his case. He cannot lose it! For Sartre the whites are always black, and no doubt this mood suits the periodic outbreaks of Yankeephobia in France. Sartre understands the American colour bar about as clearly as, say, Senator McCarthy does Communism — they both have made use of the same tactics in their attack.

Les Mains sales (1948) is a political melodrama of fierce excitement and intensity which steadily mounts until the final denouement; indeed the play might almost be a perfect model for its type, and writers such as Charles Morgan (who attempts the same hybrid form in *The Burning Glass*) might well take lessons from Sartre the dramatist. True, Sartre does not make his characters human, but in this play abstract political figures are all the better for presenting mere silhouettes; the divine right of the Communist Party policies and the necessity to liquidate deviationists when new policies are enacted require an austerity both in language and characterisation. A little of this goes a long way, but it is justified here.

The action of the play passes in Hungary towards the end of the German occupation. The Communist leader Hoederer has been instructed to negotiate with the representatives of the government an agreement which will be hotly disputed and rejected by the mass of the party. Hugo, a young bourgeois intellectual who has made his choice and his revolt, wishes instead of editing the party's underground newspaper to prove his revolt in action, not words. He is therefore sent as secretary to Hoederer, with orders to kill him before he implements his policy. But Hugo is not a militant in spite of his ideals. The idea of to kill (or not to kill) torments him. Hoederer, on the other hand, is a born revolutionary, inflexible in his purpose and decisive in action. He senses that Hugo is going to kill him, but he believes that he can overcome Hugo through humanity, for Hugo cannot shoot him in cold blood. When Hugo does kill him, it is a 'crime passionnel' — the title of the play when produced in London.

In the epilogue, two years have elapsed. Hugo has been released from prison and returns to the yoke of his party cell, where Hoederer's views have now been accepted as official policy without a murmur, and consequently instead of being a hero he is a criminal. His ideals are challenged; he can only save his life by renouncing his idealism. He prefers the Communist firing squad, since he is "not fit for salvage".

"Although the action takes place 400 years earlier, *Le Diable et le bon Dieu* may be regarded as a complement to *Les Mains sales*", Sartre has written of his intentions in his most ambitious, philosophical and iconoclastic play.

In Goetz, my hero, I have tried to create a character as far removed from the common run of his contemporaries as was Hugo in the other play, and equally torn by conflicting emotions. This time, it is a little less fine drawn. Goetz is torn because, as the bastard son of a noble and a peasant, he is rejected by both sides alike. The problem is how he is to break away from the anarchism of the right in order to throw in his lot with the Peasants' Revolt.

I have tried to show that Goetz, a free-lance captain of mercenaries and an anarchist of evil, destroys nothing when he believes he is destroying the most. He destroys human lives, but cannot disturb society or social judgments; everything he does ends, to his fury, by benefiting the rulers. When, in time, he tries to perform an act of absolute good, and gives his lands to the peasants, this is equally without significance. Whether he tries to achieve the absolute through good or through evil, he succeeds only in destroying human lives. . . .

Such an outline indicates the essential fabric of theme and ideas. Sartre has taken for his existentialist hero a celebrated captain in the Germany of the Emperor Maximilian I called Iron Hand, who sold his services to the highest bidder and suddenly made a strange choice in heading the Peasants' Revolt in Germany in 1524. The play, as Sartre conceives it, falls into two parts. In the first half Goetz is the romantic anarchist who obeys only his evil passions. The citizens of Worms have defied their Archbishop who engages Goetz to besiege the town. But Goetz longs not only to capture it, but to set the city on fire, and wipe out both its treasures and inhabitants. The citizens, for their part, kill the bishop and threaten the 200 clergy they have imprisoned. Heinrich, an apostate priest who has the trust of the people, is given by the dying bishop a key which will enable the clergy to escape from the city by an underground vault. Heinrich realises that he also has the power with this key to hand over the city to Goetz. Heinrich chooses to do this.

Goetz is determined on evil, from his own personal actions, such as threatening to hand his mistress — who adores him — over to his soldiers, to his ambition to lay waste the city. When Heinrich meets him, he discovers almost too late the character of Goetz. He speaks up, and the voice of the priest returns to him. Evil, he tells Goetz, is such an easy thing. It is good that is so difficult, if not impossible, to accomplish. Goetz falls for this argument. Throwing a dice he decides to see whether fate meant him to destroy Worms or become a saint. He is to serve God. He has cheated from the start, for the dice was weighted. The idea of doing good for a year, of playing the holy man, amuses his imagination. Heinrich is then to judge him.

The metamorphosis in the character of Goetz is complete, but in intending to do good, he only succeeds in doing evil, of bringing in the train of his actions misery and destruction. He gives his lands to his peasants and thus leads to discontent throughout the country, and to a premature peasants' revolt. He is despised even by his own peasants, and in order to win their confidence he cheats again, by cutting his hands and pretending to be a stigmatist. Already in playing the saint he has lied. Goetz plans to build a city on earth as it is in heaven, but his scheme is doomed. His domain is invaded and the peasants are massacred. The Peasants' Revolt has broken out, but he refuses to lead them to victory, for man must not fight. So the year passes and Heinrich returns. Goetz must ask himself the question whether he has done good. He knows the answer and kills Heinrich. Neither God nor the devil exists; only man in his state of nothingness. It remains for Goetz to return to armour, lead the insurgents, in order to teach man that he is alone in the universe, or, as he says, "I shall remain alone with this empty sky above me, since I have no other way of being among men".

The play lacks unity (the unities which were so important to existentialist work in 1946) but a more serious objection is the confusion in the whole of Sartre's philosophic reasoning in this play. That we can believe Goetz is incapable of doing good needs no insistence, but it seems singularly false that Goetz cannot succeed in evil. As Phillip Toynbee remarked in his review of *Lucifer and the Lord* in the *Observer:* "As the most powerful military leader of his time and place there is no good reason for doubting his power to do evil, and Sartre, to elude this obvious difficulty, indulges in a typical piece of metaphysical sleight of hand."

For Goetz, even when trying to do good, is but a doleful masquerade of evil. Nowhere in the play does Sartre allow the voice of the Church to be heard; he sets out to prove that good is impossible by already assuming it is. The absence of the voice of God in reality is a sufficient excuse and indeed explanation for the absence of the case for Christianity in the play. How Sartre despises the Church! The abuses and corruption that have at times permeated the conduct of the clergy are unsparingly underlined; scandals such as the sale of indulgences to the poor in medieval times are very definitely equated with false hopes and deception which religion offers to-day. Since Sartre is an atheist he cannot be accused of sacrilege, but he can of insincerity. Sartre weights his dice before the house lights go down and he plunges man into darkness.

*

What are we to make of this existentialist progress in Sartrian theatre? We must not mistake it for a search for solutions, for Sartre does not believe that there are any. We must, if we insist, find our own solution. We must be sceptics. For it was through the scepticism taught him by his tutor before he reached Argos that Orestes discovered individual freedom (he allowed his sister Electra to get her own way). By the time we reach Goetz, however, Sartre is not only concerned with freedom for oneself, but also wishes to extend this to include the freedom of others; man must be liberated. From abstract situations we move more and more to reality. Yet whereas the notion of 'freedom' sounds exciting in the abstract light of *Les Mouches*, its glitter fades in daylight and does not even approach, let alone replace, 'faith' in the world of reality.

Les Séquestrés d'Altona returns us to the depths of *Huis Clos*. The theme is that we are all guilty in war. A German industrialist at a period of international tension is dying from cancer; in order to assure the continuity of the business he calls on his second son and daughter-in-law to sacrifice their own lives for the family interest. But this is merely the point of departure of a four-hour play which leads us into the darkness and stench of a cave, where we are subjected to both the emotional tension and the barrage of ideas of a work both impressive and shattering. Why, for example, has Frantz, the elder son who is supposed to be "officially dead" chosen to sequest himself upstairs in his father's house? Sartre advances several explanations but each one with almost Pirandellian revelation he proves false. We enter Frantz's room, contrast the disorder with the stolid bourgeois comfort downstairs. We listen to his justification of actions still haunting him from the war which he dictates to a tape recorder. Rather than face what he believes is a war devastated Germany he lives in voluntary seclusion sharing an incestuous love with his sister. When the truth is finally revealed neither sequestration, nor love suffice, only a suicidal pact with his dying father.

We are a long way here from any faith which requires man to fight for ideals and instead suicide appears as a possible solution for a conscience which is guilty. In this very Germanic play Sartre seems to combine a certain French *clarté* with German philosophic confusion, and the combination of these cross currents go far to explaining the inconsistency which he finds in his own "logically" held political convictions. If he would long for a Communist Utopia he knows that he would himself be one of its first victims. So it seems to me is a Sartrian hero the product of confused thinking.

Their way of making men love is through hatred, or as Goetz declares, "we shall be sure of victory only when my men are more afraid of me than the enemy". It is as if having offered freedom through a revolt not unlike anarchy (free from giving or accepting orders, obeying laws, etc.) Sartre does not see beyond the blood bath any more than Marxists see beyond the withering away of the State. Condemned to be free, is this freedom really worth the having? There is and never can be absolute freedom, even for Sartre, since man is still bound to natural laws and this absurd life; the victim, whatever his existentialist will-power, to the unforeseen and unknown way. Life may very well be merely "full of sound and fury, signifying nothing". But the accent is on life. The life that Sartre proposes, a revolt in the name of an undefined freedom all too reminiscent of other great purges, is a monstrous perversion of the world; since we have been promoted to gods let us dispose of it.

TWELVE

"THIS FEVER CALLED LIVING"—
ARMAND SALACROU AND
JEAN ANOUILH

> "When the World hath once begun to use us ill, it after-
> wards continues the same Treatment with less Scruple or
> Ceremony; as men do a Whore."
>
> JONATHAN SWIFT

IN an article in *Le Figaro Littéraire* Armand Salacrou has complained that the French classical authors ill prepare people for the
absurdity of life — because tragedies like *Le Cid* are disconcert-
ingly optimistic. Perhaps the difference in religions, from monotheistic
to atheistic, does after all lie, as Schopenhauer contends, in whether
they are basically optimistic or pessimistic. In leaving the existential
pessimism of Sartre, the romantic pessimism of Salacrou and Anouilh
presents a world, if seen from a slightly different angle, in a no less
critical fever and radical despondency. Whereas Sartre strides forward
confidently, unfrightened by the void he has created, certain in a world
of uncertainty, neither Salacrou nor Anouilh can enter the existentialist paradise — for their profound regret comes from a paradise lost
which can never be recovered.

If Sartre is more concerned with philosophy and politics, Salacrou
and Anouilh look to morals. Salacrou knows instinctively that he will
never be happy until he finds God, Anouilh cannot forget that "there
is always a lost dog somewhere which will prevent me from being
happy". Salacrou is more directly concerned with religion, he understands "the necessity of God without being able to believe in God";
he is a man of faith who has lost his faith and yet cannot live without it.
Anouilh's violent fanaticism is for purity and unspoilt innocence; if

171

this has been stained, the stain can never be effaced; his plays are in fact *engagée*, not in the existential sense, but in the past, the lost purity of adolescence and childhood.

It is easy to link the name of Anouilh with that of Sartre and label him 'existentialist'; but even if, as M. Radine has observed, Anouilh used some of the main existentialist themes several years before Sartre, "as Monsieur Jourdain used prose without knowing it", his whole approach and reasoning are different. Indeed, the difference may be said to lie in the fact that Anouilh's characters do reason, while for Sartre it is the act of decision which matters; in other words, the choice, not the choosing. Anouilh refuses, Sartre revolts. Anouilh's refusal cannot in the true sense be called a revolt since it is negative, not positive. He seeks an escape from a world which has become vile and loathsome — he does not claim existentialist freedom. If Sartre depicts certain human beings as "not fit for salvage", Anouilh rejects the whole world. It is the refusal of an idealist, a perfectionist, a moralist; Anouilh delights in the romanticism of despair, where revolt comes to nothing, where the only escape and the sole absolution are to be found in death, where before the grotesqueness of life a fictional world is the safest refuge for human misery. If Anouilh was indirectly inspired by the Giraudoux universe for his shelter, he has made any parallel in life impossible, for happiness is out of bounds in a world where sin prevails, where love is banished and where man can never be redeemed. Unable to regain their lost paradise and innocence, Anouilh's characters are no longer masters of their destiny, as are those of Sartre. Nor does Anouilh, as Mr. Merlin Thomas has remarked, seek philosophical justifications, as Sartre does, to dramatic contexts. He is a moralist, not a philosopher. It is a very simple thing for which his characters search, yet vastly complex, much more so than the right to live their own lives — it is how to live in an absurd reality.

It is on the frontier of absurdity that we find the dividing line between Anouilh and Sartre; with Salacrou, more philosophic than Anouilh, less so than Sartre, standing between the two figures. Salacrou is absorbed by the practicability of how to make the most of absurdity. It is best to begin our journey to Anouilh by way of Salacrou, who is neither so bitter nor so aggressively nihilist as Anouilh, but who serves as an introduction to the mood of romantic despair. Salacrou does not believe in cruelty, he has infinite compassion, but he lingers in the shades of darkness and misery. Having rejected the possibility of an after-life he finds no comfort in Sartrian liberty. But, unlike Anouilh,

Salacrou is always ready to forgive, to have pity, and to make an attempt to understand our behaviour, since an understanding of life is beyond us. His picture of the world is both simplified and exaggerated, but he does not present the vehemence in his attack which we find in either Sartre or Anouilh. His characters are human with human frailties and failings, they do not respond to a system of philosophy, they want only to be happy without even being sure that they would know what to do with happiness should it ever arrive. Escape through death does not attract him. To Salacrou man is not God, nor is woman necessarily pure. Any man, as the title of one of his plays suggests, is merely "a man like others" and any woman, as his heroine Lucie Blondel puts it, is "a woman like others". His characters are like all the rest of us, trying to make the most of the ordinary business of life.

Salacrou, then, wishes to compromise himself with his time and period, to paraphrase a line in *L'Inconnue d'Arras*. He brings his audience as witnesses of the contemporary scene and daily problems. His characters are not exceptional beings, they are ordinary people. They know as little as anyone of how to lead a satisfactory and happy life. Salacrou does not believe in certainties; like Maugham the only thing he is certain of is that he is certain of nothing. This failure of man to find a faith becomes repetitive in all his plays, except perhaps in his tribute to the French Resistance, *Les Nuits de la Colère*, from which it is temporarily absent. His longing to know the mystery of life has the pain and the anguish of Anouilh's craving for purity; both are impossible.

Unknown and beyond understanding. But there is nothing hidden in the plays of Salacrou. Though his plays demand attention, they can be fully appreciated at one performance; they do not gradually reveal themselves like the works of Giraudoux or Claudel. They are immediately theatrical and effectively simple. Though we cannot quite apply the term 'well-made' to the experimental and often erratic technique of Salacrou, his theatre is nevertheless every minute dramatic.

Early in his career Salacrou fell under the surrealist influence, and though he found there an impasse he never rid himself of this influence. It is this which prevents his plays from becoming, to borrow from the title of Jan van Druten's play, "a camera", and himself a playwright of the boulevard. Salacrou looks not at the face, but the soul of the people he meets in the street. His characters are in every-day situations, he does not dare see more than the immediate present. The vision of Shaw or Claudel, Ibsen or Strindberg, Pirandello or Giraudoux is denied him.

If we must find him an opposite number, Salacrou takes his place somewhere above the plays of say Thornton Wilder.

Salacrou may not be a really important dramatist, but his plays do touch those problems which to-day's audience feels most acutely. He speaks to them in their language, ordinary commonplace idiom, often as ridiculous and banal as what crowds shout out at football matches. But this does not deny their serious intentions, and Salacrou does not intend his plays to be taken lightly. In his *Note sur le théâtre* (1943) he writes: "What I ask of authors, critics, the public, is, at the birth of a new work, to view it honestly, without trickery and not as means of passing the time, with the anguish of interpreting its soul. For me, it is in the theatre that at certain moments of great purity I feel nearest to approaching the inaccessible shore. And it is in the great theatrical works that I sometimes believe that I have found my salvation."

Again and again it is the religious enigma to which Salacrou returns. The concept of God in paradise and Satan in the flames of hell he finds as incomprehensible as the life of animals who 'officially' finish as they began: 'in the dark'. To answer his need, Salacrou confides, just as a Catholic finds refuge in heaven he from an early age found himself shrouded with a determinist philosophy; for him determinism became "a daily custom with as much incongruity as universal gravitation". It is not difficult to believe that this search for God can become the most terrible moral situation a man can know. In *La Terre est ronde* (the idea of a terrestial globe not suspended by any thread in the emptiness of infinity haunts the imagination of Salacrou) the futility of existence becomes a nightmare: "Do you realise that you are nothing, what was before you was nothing, and what will be after you will be nothing? All is nothing. And nothing exists, if it is not thou, the understanding of God." And how far are we from the hope that such an understanding exists. "You must not look for in my plays what I am looking for there myself", is Salacrou's reply. If Salacrou is less dogmatic than Sartre, less bitter than Anouilh, all three share a dominant pessimism. But of the three, Salacrou alone seems to feel human tears; the others have other preoccupations, liberty or escape.

*

Armand Salacrou was born at Rouen in 1899 and spent his childhood in Le Havre. His parents wished him to become a doctor and in 1917 he took his first year in medicine at Paris, and like Somerset

Maugham, came into contact with suffering humanity through his hospital experience. But student life in Paris also introduced him to an intellectual life, and in the summer vacation of 1919 he decided to abandon medicine. Instead he went to the Sorbonne, where he took his Licence in philosophy. A friend then found him a vacancy on *L'Humanité*, the Communist daily, where Salacrou was responsible for the entertainment column and the convocation of party rallies. A varied existence followed in the next few years, and in 1926 Charles Dullin offered Salacrou the secretaryship of the Atelier (it is interesting to note that Anouilh was secretary to Louis Jouvet), and to supplement his income he started a publicity agency in a small way which soon grew to mammoth proportions and made a fortune (Anouilh was also connected with a publicity agency for two years, though at the bottom of the ladder).

Meanwhile Salacrou had started his career as a dramatist. Under the strong influence of the surrealists he had written his early plays, *Le Casseur d'Assiettes*, *Tour à Terre*, and *Le Pont de l'Europe*, plays of little significance, but in which Salacrou was able to experiment and learn the craft. These attempts were ambitious, full of verbosity, wildly pessimistic, badly constructed, and made no attempt to come to terms with the theatre. But they had for at least one critic of the day the sign of better things to come — "Bear the name Salacrou in mind, I prophesy that this writer will one day speak about him again".

In 1927 Salacrou wrote his next play, *Patchouli ou les Désordres de l'Amour*, which was eventually staged, without success, by Charles Dullin at the Atelier in 1930. Indeed, the first night was a disaster, and whatever merit the play possessed certainly missed the public and critics. Dullin tried to save the play from their wrath by soliciting favourable judgments from important figures. Giraudoux found himself able to see promise in the young author, and wrote of *Patchouli*: "It is not an immature play, it is a play about youth. I listened to it with an emotion which, for the kind, was quite new." Immature or not, it was the last play written by the youthful Salacrou. With his next two plays, *Atlas Hôtel* and *Les Frénétiques*, there was a very marked development both in technique and ideas — his surrealist affair was finished and he came over in his next few plays to the side of naturalism with far happier results.

With *Atlas Hôtel* Salacrou for the first time knew success, and was even accused by the critics of "writing plays like everyone else", a reproach which was perhaps inevitable. The plays which were to follow, such as *Une Femme libre* and *L'Inconnue d'Arras*, were quickly to dispel these doubts. There is, it is true, in *Atlas Hôtel* the old triangular tale told under the burning passions and the blazing sun of Africa, and even the extraordinary erection of the hotel — half finished, with neither roof nor windows, and enmeshed with fig trees and cactus plants inside — is no more bizarre than that which audiences have been accustomed to from the days of *The Admirable Crichton* to *The Little Hut*. The hotel is a speculation of a certain Auguste, who has sacrificed everything for his enterprise. The wife of Auguste, Augustine, was formerly married to a poet who had deserted her — not for the sake of art but for pulp fiction and business rackets. Chance brings this ex-poet to Atlas Hotel where he once again tries to make love to Augustine and tries to persuade her to run away with him. In doing this he stoops to such low tricks that he loses her forever.

In both *Atlas Hôtel* and his next play *Les Frénétiques* Salacrou moves rapidly towards the naturalistic mood and his characters gradually assume more and more the reflection of ordinary people. In both these plays, however, something is missing, as if the realistic vein were alien to Salacrou's powers of imagination and thought. It was not until *Une Femme libre* that Salacrou was to emerge as one of France's rising dramatists; in this play the horizons at once expand, there is greater insight and depth to the psychology of his characters. The title "Une Femme libre" immediately suggests the theme of Ibsen's *A Doll's House*, and Salacrou's heroine Lucie Blondel has been contrasted with Nora. The comparison, while totally artificial, does at least enable us to say that Lucie Blondel is not a woman like Nora. Nora slams the door defiantly because she knows what she wants; Lucie knows nothing, except that she has her freedom like every other woman. Thus whereas Nora longs to enjoy her freedom with the sex consciousness of a suffragette, Lucie has never known anything else but freedom. When Jacques asks her where she has lived, where she belongs, she replies: "I belong to my twenty years. Don't you see? That's my country and family background I have left — my twenty years of life . . . We must just live from day to day with our age." Lucie belongs not only to her twenty years but also to the twentieth century; Nora steps bravely just a decade or so ahead of her times into the twentieth-century limelight; to-day her way is so much the way of the world that not even Ibsen, with the powers of greatness, can make *A Doll's House* anything more than a period piece, and a slightly boring one at that. If Lucie is, as M. Radine asserts, a wishy-washy Nora, she is not so far from what we might expect Nora's granddaughter to be; not an exceptional woman self-righteously leading a cause, but an ordinary woman who is frankly afraid of life and who does not know, can never know, the meaning of happiness and satisfaction. We can believe in the character of Lucie even though we cannot accept all the happenings of Salacrou's play, which is nearly shipwrecked as the result of his clumsy denouement; oh! for Ibsen, the master builder!

We meet Lucie when Paul, her fiancé, brings her to be introduced to his family, a caricature of bourgeois complacency, bigotry and prejudice. But as in so many bourgeois families there is one rebel, not her fiancé Paul (a business-man who fits well enough into the family circle and enables them to keep up their social standing with his income) but Paul's brother, Jacques, who has something of the artistic temperament. Lucie, already frightened by her frigid reception and afraid of what life has in store for her as a member of the family, meets Jacques, who warns her that one day she will take her place among the family portraits and in the family graveyard. "And we will one day be like them if we live like them", he continues, "that's what I call family life, the life amidst failures and corpses." But Jacques has made his decision; if Lucie is just beginning her life at the Miremonts, his is over there. Since there are "too many things in the world" to do and to see, he will leave the narrow little world of the Miremonts, and go out and face life. As he opens the door, Lucie decides to run away with him.

In the second act two friends of Jacques, Max and Cher Ami, wreck the happiness of Lucie with their theories of free love and freedom, in much the same way as Jacques in the first act destroyed Lucie's hopes of living with Paul. The idea of living with Jacques cannot be reconciled with the loss of freedom which that implies if she becomes his property.

JACQUES Do you believe that you love me enough to love me for always?

LUCIE Always? Let's leave the future alone.

JACQUES Give me an answer.

LUCIE Let's be content with to-day's happiness.

The third act finds Jacques and Paul reunited at their family house, both torturing one another with the memory of Lucie. In the six months that have elapsed, Lucie has become a much talked about lady about town, the type described in society paragraphs: "Mlle Lucie Blondel has just

arrived Biarritz by air, a private plane piloted by Mlle Blondel herself
more sportive than ever". It is Aunt Adrienne, who has somewhat
surprisingly taken a liking for Lucie, who recalls her to the house —
she writes her that Jacques is dying, and calling for her. When Lucie
arrives she meets Jacques, who is much taken aback, since he knows
nothing about the letter. The questions pour out, why did you leave
me? — what have you been doing? Lucie tells him that she feared that
one day they would no longer love each other, but suddenly pleads with
him to run away with her again. She is willing to renounce her career.
But Jacques hesitates. He cannot forget the other men she has given
herself to since she left him (are they as miserable as I, he wonders)
and realises that it is through the many that she feels free. There
is no hope for their love. Jacques cannot accept Lucie's assurance that
they could be happy. Paul enters the room, but does not see Lucie.
Jacques tells him that Lucie can no longer mean anything for them;
that if she came to see them, they would have to tell her "You cannot
stay here and we cannot follow"; that "she wanted freedom and must
therefore pay for her freedom". At these words Lucie rushes from the
room in tears, and the brothers once again resume their 'battle'. The
three are condemned to solitude and suffering.

   In his next play, *L'Inconnue d'Arras*, Salacrou was to turn away from
naturalism towards a surrealist approach suggested by an original idea
of a man, committing suicide because of his wife's infidelity, reliving
his entire life in the fragment of a second between the pressing of the
trigger and his death. So the play presents the characters who influenced
the husband, Ulysse, in his life; the ghosts of his father, his young
grandfather (killed at the age of twenty), his mother, his old schoolmaster, the women he has known in his life, appear in short episodes.
Among the women is the unknown girl he met one winter's night near
the battlefield at Arras during the 1914 war. She had been abandoned
and he had taken her into an empty house, where he had put his coat
over her. This episode, which forms a vital link in the play, reveals
that the husband had secretly been in love with this unknown woman
all the rest of his life. She had told him that three days previously she
had come to Arras to look for her sister, but the town had been evacu-
ated. She was frightened and hungry and called out to him, and when
she kissed him after he had given her his overcoat, he had punched her
face — because she smelt of alcohol. Later that night Ulysse had returned with the intention of raping her, but finding her asleep, had been
filled with pity and had left her food and drink. Returning the next day

she had gone, and he had been searching for her ever since. He will never know her mystery or her name.

Salacrou uses the episodes to express some of his essential ideas; but it is a play of promise rather than fulfilment. From a technical viewpoint the episodes are expertly handled, but there is an unfortunate tendency to baffle the audience, so that even for some time after the rise of the curtain they are not quite sure whether the intention is farce, mock melodrama or grim humour.

Shortly afterwards Salacrou wrote *Un Homme comme les Autres,* where he becomes decidedly more interested in moral problems. His original idea, he tells us, was to write a play about a husband who is worshipped by his wife, a husband who in the eyes of his wife can do no wrong, but who in fact is like any other husband. In order to reciprocate the love of his wife, the husband longs to be loved for what he is. But when he tells her his wish, she cannot forgive him for not being what he is not! To this idea Salacrou has introduced a sub-plot of a young man who attempts to strangle an old lady for robbery, since he needs money to satisfy the expensive tastes of his girl friend. The man is sentenced to two years' imprisonment and when it is served he realises that he never loved the girl and cannot understand how he ever acted as he did. Forgiveness follows violence!

In *La Terre est ronde* Salacrou gives us his most important, as well as his most ambitious play to date; it is a passionate debate between reason and religion (since Salacrou is an agnostic it is a choice of 'either/or'), an intellectual and spiritual exercise which results in a futile victory of reason, reassuring us that the earth is but a round ball spinning in infinity as purposeless as are the lives of its inhabitants. Though written in 1938, the play has the full-fledged post-world-war pessimism of the nihilist school. Both *Le Diable et le bon Dieu* and *La Terre est ronde* lead us to the same *angoisse,* the 'all is for nothing' labyrinth; in the shades of such futility Charon is no more to be expected than Samuel Beckett's Monsieur Godot.

La Terre est ronde is a contemporary play merely dressed up in historical guise; like Goetz in Sartre's play, Savonarola cannot succeed in doing good, however much he tries. Goetz could not build his city in the sun because he was a man of evil; no more can Savonarola offer Florence, the pure and unspoilt 'flower', to God, because he hates man, the creation of God. In Savonarola's character there are more recent echoes, as M. José van den Esch stresses in his study of Salacrou, the realisation by the audiences who saw the play in 1938 that the 'Christ is King' greeting of Savonarola's was no more sincere that the 'Heil Hitler' that the Nazi mobs were then chanting.

The central character, however, is not Savonarola but Silvio, an intelligent young Florentine who is in love with Lucciana, but who cannot bring himself to marry her because he is worried about the mystery of life, and feels he must discover unknown lands to expand man's knowledge. Alas, Lucciana only loves Silvio without understanding his thirst for 'the reason why'; she can offer him her love, but she cannot satisfy more than his flesh. Because of this she must lose him. Silvio tells her one day: "I'm twenty-three and I know that people no longer marry, at any rate since this morning. I've learnt about an extraordinary happening. You see, Lucciana, it seems that the earth is round." Silvio does not leave on his voyage of discovery; instead he liberates himself by joining the cause of Savonarola, who is able to answer all his uncertainties. Silvio and Lucciana are still in love, but Silvio wishes their love to be something spiritual, and tries to persuade her to enter a convent. Meanwhile the public is already stirring against Savonarola, and demands that he should give them proof of his powers by a miracle: that he survive being burnt at the stake. Silvio cannot escape either, for he loves God as much as Lucciana. The final scene of the play is Salacrou's supreme achievement as a dramatist, and one of the best-written scenes in contemporary drama.

Salacrou's subsequent career has not maintained this standard, and the only other play of importance he has given us — a work which stands in isolation from the rest of his writing — is the tribute to the French Resistance *Les Nuits de la Colère*. The play, produced in 1946, admirably reflects the anger, heroism, revolt, degradation, felt by the members of the Resistance against the treachery, cowardice and decadence of those who either actively collaborated with the Germans, or those who accepted, who believed it possible to stay neutral, who in fact compromised with the Germans of the "Milice" while pretending they did not understand what was happening, what they were doing. But the anger of the Resistance tolerated no compromise. The play is a brilliant documentary, as realist in its selection of episodes (Salacrou uses the surrealist technique he had already tried out in *L'Inconnue d'Arras*) as any of the great Italian neo-realist films of the period. The play has but one purpose, as had the members of the Resistance. There is no place for religious or political controversy, the characters are either for or against; they are agreed to accept or revolt. The 'how to live?' which Salacrou continuously asks in his other plays, is here given

TENNESSEE WILLIAMS

ARTHUR MILLER

meaning. The purpose of their lives is realised in their death, so that the men who fell in the Resistance did so in order that their children would be happy, happy because free, and would never have cause to despair of life since in the darkest days of the occupation they in the Resistance had given their lives and had been able to live 'honourably'.

The action of the play passes in Chartres in 1944. A chemist, Bernard Bazine, married to a highly practical but extremely unimaginative Frenchwoman Pierrette, has chosen to live in Chartres with his three children in order that their lives may be as placid, imperturbable and have the same serene sense of permanency as that of the cathedral itself. One day, however, Bernard's oldest friend Jean, who is a member of the Resistance, seeks refuge in his house. He has just blown up a train carrying petrol supplies, and is wounded. Bernard and Pierrette panic. They hear the German patrols searching for Jean. He will bring an end to their happiness, he threatens their own lives and that of their children; they are giving shelter to a dangerous criminal, a man who blows up trains and destroys life, a man who breaks the armistice. Pierrette informs a collaborator and they naïvely believe that in handing over Jean he will be given a fair trial according to French law. When the curtain rises the Resistance have come to avenge the betrayal, and they kill Bernard. They also kill Pisançon, a collaborator, who as he dies shoots Rivoire, leader of the Resistance. The play then takes on the form of a dialogue between the traitors, the acceptors, and the resisters. There is also the parallel between the living and the dead. Rivoire is dead, as is Pisançon, the traitor, but whereas Pisançon believes that he has died for nothing, Rivoire has the certainty that his life has been a perfect success.

Les Nuits de la Colère is a mirror of the times through which France suffered. It is a record, just as *Journey's End* is a testament of the first world war for British audiences. Both plays have made a tremendous impact on their public, who relived the horror of those years in the auditorium. For Rivoire, the anger of *Les Nuits de la Colère* will never die; but will subsequent generations understand the reality of his anger? As a document, the play is witness that these things did happen; but it is more difficult to class it in theatrical literature.

Neither *L'Archipel Lenoir* nor *Dieu le savait* merits serious consideration. The former is a savage satire on how a rich family is driven nearly frantic at the thought of scandal, the latter is a highly improbable story dating from the Resistance, but in which courage gives way to sordid despair and fatalism. More recently *Le Miroir* and *Une femme*

trop honnête have shown that Salacrou is out of touch with to-day's
public, though his place among France's leading contemporary
dramatists is assured. His work has a distinctive originality, and his
virtuosity in describing the uncertainty of our times in terms of the
theatre is never absent from his work. But one fears he is anchored to
fatalism without hope.

However much the plays of Salacrou may disturb us, the pattern of
life they present is depressingly clear; it is never far removed from the
doldrums from which even the most optimistic of us occasionally suffer.
The world of Jean Anouilh is at once more extreme, more mysterious
and harder to understand than that of Salacrou. In the beginning were
purity and happiness; they remain the axis of Anouilh's theatre, and our
misfortune, suffering and *malaise* are a result of falling outside the orbit
of their power. We have rejected the natural order by growing up to
worship false values, to compromise, to lie, sin, be sophisticated. . . .
The same themes are to be found again and again in Anouilh's plays,
his obsessions grow work by work, varying in shade only in their
relation to 'pièces noires', 'pièces roses', or 'pièces brillantes' in which,
Shavian fashion, he groups them. Those who say an author is a man
who repeats the same things throughout his life under twenty or so
different forms may point to Anouilh, but this would be unfair.
Anouilh is less concerned with themes than working in a tradition, and
the links between him and the French classical tradition, as Mr. Merlin
Thomas has stressed in a talk on the B.B.C. Third Programme, are very
close. Again and again with mounting bitterness he returns to the same
moral problems, which at the age of fifty have produced some of
the most virulent attacks ever made on bourgeois hypocrisy and
the corruption of society. Yet though this acrimony goes at times as
far as the human mind can stand, it is those characters he brings in
from outside like ventilation in a stuffy salon that gain our sympathy
and enable us to share the romanticism for purity and the struggle for
moral values. But alas, there is no escape for the heroes and heroines of
Anouilh, for in a world which has become so debased that no salvation
is worth the taking, a brutal refusal is the only way. And even in the
artificial fantasies of his *pièces roses,* escape and happiness always in
the end bring us to an impasse.

And Anouilh the man? About his private life he has always been shy
in giving details, though we do know that he has never forgiven
society for his having known the meaning of poverty in his youth. But
his adult life appears to have been happy—a successful dramatist at an

early age, a marriage to the woman of his dreams, and fortune at the same time as world critical renown. In Hubert Gignoux's study of Anouilh we learn the following bare outline: Anouilh was born at Bordeaux in 1910, and when young came to Paris. After a year and a half in the Law Faculty at Paris, Anouilh passed two years in an advertising firm, "where I learned to be ingenious and exact, lessons that took for me the place of literary studies". After the production of *L'Hermine* (1932) he decided to live only by writing plays, with a few odd film-scripts. He has never regretted that choice, and throughout his career he has rejected anything in the way of journalism, whether writing or the granting of interviews. "I shall keep the details of my life to myself." That is a more difficult ambition for a French literary figure than for an Anglo-Saxon.

In Anouilh's first play, *L'Hermine*, produced when he was only twenty-one, we have already all the features and tones to which we have grown accustomed in his subsequent work, indeed, in all his plays up to the present. The world is divided into rich and poor; for those who have money everything is possible, even happiness; for the rest everything is denied. *L'Hermine* tells of a poor young man, Franz, who falls in love with Monime (the first of Anouilh's heroines, a picture of perfection which only a lover is likely to accept and it is indeed the explanation for the idealisation of his love), a rich heiress whose family, ruled by the old Duchess of Granat, would never permit the marriage. Franz seeks money from an industrialist, Bentz, but when he is refused help he resorts to what seems to him the only solution, the murder of the Duchess. In spite of Monime's horror at the suggestion, he kills the old lady, although some moments previously he has learnt that Bentz has agreed to help him. He has killed her all the same. Now they have all the money they need, but it is too late. Monime tells him she can no longer be his wife, and Franz, with nothing left to live for, gives himself up to the police.

The next play Anouilh wrote was *Le Bal des Voleurs*, an exuberant high-spirited 'comedy-ballet' belonging to the most wild of his 'let's pretend' humours he calls *rose*. As this play was not performed until six years later, it is his next produced play — the second of his *pièces noires* — *La Sauvage*, that we shall consider. For *La Sauvage* is a work of considerable importance, less mature perhaps than subsequent works, but of great dramatic vision and power. The thirst for purity is already a driving passion, from which there is no escape. This purity is personified in Thérèse, a poor girl who plays the violin (and badly) in her father's second-rate café band. Her mother, a monstrous creature who is the pianist's mistress and schemes when she has the chance to sell her daughter's honour to the highest bidder, plays the 'cello; such is the world into which Thérèse has been born, and from which she can never escape. A world of disgust and shame. One day she meets a true artist, Florent, a musician of talent. He is rich, and could lead her into another world, the best of possible worlds. But Thérèse knows that she must refuse this happiness, because those who have known shame and misery can never escape from its punishment. What is done is done, and to-morrow will be too late. Only when Thérèse manages to make Florent miserable by telling him in sordid details and lies about previous lovers, does she momentarily believe she could be happy. Florent, however, settles back to his work and happiness, and on the eve of the wedding day as Thérèse listens to the music he plays at the piano she realises that she is listening to the sounds of a distant world which is barred to people like her. It is not for her to embark on the pilgrimage to the Isle of Cytherea. She instinctively knows that the secret of happiness is denied her by destiny.

For his next *pièce noire*, *Le Voyageur sans Bagage* (1936), Anouilh took the subject of a soldier who loses his memory in the war (theme dear to Giraudoux) and little by little discovers the horror of his 'forgotten' past. His nature revolts, and in running away from his family he is running away from himself.

Eurydice (1941), like Thérèse, is another of Anouilh's heroines. The Greek legend of Orpheus and Eurydice becomes the tale where true love is doomed, where the lovers flee from the impossibility of this world to find happiness and purity in death. Life is the tragedy, death the happy ending. The play opens in the buffet of a French provincial railway station. Orpheus, son of a down-and-out musician (like Thérèse's father, a common and vulgar man, but not a bad soul), meets Eurydice, daughter of a withering actress in a seedy theatrical touring company, and falling in love at first sight, they run away to a cheap hotel in Marseilles. Eurydice, however, cannot escape her past, and when she receives a note from the manager of the touring company, whose mistress she had been, she runs away from Orpheus. The bus she takes crashes and she is killed. A mysterious messenger of Death, Monsieur Henri, offers to lead Orpheus back to Eurydice, according to the legend, provided he promises not to look at her until dawn. When, however, Orpheus meets Eurydice, he must know the truth about why she ran away, and looks into her eyes. Eurydice disappears, and

Orpheus tells M. Henri that he cannot live without her. M. Henri advises Orpheus to meet her in death, forever. The father of Orpheus wakes up and asks where Orpheus is. M. Henri merely whispers "He is with Eurydice — at last."

Eurydice is a very typical example of Anouilh's style; it is a symbolic theatre, where the classical parallels are simplified and modified to moral purposes. The language is direct, the sentences short, the words bitter. The characters talk, not like reasonable adults, but like squabbling children. And of course Anouilh's theatre is a nostalgic longing for the lost innocence of childhood — those who have never grown up to lie and cheat. But these children are not masters of their own destiny; they live in a world where the power to find love is impossible. Not knowing who they are or what they are to do, the characters of Anouilh are intended as an approximation to the complete powerlessness of modern man; they stand naked before life, knowing nothing and unable to alter destiny. There only remains for them solitude, violence and refusal.

The *pièces roses* which Anouilh was writing at the same time present a juggling with reality and illusion, a topsy-turvy mélange of fact and fable, plays acted within a play, mistaken identities and what have you, situations in which one is never sure whether or not the whole delicate façade is going to crumble and the masquerade is to be disowned. The *pièces roses* are more than a divertissement, for behind the transparent veil of make-believe, reality is never absent; it is for Anouilh the supreme tragedy and the ironical joke. The influence of Pirandello is very marked in these plays, and via Pirandello, the blend of the serious and fantastic that we find in Jean Giraudoux. In *Léocadia* (1939) the theme is how a poor milliner Amanda tries to take the place of Léocadia, a sophisticated enchantress with whom Prince Albert believes he was desperately in love. She shatters for him the sentimentalised memory of the past by being Amanda living, and not Léocadia, dead.

None of his *pièces roses*, however, comes anywhere near the standard reached in *Antigone* (1942) which is Anouilh's best play to date. Once again Anouilh has been able through Greek drama to discover a heroine who could answer his summons for purity, who would reject compromise, who was born to say 'no'. The Antigone of Anouilh cannot accept any life other than the life she would have chosen to live.

The play, written during the war and produced while Paris was still under the German occupation, was immediately topical, and being overtly political, was capable of interpretation by either side as a justification for acceptance or rebellion. Anouilh, of course, was very much on the side of Antigone, but he stated the other case persuasively enough for the play to cause a controversy and even to be branded as a Nazi play.

The problems which Anouilh had raised in his previous works are concentrated here in two characters: Creon, who stands for order, tradition, observance of the law; and Antigone, who believes in opposition and in doing what she thinks right. For Antigone the only happiness that is possible is total happiness; for Creon happiness is purely relative. Both are in exactly the same *angoisse*, only they do not see their way out in the same fashion. Antigone, with her passion for purity, cannot accept reality. You cannot both accept the world such as it is and retain your ideal. She belongs to her solitude, and must die for herself. She does not even know why she must die. That vague word 'freedom'.

The Greek values of the play are cast aside and the doubts of the contemporary world substituted. Antigone sees in the modern compromise of Creon only false values. Nevertheless the arguments Creon uses are so convincing that he almost persuades Antigone to save herself. He uses the common-sense approach, so reasonable that the obstinancy of Antigone would seem ridiculous to most modern men. Yet we know that Antigone is right even if few of us would have the courage to reject such a reasonable argument. Moreover, Creon also knows that she is right, for she has belief, whereas he believes in nothing. And to live for nothing is the modern tragedy.

Somehow the plays since *Antigone* have not retained the same urgency and purity. As they have become more professionally 'slick' they have tended to create a picture which no longer rings true. It is easy to wallow in the sordid, to say life is very ugly, but how tired we get of hearing these endless repetitions of exaggerated ugliness. There is always, it is true, escape, but the highly successful *L'Invitation au Château* proves little except that Anouilh is a clever entertainer who can at any time turn his gloomier thoughts rose coloured and write a play which merely marks time.

In *Ardèle* (1948) we find the anger of youthful idealism and revolt has given way to middle-age frustration, collapse and hatred. Nathalie has accepted life, she has accepted Maxime, although she really loved his younger brother Nicolas. *Ardèle* is not a tragedy of lost innocence, it is a bitter, ironical tirade against lust, in which even the youngster Toto, aged ten, and his cousin Marie-Christine, the Countess's daughter of the same age, have been corrupted and imitate the behaviour of the adults. As for perfect love, we are invited to believe in its realisation in two hunchbacks who end by committing suicide. The whole play is ferocious to the point of explosion, a strange concoction of farce and pathos, the former intended to shock you into the latter. Along that road Anouilh can go no further. Already he is middle-aged in thought, and his romanticism of youth has been finally forgotten.

How different is *Colombe* (1950) from Thérèse! Colombe the flower girl only wants to be happy and make others happy. Julien, the 'pure' character in the play, brings Colombe to see his mother, a famous actress with whom he is not on speaking terms, because he wishes his wife to be looked after while he does his military service. His mother takes Colombe into her company and gives her a small part. Soon Colombe is surrounded by admirers, and after preserving her honour for a while, is eventually seduced by Paul, Julien's brother. Julien returns and after learning the truth asks for an explanation. Colombe replies:

> Oh, how difficult everything is with you! I have to think six times before I dare open my mouth, and to me it all seems so simple. Everyone's kind and doing their best; and all I ask of life is . . . a little happiness . . . just happiness.

Thus purity has capitulated; no longer do the characters revolt, nor do they any longer hold our sympathy enabling us to share their thoughts and actions. Julien is as caricatured in his simple honesty, Colombe in her innocence (which leads her to compromise) as are the intentional caricatures, the cynical Paul or the hysterical Madame Alexandra. It may be every character was intentionally made repulsive; at any rate we have here the savage cynicism of middle age replacing the youthful refusal of *La Sauvage*.

La Valse des Toréadors (1951) explores further the history of General Saint-Pé, who was a character in *Ardèle*. As well as the general's wife, whom the general does not love, we meet an aging lady, Ghislaine de Sainte-Euverte. The general has been in love with Ghislaine since the time in his youth when they waltzed together at the Saumur Cavalry School ball. That was the only time the general had ever known the meaning of love and discovered he had a soul; yet the relationship was purely platonic. The play becomes a tragic study of this true love, but the style is of course in the bitter farce according to the later

Anouilh style. We have the spectacle of both Ghislaine and the general's wife trying to commit suicide at the same time. Then there are the general's two impossibly ugly daughters trying to flirt with the general's secretary. In the end Ghislaine goes off with the secretary, who turns out to be the general's son (he was a foundling) and the general resigns himself to stay with his mad wife and make love as opportunity presents itself to the new maid in order that he may be a "little less lonely in the darkness of the world". There is a strong suggestion in the play that man can preserve his soul in spite of everything, and the play ends on a note of resignation. This acceptance through remorse is a far cry from the *pièces noires*.

Anouilh's portrait of Joan of Arc, *L'Alouette* ("The Lark" in the translation by Christopher Fry, seen in London), has been both enthusiastically praised (M. Jacques Lemarchand in *Le Figaro Littéraire* compared it to the *Cyrano de Bergerac* of the half century) while other French critics have dismissed it as a pot boiler. It might be suggested that the play is effective theatre, but falls a good way short of being a masterpiece, or even "better than Shaw".

The opening of the play recalls the mood of *Antigone*, a bare stage, with neutral décor, benches, a footstool for Joan, a throne, bundles of sticks . . . one by one the characters saunter on to the stage, then Joan. Finally Warwick, a debonair young Englishman, enters with Cauchon, the judge. The whole introduction is reminiscent of *Antigone* while the opening words of Warwick have the startling directness of Anouilh's style:

> Are we all here? Good. Then let's start the trial without delay. The quicker she's tried and burnt, the better it will be for everyone.

Cauchon restrains his exuberance; there is a whole story to enact, the whole of Joan's short life. And so we are introduced to the various episodes in the history of Joan of Arc; her father who does not believe in voices, but believes it's the soldiers his healthy teen-age daughter wishes to go with, and he corrects her with a good healthy beating. Then there are the stages when Joan flatters and outwits captains and persuades them to let her ride to see the Dauphin. The famous scene follows when Joan recognises the Dauphin in his disguise. Perhaps even more remarkable is the way she addresses the Dauphin, 'dearing' him with the French 'tu' and convincing him both of his duty to rule and to appoint her head of the army. Thus we reach the end of the first half of the play, which in book form goes directly into the second part without a break.

Anouilh's conception of Joan is the most French of all the studies made of her — that of a French peasant girl. He is not interested in the 'miracle'. For him, the mystery of Joan is largely explained because the social, political and military situations were ripe. If it had not been Joan, it would have been someone else. To use his own words in the programme introduction of the Paris production, there were candidates before and after her. Anouilh is careful, however, not to offend the Catholic canonisation of Joan. He stresses that "Joan is a saint who died in a political episode; God did not necessarily take sides against Henry VI of Lancaster". No other play about Joan has been so concerned with national characters. Joan is the epitome of the simple, honest, French country girl. Her mother and father are to be found all over France to-day; practical, hard-working, thrifty people. Warwick is the caricature of an English 'gentleman', not given to logical thinking but insisting on the practical necessity of his actions. The policy of His Majesty's Government demands that Joan should be burnt. Later on in the play he tells Joan that it is stupid for her to be burnt (the argument of Creon in *Antigone*). For the policy of His Majesty's Government, solemn renunciation is exactly the same thing. Joan refuses. Warwick continues:

A useless suffering. Something ugly. No really, it wouldn't have done. It would even have been, as I said, a little vulgar and belonging to the mob, stupid to suffer a lingering death in order to be seen by everyone and cry defiance on the pyre.

Joan protests mildly that she is of the mob and foolish. Warwick then shrugs his shoulders and complains: "How sordid this all is. And vulgar. Of course you never can have dealing with these French."

Apart from this scene, the second half of the play is a long-winded and bitter disappointment after a more than promising beginning. Only in the very end does Anouilh again stir the audience by at the last minute saving Joan from the stake, since the story of Joan of Arc is a joyous occasion. And as far as His Majesty's Government are concerned, Warwick declares that Joan is already burnt and its political objective achieved.

The play is more than competent, but considerably below the standard that Anouilh might have reached had he written another

Antigone. There are delightful episodes in it, but somehow it lacks a driving force. This is expecially noticeable in reading, since the play was so beautifully acted by Madame Suzanne Flon in its original Paris production, and Dorothy Tutin also succeeded in the rôle in London.

L'Alouette, Anouilh told Mr. Stephen Pollak (an interview described in a B.B.C. talk), was a 'challenge' which he had to write, as Joan has become a challenge to all French writers. His more recent works, *Cécile, ou l'Ecole des Pères* (1954) and *Ornifle* (1955) seem to bear out Anouilh's inclination (as described by Mr. Pollak) to concentrate more on comedies. We are promised however that one day he will give us his version of *Oreste*, a fragment of which he wrote back in 1942.

Cécile is an amusing, harmless *jeu d'esprit;* everything is as false as false can be, and especially the ending, when Araminthe, Cécile's young and attractive governess, accepts the proposal of Cécile's father. Gone for the moment are Anouilh's obsessions (a passing reminder of poverty is quickly dismissed) but they return in *Ornifle*, his "comedy portrait" of a present-day Don Juan. After various episodes have emphasised Ornifle's debauchery a young man arrives on the scene clothed in black. This figure of death is Ornifle's son who has come to take vengeance on his father for abandoning his mother — he pulls out his revolver and fires. Although his revolver has been emptied by Marguerite, his fiancée, Ornifle collapses with a heart attack. This play was not well received by the Paris critics. M. Gabriel Marcel, writing in *Les Nouvelles Littéraires* describes the play as meandering beyond the borders of vaudeville in a kind of no man's land where plays which lack credulity and style belong, "an insipid piece of absurdity never before known in Anouilh's plays".

After *Pauvre Bitos*, a wild domestic satire described as "not for export" Anouilh continued to mirror the feelings of the time in *L'Hurluberlu*, another satire, but more in the *pièce-rose* vein. The General of this play is a most appealing character. Having been prematurely, and we gather, unwillingly retired, he devotes his energies to helping overthrow the republic with a spirit of reforming zeal. There is no shortage of suitable targets in France, whether it be the Fourth or the Fifth Republic, and then of course there is Anouilh's own tried favourite, the army. His range also includes the aristocracy and the *avant-garde* plays of Ionesco and Beckett. As the play develops, personal issues become more important. The general's young wife is bored, and his inability to understand her point of view drives his eldest daughter from the house. Gradually the family disintegrates, the revolutionaries also desert him, until he is left with only his small son Toto. *L'Hurluberlu* is hardly one of Anouilh's best plays, but as the critic of *L'Express* commented, as a result of it Anouilh will become, whether he likes it or not, "the Molière of President Coty".

Hardly had *L'Express* printed this when Anouilh's "scenario with dialogue" *La Petite Molière* was presented by Jean-Louis Barrault at the Bordeaux Festival; the production has subsequently gone into Barrault's repertory at the Odéon. Originally written as a film script (in collaboration with Roland Laudenbach) and adapted by Barrault to the stage, the play (and play it is, in spite of Anouilh's description) tells the story of Molière and his troupe of actors together with both the worry of building up such a company and also inevitable female entanglements.

The season 1959–60 is more than ever an Anouilh one in Paris with his *L'Hurluberlu* (held over from 1958); *La Petite Molière,* a double bill consisting of *La Foire d'empoigne* and *Madame de* offered as the 1959 "Hommage à Molière" at the Comédie Francaise, and finally the production at the Théâtre Montparnasse-Gaston Baty of *Thomas Beckett, ou l'honneur de Dieu.* All this at the same time, there is no doubt that Anouilh has conquered the public. Each year he seems to excel himself as the man of the theatre *par excellence.* In the mood of his plays he seems to be in close touch with the spirit of the French nation; and to understand and serve the desires of his large and ever increasing following.

Is the trend, then, one toward the boulevards? Is Anouilh ready to accept his rôle as being only "to distract and entertain" (as reported in the French periodical *Opéra*), just as he has always done in writing for the films? If this should be the case, then consideration of him as a serious dramatist may as well end here, and we may find Anouilh one day classed in the tradition of Victorian writers such as W. S. Gilbert, Pinero, and Henry Arthur Jones, had they had a French upbringing and lived in a world run riot. Of course, everything would depend on the coloured spectacles they might have chosen. . . .

THIRTEEN

BROADWAY CORTEGE—TENNESSEE WILLIAMS AND ARTHUR MILLER

> "People in America of course live in all sorts of fashions, because they are foreigners, or unlucky, or depraved, or without ambition; people live like that, but *Americans* live in white detached houses with green shutters. Rigidly, blindly, the dream takes precedence."
>
> Margaret Mead, *Male and Female*

THERE are two United States — the legend and the reality (just as there are always two Presidents — the institution and the man). "America" is an idealisation symbolised by the Statue of Liberty; America is a blue print of a nation where many complex questions have still to be solved. The majority of Americans never doubt "the great adventure"; they are, to use M. André Siegfried's phrase, "congenital optimists"; "Never take 'no' for an answer". "The difficult we do at once, the impossible takes a little longer", this is the soul of 'American dynamism', the very spirit of the nation. Everyone is fully geared to 'lick' the system, the childhood hero becomes the man who "started with the clothes on his back and ended up with diamond mines". The American way of life is the acme of civilisation and supersedes all the cultural heritage of the immigrants she absorbs; children of immigrants can say "I am a one hundred per cent. American, born and raised in the greatest country on earth and proud as hell of it". Confidence spirals upwards in relation to the dizzy climb of the trade cycle, only in a major catastrophe such as when the bottom falls out of the market or when their sons do not return home from the war does a different mood take possession, the "what the hell does it all add up to?" despondency. "Do you feel your-self to be spiritually unprepared for the age of exploding atoms? Do you distrust the newspapers? Are you suspicious of governments? Does further progress appear impossible to you?" The voice of doubt momentarily replaces the Voice of "America", the very foundations of the ideal are shaken in the eruption. The transformation of society and individuals "when big wheels crack on this street" is "like the fall of a capital city, the destruction of Carthage, the sack of Rome by the white-eyed giants from the North". The question is whispered "Could it happen to me?" and the echo resounds on all sides "YES". The gap between the heaven of the ideal and the *terra incognita* of reality shatters the illusion of the pioneer's dream. The man who set out to 'lick' the system eventually realises "I'm a dime a dozen, and so are you"; "You were never anything but a hard-working drummer who landed in the ash-can like all the rest of them!"

The above paragraph is an attempt to suggest the American scene as presented in the plays of Tennessee Williams and Arthur Miller, and typical samples of their dialogue have been taken at random to paint the picture. If the mood is a parallel to the European school for pessi-mism, it is very different from the philosophical equations we find in existentialist pessimism or the romantic courting of death. We have here a typically American pessimism, the result of a deliberate optimism *manqué*. O'Neill's gloomy pessimism was much more in the European tradition, with Williams and Miller the American playwright becomes 100 per cent. American. If Tennessee Williams looked to Pirandello and Arthur Miller to Ibsen for their masters, they have so absorbed and integrated their teachings into the American way of life that they have already the appearance of having started an American school in its own right.

It is almost inevitable to link the names of Williams and Miller to-gether, just as in the past one spoke of Ibsen and Björnsen; it is too early to predict which name (if either) will come first, or whether, after their brief blaze of Broadway glory, they will disappear from the playbills. Though the two men may have a similar outlook, or should we rather say though they are both sensitive interpreters of the Ameri-can mood, their work shows the difference of their own personalities and their artistic approach. Tennessee Williams is the poet who delights in language and symbolism and a non-naturalistic style of production; Arthur Miller is the prose writer in the tradition of the social-purpose plays of Ibsen, he is a moralist and prefers realistic stage conventions (though in *Death of a Salesman* he permitted the introduction of certain non-naturalist elements suitable to a dream play).

Miller was born in 1916, two years after Tennessee Williams, and both playwrights worked for many years without success and achieved fame at the same age. Williams is a Southerner while Miller was born in New York City. While writing their early works, both men tried various odd jobs and Williams roamed extensively in America and Mexico. Just before the war the Group Theatre awarded Williams a cash prize for four of his one-act plays entitled *American Blues*, which were concerned with the recent American depression. One of his early plays received professional production, *The Battle of Angels*, but was abandoned on the road in Boston and never reached Broadway. (In 1957 Williams rewrote *The Battle of Angels* under the title *Orpheus Descending*, this time a success in New York, London and Paris.) In 1940 Williams was awarded a Rockefeller Foundation Fellowship and a 1,000-dollar grant for work in drama by the American Academy and National Institute of Arts and Letters. It was not until 1945 that, with the production of *The Glass Menagerie*, Williams made his name.

Arthur Miller had one of his early plays, *The Man Who Had All the Luck*, produced on Broadway in 1944, but this proved a failure. The following year he achieved prominence as a novelist with his anti-Semitic theme *Focus*. In January, 1947, Miller established his reputation with the production of *All My Sons*. At the end of the same year Williams gained his second outstanding success with *A Streetcar named Desire*, and at the beginning of 1949 Miller achieved an equal triumph with *Death of a Salesman*. Since then Miller has written a highly topical play, *The Crucible*; Williams was active turning out *Summer and Smoke* (1948), *The Rose Tattoo* (1951) and *Camino Real* (1953), but not until *Cat on a Hot Tin Roof* did Williams repeat the success of *Streetcar* or *The Glass Menagerie*.

These two young Americans are writing American folk tragedies of the twentieth century. It is as if the society in which they live whips them into indignation, and their plays have a primitive driving force which is a concomitant to life where materialism is master. In the plays of Williams the spiritual is rejected and nothing remains but animal motivations, the instinctive blind groping to follow the system and take what life offers before the realisation of futility. The price we pay, says Williams in *Camino Real*, is "desperation — with cash here! Without cash there!" True, there's a victory in life to be won in this society, and the possibility of victory, as Miller stresses, is essential

o tragedy. But is this victory not like a victory in modern war, and
however much we shake our heads at the world we live in, is this the
true meaning of tragedy? There is a feeling in these plays of a debased
tragedy, which does not inspire our highest emotions and which
merely makes us weep on each other's shoulders.

*

The broken image of Pirandello's theatre, the illusion so carefully
nursed and brutally destroyed, the unfortunate victim unable to face
the consequences of truth, this is the dramatic situation which
Tennessee Williams evokes throughout his work. Often the image is
broken through the use of a symbol, which expresses directly the
author's intent. "We all have in our conscious and unconscious minds
a great vocabulary of images," Tennessee Williams has written, "and
I think all human communication is based on these images as are our
dreams; and a symbol in a play has only one legitimate purpose, which
is to say a thing more directly and simply and beautifully than it could
be said in words." So in his first success, *The Glass Menagerie*, Williams
has shown how a cripple girl, Laura, nurses the illusion of her own
fragile childhood through a collection of little glass animals, one of
which is different from the others by having a horn. When this horn is
broken, she sees the symbol as her chance to live an ordinary life.

The idea of a woman coming to terms with life, and shattering the
image which is no longer possible in the disintegration of society and
the death of the old aristocracy, is the theme of *A Streetcar named
Desire* and is also developed in *Summer and Smoke*. In *Streetcar* Stella
and Blanche du Bois are from an old Southern family which has fallen
on hard times. Stella has secured her future by marrying a great beast
of a man, passionate and uncouth, who eats "more like an animal"
than a human, and acts with primitive possessiveness of her. Stella has
reconciled herself to being his slave because she has found sexual
satisfaction. Blanche, on the other hand, has seen the decay of her
aristocratic upbringing and has had a disastrous tragedy in her first
experience of sex; she has fallen to prostitution and drink, but clings
desperately to her shaken respectability and the possibility of leading
a normal life and finding a decent husband. At her sister's house she
nearly finds her salvation, but her sister's husband, who recognises her
for what she is, brings about her final mental collapse and madness.

The character of Blanche is complex; although a fallen woman she has never lost traces of the gentility of her upbringing and her need for kindness and — to quote the final words in the play as she is carted off to a mental home — "the goodness of strangers". She seeks protection from the harsh and revealing light of reality (admirably symbolised by her desire to hang Chinese lampshades round naked bulbs), but not even her sister can protect her from the inhumanity of strangers. The play asks to be considered as a tragedy, but it is a tragedy of a heroine who has fallen from the start. We are all responsible for Blanche and detest a society which has not given her a chance to save herself, and spiritual values are lacking for any other kind of redemption. It is a tragedy of society, not of an individual.

In *Summer and Smoke* Tennessee Williams seems to return to the theme of *The Glass Menagerie*, the longing of a young woman to lead a normal life, and this time, a normal sex life. The play reveals the failure of Alma to find satisfaction of both sex and spiritual values in the man she loves. Her lover is as frightened of her soul as she is of his body; he could not feel "decent enough" to touch her. Since she cannot find true love, she destroys her spiritual quest and gives herself to the first travelling salesman she meets. Tennessee Williams makes effective use of symbolism in this play by spotlighting an anatomy chart on the wall of a doctor's study:

JOHN Your name is Alma, and Alma is Spanish for soul. Sometime I'd like to show you a chart of the human anatomy that I have in the office. It shows what our insides are like and maybe you can show me where the beautiful soul is located on the chart.

His next play, *The Rose Tattoo*, is a disappointment and seems more to provide effective theatrical tricks than reveal genuine drama out of a very Pirandellian plot. There remains a curiosity, *Camino Real*, and of course Tennessee Williams's most recent play *Cat on a Hot Tin Roof*. Unfortunately *Camino Real*, Williams's most ambitious play, must be called a failure, but a frankly worth-while failure. The play baffled its audiences during its short run and numerous people at each performance stamped out and demanded their money back at the box-office. Those in favour of the play claimed that the audience refused to go half-way to meet a highly original and different type of play. It seems in my view that *Camino Real* is an exciting idea, but that in the play Williams has given us no more than a bare scenario, which could be made into a cycle of plays. In its present form the play has a crudity of harsh and strident paints which may well be the intention, but it is achieved at a sacrifice of characterisation. *Camino Real* must be judged in its total effect; it is not immediately communicative and the symbols do confuse instead of illuminating and simplifying the author's signposts.

Camino Real is presented to us as a town square or *plaza* surrounded by an ancient wall beyond which lies a desert called Terra Incognita. This desert is the only way of escape, and it is a way which requires the courage which so few possess. In the square itself on the left lies the luxury side of the street, containing the fashionable Siete Mares Hotel; opposite the hotel is Skid Row, which contains the Gipsy's gaudy stall, the Loan Shark's establishment, and a 'flea-bag' hotel, "Ritz Men Only". To the right there are a pair of arches which give entrance to the Dead End streets. Camino Real is a port through which travellers pass. Our first travellers are none other than Don Quixote and Sancho Panza. Sancho reads in his chart that at Camino Real he should halt, and turn back, "for the spring of humanity has gone dry in this place". Sancho decides to turn back leaving Quixote to his dreams. We then meet all kinds of travellers from all nations; some stay at the luxury hotel and others in "Ritz Men Only" but the price they pay for both is that of frustration. They are robbed of their money and their papers; they seek an escape, but they have not the courage. The mysterious plane, the Fugitive, arrives, but we know it will crash. And meanwhile the Street-cleaners eliminate all those who are on their lists with the horrific Belsen extermination thoroughness:

> Now do you want to know what is done to a body from which the soul has departed on the Camino Real! — its disposition depends on what the Street-cleaners happen to find in its pockets. If its pockets are empty . . . the 'stiff' is wheeled straight off to the Laboratory. And there the individual becomes an undistinguished member of a collectivist stage. His chemical components are separated and poured into vats containing the corresponding elements of countless others. If any of his vital organs or parts are at all unique in size or structure, they're placed on exhibition in bottles containing a very foul-smelling solution called formaldehyde. There is a charge of admission to this museum. The proceeds go to the maintenance of the military police.

O

Such is Camino Real. Man here has become a guinea-pig, and when he protests, he is reminded that "we are all of us guinea-pigs in the laboratory of God". "I don't make it out," exclaims our bewildered man. "Who does?" replies the Gipsy, "The Camino Real is a funny paper read backwards!"

As can be seen from the idea, this is more a synopsis for an imaginative *mise en scène* and it is a play of silhouettes and atmosphere. Pessimism of course predominates, but there is a way out across the desert which the young American traveller Kilroy decides to explore, accompanied by Don Quixote. *Camino Real* is the rendezvous of man's inhumanity to man, but courage to face the unknown way is what matters.

What are we to make of *Cat on a Hot Tin Roof* (1955)? It has been observed by critics that Williams uses the fourth wall as a mirror, and that this expressionistic treatment is often in bold contrast to the realism of the script so as to shock an audience into attention. The mirror in *Cat on a Hot Tin Roof* reflects the most bitter, cruel, sensual of Williams's interpretations: a play of emotions where again all repressions are swept aside, and what remains is the stark animal ferocity of an individual's loneliness, his inability to face responsibilities he owes not only to others, but to himself. Here is a tragedy which is denied a tragic ending; here are characters whose experiences we suffer but whose sympathies we can never share.

Maggie loves her husband Brick, but her relationship with him becomes increasingly like that of a cat on a hot tin roof. Brick seems to live in a dream world (through the bottle) in an attempt to recapture the memory of his college days when he was a success as a football player. It is only since the death of his college mate Skipper that Brick has taken to drink, and it is more than hinted that this may have been due to homosexual relations, which would also explain why he and Maggie cannot live as husband and wife. It is, however, important for them to have a child, for Brick's father is dying from cancer (a fact that the father does not know) and Brick's brother and wife, who have four children, are scheming to get control of the estate for themselves. When the accusations are let loose truths are revealed, and as a climax Maggie tries to save the situation by saying she is pregnant. The play ends with Brick accepting the challenge to make good her lie.

The plot, however, is not important; it is merely the skeleton which signposts Williams's universe. It is a world of harsh, strident colours, where normality is non-existent, and where abnormality is the essential means of the discovery of oneself. In *Orpheus Descending* (1957) Williams returned to a play he wrote in 1940 *The Battle of Angels*. In a preface to his new version he describes how he spent a summer with a clarinet player who eventually became moody and suddenly disappeared. That was in 1939, and over the years Williams has brooded on this theme. "A play is never an old one" he comments "until you quit working on it and I have never quit working on this one, not even now." It is interesting that *Orpheus Descending* should contain the quintessence of all Williams's other work, his merits and his failings. Set in the decadent South, in a small town where passions smoulder and corruption is rampant, Orpheus is a guitar player who was once corrupted and would free himself, like an Anouilh hero, from the stains. He believes that by refusing all commitments and entanglements he has shaken himself free, but he has forgotten that he is a man and underrated those forces of desire which will overpower him. He successfully keeps at bay the advances of a nymphomaniac, but surrenders to the lonely passionate storekeeper herself trapped into a marriage with an elderly sadist who with other members of the Ku-Klux-Klan burnt out her father. Her husband has not escaped his punishment, he is dying from cancer. So she watches him in his agony, dreaming of her revenge and all the things she will do. She clings desperately to the guitarist for the love she has been deprived of and for the children she wishes to bear. Meanwhile the guitarist has not avoided other human contacts. A kindly but unwise gesture to the sheriff's wife, a religious fanatic, alerts the lynch mob who warn him not to remain overnight in the town. But he stays for the sake of the "lady". The husband in his last breath shoots his wife and accuses the guitarist of murder. It is too late, the dogs are howling for his blood. As he is thrown to them all that he leaves behind is his serpent-skin jacket, which the nymphomaniac keeps as a souvenir. Nobody wants the guitar.

In spite of some powerful scenes the play is far too long for sustained melodrama, the characters too exaggerated for tragedy. We breath a claustrophobic atmosphere of romanticism, we are obsessed with a puritanical frenzy where there is no forgiveness for those transgressors more sinned against than sinning.

Garden District (1958) consists of two one act plays, a curtain raiser *Something Unspoken* where a wealthy Southern spinster sits beside the telephone concerned only with her small world of club politics, and *Suddenly Last Summer*, a nightmare of hypnotic power. Here again the theme is sexual maladjustment in a luxuriant mansion in New Orleans with

> . . . a fantastic garden more like a tropical jungle, or forest, in the prehistoric age of giant fern-forests when living creatures had flippers turning to limbs and scales to skin. The colours of this jungle-garden are violent, especially since it is steaming with heat after rain. There are massive tree-flowers that suggest organs of a body, torn out, still glistening with undried blood; there are harsh cries and sibilant hissings and thrashing sounds in the garden as if it were inhabited by beasts, serpents and birds, all of savage nature.

We are in for shock treatment. A mother with an obsession for her dead son, who was taken from her in his last summer by a girl who witnessed his death. She has described his terrifying death and will tell the story once again, face to face with the mother and a doctor, who has been ordered to operate and remove it from her mind. Under the influence of a drug she describes how they were dining in a restaurant on one of "those white blazing days in Cabeza de Lobo" surrounded by beggar boys banging on jagged tin cans, until in trying to escape he was pursued by them up a hill. When she arrived with waiters and the police at the spot where he had disappeared they found him lying naked and devoured. The featherless little black sparrows had

> . . . torn or cut parts of him away with their hands or knives or maybe those jagged tin cans they made music with, they had torn bits of him away and stuffed them into those gobbling fierce little empty black mouths of theirs.

The doctor is not so sure that this can be removed from her mind, for the play ends on his words "I think we ought at least to consider the possibility that the girl's story could be true."

The hero of *Sweet Bird of Success* (1959) is a blond gigolo called Chance Wayne. He returns to a small town in the Deep South where as a youth he had had a sweetheart called Heavenly, daughter of the political boss Finley who had chased him out. He hopes he is returning in different circumstances, under the wing of an ageing beauty queen who is approaching middle age with the help of hashish and other drugs. Chance sees in her merely a hope of gaining a foothold in the movies—she has just made a film which proves to be the means of her come-back at the end of the play—and the possibility of pursuing the stage career of a Don Juan. His return is rather different from what he had imagined, for as a result of his infecting her with veneral disease Heavenly has had her sexual organs removed. Chance falls into the hands of Finley's henchmen and takes his punishment of castration.

Physical mutilation seems to be the dominant theme in all these latest plays, whether cannabilistic as in *Suddenly Last Summer*, devoured by dogs as in *Orpheus Descending* or castration. This makes one wonder whether Williams is not deliberately cultivating sensationalism, with the applause of the critics, finding that the hysterical frenzied hara-kiri of his own heroes is more rewarding than tenderness, warmth and understanding. As Williams has admitted "I prefer tenderness, but brutality seems to make better copy."

*

The plays of Arthur Miller are also concerned with the twentieth-century tragedy, the tragedy of the common man. He is more concerned with the direct social conflict, which we find in all his three main works, *All My Sons*, *Death of a Salesman* and *The Crucible*. The first play is an accusation against war profiteers, the second accuses a system which causes the death of those who try to keep up with it, and the last accuses the hysterical witch-hunting mania which provoked the trials at Salem in 1692, and was clearly directed at the modern witch-hunting intolerance which had reached its peak in America when the play was produced in 1953.

Arthur Miller believes that the common man is as "apt a subject for tragedy in its highest sense as kings were". One wonders, however, whether *Death of a Salesman* does not fall a good deal short of its writer's intentions. The question is surely not whether we are writing about 'kings' or 'ordinary men', but 'ordinary men' and 'exceptional men', or if you prefer, 'ordinary exceptional men'. It is, or so it seems to this writer, very doubtful whether pure tragedy does not require an extraordinary mind to enable it to make us realise the true perspective of tragedy. Arthur Miller has since admitted that his character Willy Loman "lacks sufficient insight into this situation, which would have made him a greater, more significant figure". Is not the tragic situation always elusive to those whose horizon is limited, bourgeois, and narrow-minded? That is the reason why there is so little tragedy in modern drama.

Death of a Salesman is nevertheless a very remarkable play, and if we don't make the claim for it to be a tragedy, we can safely claim that it is a most interesting psychoanalytic study of an ordinary man. Though the whole impression of the play is of stark realism and the dialogue is purely colloquial, it is conceived as a dream play, and characters and sequences overlap in the style of a carefully thought-out cinema montage. Willy Loman, the salesman, is caught up in the system he tried to 'lick'; he is a failure as a salesman and as a father. The two are related, for his elder son had found Willy out while he was still at school — the God-like mask had fallen from Willy's face when his son discovered him being unfaithful to his mother. Willy's own failure is all the more bitter to him because of the memory of Ben, his elder brother, who at seventeen walked into the jungle, and came out at the age of twenty-one, and he was rich! Willy, on the other hand, never a successful salesman at the height of his career, has been burdened by debts, paying a twenty-five-year mortgage for his house, for his refrigerator, his car, all the 'necessities' of the system — at the cost of his own life. The day arrives when he can face the world no longer, when no one knows him and even his old firm refuse to employ him. He suddenly grasps the futility of his own life. Meanwhile his elder son has been a wanderer (like Ben) and his younger son is also a salesman who has probably the same fate in store for him at the end of his life as has Willy now. Eventually, nagged on by the vision of his elder brother Ben (whom we are told is dead), he decides to join him in the adventure in the jungle "which is dark, but full of diamonds", and from which one never returns.

The searching pyschological study of a character was not attempted by Miller in his next play, *The Crucible*, which is a kind of modern parable. Arthur Miller has explained that in this play he was not attempting "to give people a sense of reality in depth" as in *Death of a Salesman*, but to write a play where "the characters were special people who could give voice to the things which were inside them". *The Crucible* is about organised terror, where theme not character is all-important, and where in fact his characters are inclined to become mere spokesmen for his plot. Thus, whereas the characters do not come before us as individuals but as martyrs for the author's moral purpose and sense of justice, the play admirably succeeds in its intensely dramatic exposition of theme and the forcefulness of its writing. The message of the play, a timely reminder of the historical facts of the Salem witch trials, carried out with so much bigotry and zealous intolerance and blindness, comes across without turning the stage into a pulpit, for the historical facts themselves have dramatic unity. It is interesting to remember also that twenty years after the executions, the government recognised that a miscarriage of justice had been done and gave compensation to the victims still alive. Thus the defeat of an ideal was turned into a moral victory. What is to be admired most in the play is the sweep of Miller's convictions, the power of his faith and the urgency of the subject matter. But whether the play will survive on its own merits and the fall of McCarthy is another question.

In *A View from the Bridge* (1955) Arthur Miller returns to his theme of tragedy and the common man. *A View from the Bridge* is the second of two plays which he links with this general title, the first play, *A Memory of Two Mondays*, setting a sombre mood in anticipation of the second which, in its Broadway production, proved the main event of the evening. Set in Red Hook, on the bay seaward from Brooklyn Bridge, *A View from the Bridge* shows the reaction of longshoreman Eddie Carbone to the arrival of two Italian immigrants (and illegal immigrants) to his house. Eddie has unconsciously grown to adore his first wife's seventeen-year-old neice Catherine, and when she takes an interest in Rodolpho, one of the immigrants, he determines to stop this by fair means or foul. He tries to show Catherine that Rodolpho is effeminate, that he is only wanting to marry her so that he can become an American citizen and regularize his illegal entry. When Eddie finds he cannot shake her even by humiliating Rodolpho in front of her, he denounces Rodolpho and his companion Marco to the immigration authorities. Marco in turn denounces Eddie to his neighbours, and it is against Marco that Eddie draws a knife and is killed in the ensuing fight. Such a rough sketch of the action gives little justice to the subjective complexity of the theme. For here a tragic canvas comes to terms with the man in the street.

The future of Miller and Williams will be watched with interest, for with all their obsessions and pessimism, they are among the most original writers in the theatre to-day. Neither panders to the fashions of Broadway and both have, in their way, 'licked' that system. Both, however, have yet to offer a play where there is breadth of vision, imagination free from obsession, allied to the tragic force not of environment, but of life.

FOURTEEN

THE LITTLE WORLD OF JOHN OSBORNE

LOOKING back on Raffles after half a century George Orwell remarked: "all he has is a set of reflexes — the nervous system, as it were, of a gentleman. Give him a sharp tap on this reflex or that (they are called "sport", "pal", "woman", "king and country" and so forth), and you get a predictable reaction." Orwell went on in this essay to compare the morals of Raffles with those of Miss Blandish, observing (in 1944) that in Mr. Chase's book there are no gentlemen and no taboos. The English novel had achieved its emancipation and Freud and Machiavelli had reached the outer suburbs. But the theatre did not follow suit in the post-war years; the plays presented tended to be as polite as restrictions and rationing seemed drab. The most that the new social revolution of the Labour Government achieved was echoed in the verbal tinklings of Priestley's *Linden Tree*, and soon Priestley was to cast himself into the wilderness. Long runs by star-studded casts were the order of the day, they had the formality of an eighteenth-century conversation picture where one could marvel at the way a famous actress would delicately finger a cream cake without making her fingers sticky. It was Charles Morgan who commented in a preface to *The Flashing Stream* (1938) that while English people in life recognized and even enjoyed "great variety among those whom they love and admire, in the theatre, where they sit in mass, they assume more than their fair share of the intolerance and hysteria of the masses."

This was to be the case until 1956, and it is perhaps largely due to the spread of television that things are different to-day. The Television Playhouse, whether B.B.C. or I.T.V., with its several million viewers, constitutes, as Ted Willis puts it, "the most vital, the most alive, and probably the most useful section of the community . . . but they are often limited by social conventions which are narrow in the extreme." To which Dr. Tyrone Guthrie has added that the drama has been

JOHN OSBORNE

Eugène Ionesco

relieved, thanks to television, of the onus of popular entertainment. All these circumstances aided the entry of Jimmy Porter on to the stage of the Royal Court Theatre, London May 8th, 1956, a decisive date which marks a turning point in recent theatrical history. Until there was a change in the intellectual climate, the blowing away of the cobwebs, a creation of a new sort of atmosphere in the theatre, there was little hope for the blistering honesty of a Jimmy Porter to succeed in the English theatre. A return to a direct language without polite euphemisms would only be acceptable to English audiences and critics from characters in Shakespeare and Chechov, but not, as Osborne commented, "from one who speaks out of the real despairs, frustrations, and sufferings of the age we are living in, now, at this moment." Times had changed. For the first time the audience is ready, so enter Jimmy Porter, or if you prefer, John Osborne, for we cannot help feeling that Osborne has painted a reflection of his adolescence in his very articulate hero. This ending of a theatrical stalemate, the raising of the dust to disclose a different approach to theatre, a vocal movement in embryo, was an exciting moment. Even if *Look Back in Anger* was not the best play of the decade, it can be called the most important, for whatever may be the shortcomings of Osborne, a play which establishes a new intellectual climate, a return to a directness of language long absent, can have an important influence on the future.

How then, would Jimmy Porter fit the Raffles description? We must quickly eliminate the "gentleman", the "Christian gentleman" of public schools. Like Raffles Jimmy Porter has no moral code, no religion, but unlike Raffles, he has a strongly developed social conscience. Give him a sharp tap on the reflexes of his nervous system and you get the predictable obsessions, against society, the Church of England, the Press, women, and himself. "Damn you, damn both of you, damn them all . . ."; "when you see a woman in front of her bedroom mirror, you realise what a refined sort of butcher she is . . . thank God they don't have many woman surgeons! those primitive hands would have your guts out in no time. . . ."; "No, as far as Michelangelo Brigade's concerned, I must be a sort of right wing deviationist . . ."; "I've no public school scruples about hitting girls . . ." and so on.

Jimmy Porter is introduced as a young man about twenty-five, "a disconcerting mixture of sincerity and cheerful malice, of tenderness and freebooting cruelty; restless, importunate, full of pride, a combination which alienates the sensitive and insensitive alike. Blistering honesty, or apparent honesty, like his, makes few friends. To many he may seem sensitive to the point of vulgarity. To others, he is simply a loudmouth. To be as vehement as he, is to be almost non-committal." Here we have an egoistical battering-ram, an enigmatic character who however much he has to offer, is constantly misunderstood. He deliberately will set out to shock, he has the utmost contempt for all bourgeois values, his favourite words are "phoney" and "wet". A portrait of a character of contradictions, a complex mixed-up mind, full of fire and fury and not simply the louse he might appear — at least superficially. "I may write a book about us all" he exclaims "written in flames a mile high. And it won't be recollected in tranquillity either, picking daffodils with Auntie Wordsworth. It'll be recollected in fire, and blood. My blood."

Cliff, who shares the flat with Jimmy and his wife, Alison, is a different character altogether. One is largely indifferent to his existence. Alison is the most elusive personality. She is tuned in a different key. According to Osborne "she really is incapable of loyalty, even to herself. She is caught between two uncertain worlds and cannot bring herself to declare her allegiances." Alison is something of a pipe-dream, too good to be true in this environment. She does not seem to have a mind of her own, but is ready to be moulded, by her parents in their status of upper-middle class comfort and boredom from which she has fled, or moulded by the squalid and frustrating existence she shares with Jimmy. She is ready to renounce everything: "I don't want to be a saint, I want to be a lost cause. I want to be corrupt and futile! . . . Don't you see, I'm in the mud at last! I'm grovelling! I'm crawling!"

This is the only stage at which Jimmy is willing to be at one with her, it is the culmination of a blind rage of invective, ridiculing her parents, her snobberies, and everything she could cling to for an anchor. He drives her away and she returns home. She is pregnant and has a miscarriage. While they are separated Jimmy carries on an affair with Alison's actress friend, Helena. But Jimmy and Alison are made for one another, and there is no solution for either of them. Alison returns knowing that there will be more fights, that they will destroy one another, and that only in a lover's fantasy of playing bear and squirrel will they ever find happiness. Osborne asserts that this ending of the play should be ironic, not sentimental, that as "little furry creatures with little furry brains, full of dumb uncomplicated affection for each other," they are merely following "a common pattern of behaviour among sensitive, intelligent people." Be this as it may, coming as an anti-climax to what has gone before it is difficult to avoid the feeling that this is both whimsy and sentimentality.

Look Back in Anger is a play where the characters take over, and one character in particular. Osborne's dialogue, a non-stop outburst of bad manners delivered with the brutality of the blackboard-jungle school, has a magnetism about it which holds audiences who are far removed from the world of the angry young men, American and French audiences, for example. True there is little to admire in the character of Jimmy Porter, far less than that of Amis's *Lucky Jim* who is perhaps a prototype of the new provincialism. One would hardly wish to have Jimmy Porter as a friend or an acquaintance, with his odious loudmouth egoism, and would quickly consign his destiny to a place in the James Dean mythology.

Nevertheless *Look Back in Anger* swept the theatre like an electrical storm front and the weather changed from drizzle to gale. Osborne's next play was *The Entertainer*, performed at the Royal Court in 1957, but an interesting play *Epitaph for George Dillon*, which Osborne had written together with Anthony Creighton before *Look Back in Anger*, remained unproduced until 1958. If Jimmy Porter is not exactly a young man who endears you to him, there are moments in both *The Entertainer* and *Epitaph for George Dillon* when we have some sympathy. George Dillon may have compromised with a system, but he has not opted out of life. He is a down-and-out actor who has written a play, but success is only possible by rejecting ideals and accepting the seedy standards of Barney Edwards, a show-business impressario. Thus the title of George's play is changed to 'Telephone Tart'; as for George Dillon himself, he recovers from tuberculosis to be crushed by a much more insidious disease.

Of the plays Osborne has written to date, *Epitaph for George Dillon* is the most convincing piece of theatre. Certainly the best constructed, it alone has a harmony, it rings true. The anger is controlled, not self-pity or sheer temper for the sake of hitting at any sitting target, but an indignation which is felt. Perhaps Creighton was the restraining influence.

Osborne however considers *The Entertainer* to be his best play; it is a very ambitious one. Technically there is a marked Brechtian influence, borrowed and submerged until the result bears only Osborne's own signature. In turning to the music hall and the fortunes of a family steeped in its traditions, Osborne writes:

The music hall is dying, and, with it, a significant part of England. Some of the heart of England has gone; something that once belonged to everyone, for this was truly folk art. In writing this play I have not used some of the techniques of the music hall in order to exploit an effective trick, but because I believe that these can solve some of the eternal problems of time and space that face the dramatist, and, also, it has been relevant to the story and setting. Not only has this technique its own traditions, its own convention and symbol, its own mystique, it cuts right across the restrictions of the so-called naturalistic stage. Its contact is immediate, vital and direct.

Much of the success of the play in performance was undoubtedly due to the virtuoso performance of Sir Laurence Olivier, as the dud music-hall comic Archie Rice. The audience Archie has to play to are "dead behind the eyes. They pay their one and sixpence and defy you to entertain them." In vain he goes through the whole patter of brash vulgar jokes and jingoistic songs, and as he does so he enacts his own failure, his own unbelief. The turns are broken up by a series of scenes depicting a contemporary tragedy, a portrait of three generations of the Rice family. First there is Billy, the grandfather, a grand 'old-timer', lingering in the golden memories of the Edwardian era. Then there is Archie and his sozzled wife Phoebe, and their children Frank, who has just served six months in prison as a conscientious objector, in contrast to his brother, who dies out in Egypt, a hero without a cause, and a reminder of the crazy Suez adventure of 1956, which took place before Osborne finished the play.

"Nothing touches me, emotion is dead", Archie Rice claims. But Osborne's own emotions are very much alive, and the fault of the political satire is that too much is felt, too little thought. Out of characters of flesh and blood he nowhere offers hope of their rising from their misery. They believe honesty eliminates belief. The younger generation are as complete a failure as their parents. The lights grow dimmer, the repetition of the music-hall patter becomes more stale. The laughter turns hollow, sour, the tragedy is unrelieved even by Rock 'n' Roll and a Britannia in the nude.

It is interesting to compare the mood and theme of Osborne's pessimism with the way Chaplin treated *Limelight* — truly a film of our time. In *Limelight* it will be recalled that a once famous clown Calvero has lost his ability to make people laugh. And a gifted young dancer has become paralysed. Both have faith in each other. Chaplin's characters are pure, the clown is no vulgar down-and-out, he has known how to make the whole world laugh, he can still make us in the audience laugh. They are characters who transcend their environment and become universal. Osborne's characters, on the other hand, are shut in their own little world, from which they cannot, will not, escape. Canada is available, but Archie Rice refuses. For the young perhaps there is emigration.

The Rice family are thus outside society. Slaves of their own conventions they feel they have been badly done by, yet one wonders what exactly life should have offered them. Like Sartrian disciples, they were thrown into the world from nowhere, and with nowhere to go. They wander around No Hope Alley.

There remains Osborne's musical *The World of Paul Slickey*, or should one say rather the "battle" over Paul Slickey. There is no doubt about the failure, albeit an ambitious one. "There's no such thing as failure", says George Dillon, "just waiting for success." For Osborne to write a successful musical he will have to study rather more closely the technique, and not imagine that blind swiping at whatever tilt catches his eye is necessarily better than the tinkling musicals of the Ruritania kind. Being like the proverbial Irishman, and agin' everything, becomes merely dull, and the trouble with a bore is that he never knows or imagines that he himself ever could be one. To write a musical of our times Osborne will have to take rather more pains and trouble over the marshalling of his material.

Paul Slickey is one of Osborne's despised columnists on the "Daily Racket". Strangely enough he comes from one of England's stately mansions, he belongs to the despised class he writes about. If he started off being a decent fellow, society has cured him. As his newspaper boss goads him on to write more and more scurrilously, so Osborne himself launches out at the Crown, the Church, the Press, stately homes, pop singers, the Royal Academy of Dramatic Art, and women, among other topics. The climax drags on interminably as the cast change their sex. And at all this Osborne fires wildly without aim; unfortunately a hit here and there goes almost unnoticed in the general pandemonium. There are good lines in Slickey, and good characters. Even the much discussed rock 'n' roll funeral scene was not in bad taste, many a Highland funeral, at any rate, has been a merry social gathering with whisky galore. What Osborne failed to do was to find a workable technique, a plan of action for song, dance and devastating satire, instead of which one feels like crying *basta, basta* to this verbose jumble-sale.

Three plays and a musical, and Osborne's anger, hatred, obsessions grow work by work. In an American programme note he has poured vitriol on the rank and file of British playgoers. When he was booed at the opening of *The World of Paul Slickey* he replied, "It's a distinction to be booed by some people." The danger is that he will narrow down the audience until he is writing for a small number of the converted, and the rest can like it or lump it. It is the narrow world rather than the world with unlimited horizons and timelessness. Yet unless Osborne can encompass the wider canvas, unless his feelings turn towards something constructive, towards in fact a greater humanism, there will be a danger that his plays will be merely the reflection of a decade, as dated as for example Coward's *The Vortex*. Anger can so easily turn to genuine hatred of the chip on the shoulder variety, and this is hardly what Osborne can be looking forward to when he writes of hoping for "an exciting, creative time, so let the scribblers scratch and England bleed; there will be singing one day." As he is unlikely to care to remember a biblical quotation, might not the title of Clifford Odet's play *Awake and Sing* suggest a way, and we will apply the rest of the saying "all ye who dwell in the dust", to the characters who live and suffer in John Osborne's world.

THE STATE OF THE DRAMA

Britain—U.S.A.—France—Other Countries

"Just as many people outside the theatre world are content to do second-rate work, so you have to see many indifferent plays and films. . . . We are all human, and often fail to reach the standards at which we aim. But the important thing is to aim high."

SIR C. B. COCHRAN, *Cock-a-Doodle-Do*

FIFTEEN

BRITAIN

Christopher Fry; Graham Greene; James Bridie; Sean O'Casey; J. B. Priestley; Charles Morgan; Brendan Behan; John Whiting; Peter Ustinov; Terence Rattigan; Shelagh Delaney, Auden and Isherwood, Arnold Wesker.

A NEW DRAMA OR WE FAINT!" — this 'money or your life!' call for help was the title of a theatre book published in 1853. A century later we had grown more used to sleeping in the theatre than fainting, even stage villains had become as genteel as the rest of our theatre. Playgoing had become dull, it was a safety-first theatre where passions were hinted at rather than experienced. Revivals were the order of the day and the young playwright had almost been squeezed out of the West End. It was a theatre which fought shy of all continental influences, keeping within the narrow conventions of its own naturalism. Since 1956 things have changed and the situation is now considerably brighter. While there is still much that West End managements could and should do to encourage the playwright of promise, there was probably never any time in the past century when the playwright had a better chance of seeing his work performed. It now remains for the dramatists to create this new drama which we so badly need.

The English Stage Company at the Royal Court Theatre has given a lead in finding new writers, but another sign of the times is the opening of new theatres. Bernard Miles's new Mermaid Theatre at Puddle Dock, built on the site of a blitzed warehouse, promises a repertory to include everything, and aims at killing the idea of highbrow and low-brow drama; plays will be judged as good or bad in their own field. Another new theatre of promise is in the provinces, the Belgrade at Coventry.

The Arts Theatre Club, the Lyric Hammersmith, and Theatre Workshop continue to bring a theatre that matters to their audiences, and in the provinces many provincial repertory theatres have found a public which takes its plays more seriously than many West-end audiences. The dominant pattern, however, is shaped by the West End of London, where thirty-nine theatres are usually open the whole year round. In a Fabian pamphlet on the British Theatre by Mr. Richard Findlater, it is noted that these theatres have on sale about 42,000 seats per night, of which nearly a third are in seven buildings reserved for musicals, variety, opera and ballet. All but four of London's theatres are let out to hire (except the Old Vic, Sadler's Wells, the Royal Opera House, Covent Garden, and the Royal Court) to one of twenty-five managements. Half of these are concerned with the legitimate drama, where plays are classified in box-office terms as 'hits' or 'flops'.

In these circumstances perhaps it is understandable that the theatre in Britain is neither brilliant, nor is it a corpse. And there are managements of imagination who do from time to time produce plays which might seem doubtful box-office propositions; it is then doubly rewarding when they find that in spite of everything they have found a 'hit'.

(I) CHRISTOPHER FRY

Until Osborne the most talked about English playwright was undoubtedly Christopher Fry, a verse dramatist whose very success has done much to make box-office managers share his belief that "reality is incredible, reality is a whirlwind". Indeed it is, for such a bacchanalia of words and thesaurus of fine phrases have not been heard in our language-starved theatre for many a long century. No wonder at the enthusiasm of the rejoicing, the sincerity that made many compare his plays with the tradition of the Elizabethan masters; premature, yes, but at least it indicated that not everyone was complacent about the dreary monotone of the naturalistic drama. It proved there was a large public ready to support any worth-while attempt to find a way out towards poetry and imagination. Fry has now given us sufficient work (three religious plays, one tragedy and four comedies) to enable the pattern of his development to be viewed in perspective with the trend of the modern drama we have been considering, though obviously such a judgment will merely be an interim one; Fry is still in his forties.

What strikes one first in the plays of Fry is his completely idiosyncratic style and his felicity for words; his language has a dazzle which seems to be almost an end in itself and is nearly blinding when, striving to ignore it, an attempt is made to understand the essential Fry. In a lecture to the Critics' Circle Fry has defended his use of words by declaring that while sometimes in his comedies the words are "an ornament on the meaning and not the meaning itself", "almost as often I have meant the ornament to be, dramatically or comedically, an essential part of the meaning". Since writer and critic must "start with the same premise" we must bear his words in mind. Fry's plays are moods, perhaps even "the stuff that dreams are made of", they are climatic but not dramatic. In these gay flights of fancy there is no attempt to build up dramatic sequences or lead the audience to antici-pate events; there seems to be no direction in the flight and no more than a hint occasionally as to meaning and intentions. Nothing is defined.

In a talk on the background of his plays given by the B.B.C. Third Programme Fry has explained that he is attempting to combine the reality of amazement which is the province of poetry with the reality that is prose. What is different between the two realities, he contends, is 'implication'. "What I am trying to say is that a spade is never so merely a spade as the word spade would imply. I am asking for the sudden dramatic appearance of a spade in time and space, but I am equally asking for a spade which I can dig with. I am asking — now I come to think of it — I am asking for both kinds of realism at once." Now, in attempting this, it seems to this critic that Fry has completely failed to realise his aim. There are no contrasts with Fry, no planes of reality (as with Pirandello, Claudel, Giraudoux). There is but one dominant mood, bewilderment, which remains constant, with neither emotion, drama nor character, whether the play be comedy or tragedy, spring or autumn. All Fry's plays have a unity of mood, and this mood, it might be suggested, is not a combination of the reality of poetry and prose, but merely an embellishment of ordinary prose.

For Fry "we are plunged into an existence fantastic to the point of nightmare, and however hard we rationalise, or however firm our religious faith, however closely we dog the heels of science or wheel among the stars of mysticism, we cannot really make head or tail of of it." But the exploration of amazement, the "how lost, how amazed, how miraculous we are", which may certainly be considered the province of poetry, should yield a poetic vision of life, illuminating ideas, contrasts and ambiguities rather than shrouding them with a mist against which our sensitivities and our mind eventually rebel. Giraudoux also attempts to see reality in terms of amazement, but he succeeds through his ability to contrast the irrationality of the real with the rationality of the illusory. Fry's reality, on the other hand, never shows much spirit in venturing beyond the frontiers of naturalistic comedy. And this mood, a lingering swan song, extends until death, whether at the stake or like the death of the Countess in *The Dark is Light Enough*. The business of the play is never to be dramatic, nor to present life-size characters with whom we can share a bond of sympathy. The business is in words, like in an Oscar Wilde play, and while hints may be dropped with the epigrams, these tend to exclude discussion of more serious subjects which the theme itself provokes. We have a flow of words with which we may luxuriate as if in a steam sauna; but it is given to other races to have the courage to roll in the snow afterwards.

All this seems to me a direct negation of theatre, because it eliminates the dramatic, and consequently cannot claim to belong to the tradition of dramatic poetry, as can Eliot, for example. And it has led in Fry's most recent work, *The Dark is Light Enough*, to a kind of poetic monologue, devoid of action and not overflowing with imagination. But these same faults were to be found in Fry's best play *The Lady's Not for Burning*, though in this case the originality of the plot, the natural inspiration of its treatment and the sparkle of some of the phrases could not help to excite and blind the realisation that we were moving towards a dramatic stalemate.

The plot of *The Lady's Not for Burning* is probably familiar to readers; a young girl, suspected of witchcraft, is condemned to be burned at the stake (the period is the fifteenth century) and a young man, tired of the hypocrisy of the world in general and human beings in particular, demands that the local mayor should have him hanged. The girl pleads with him the cause for life, and through her love she persuades him to go on living. The appearance of the rag-man whom the girl was supposed to have turned into a dog saves her from the stake, and unofficially they are pardoned. It is interesting to compare this play (Fry's best) with Giraudoux's *Intermezzo* which treats a similar theme. With Giraudoux we have a perfect blending of the planes of reality, a poetic vision allied to the intellect. With Fry, however pleasing the poetical phrases and certain passages may be to the ear, the need for character study, a clearer, surer vision, a willingness to call a spade a shovel, becomes increasingly embarrassing. No, Fry is not the English Giraudoux, as some have called him, for his is essentially the naturalistic theatre, not Giraudoux's anti-naturalist style where lightness of touch is its own revealer. No serious dramatist can, however, afford to marvel about the mystery of the creation throughout his career without asking the audience to share with him his interpretation.

If we turn to Fry's most serious work *A Sleep of Prisoners,* which might be described as a passion play as it was originally produced in the University Church at Oxford (and later at St. Thomas's Church, Regent Street), we realise how completely at sea Fry can be when forceful exposition of ideas and meaning is required. This was the play which was to cause such a furore when produced by Jean-Louis Barrault in Paris, where the audience failed to follow it although they listened to it for the first half hour without interruption, and only, to quote one French critic, "after they had been most insufferably bored that can be imagined" did they show their dislike of the piece. Mr. Robert Kemp, drama critic of *Le Monde,* described the play the following day as "invincibly boring" and a "string of inflated small talk". Nor was it purely a failure of translation, for the play, in my experience at any rate, fails completely to come across in English. This is all the more surprising as Fry has had a long training in the theatre and is not like Eliot, for example, an academician. Be that as it may, Fry explains in an introductory dedication that in *A Sleep of Prisoners* he is concerned with "the growth of vision; the increased perception of what makes for life and what makes for death". He continues: "In *A Sleep of Prisoners* I have tried to make a more simple statement, though in a complicated design, where each of four men is seen through the sleeping thoughts of the others, and each, in his own dream, speaks as at heart he is, not as he believes himself to be." Alas, the complicated design, the verbosity (in spite of a more urgent sense in the poetry), results in complete confusion. No doubt the audience realises that these four English soldiers, locked in a bombed church and thrown in each other's company, have in the dreams they enact from biblical sources, such as Cain's murder of Abel, some sort of allegorical significance, but just what, would defeat any average audience of intelligent playgoers. A clear driving force, a simple pacific message instead of the contrived rhetoric at the end, might have made *A Sleep of Prisoners* into a memorable work. As it is it is too complex and obscure to be readily appreciated on the level at which it invites to be judged.

The Dark is Light Enough may be considered as a sequel to *A Sleep of Prisoners.* Again the play is an appeal for pacificism, and we have the prospect of the end of the civilisation we know. The Countess Rosmarin Ostenburg, living in a country in revolution (the Austro-Hungarian Empire during 1848–49) is a supremely Christian lady, endowed with wisdom and charm and the firm conviction of divine non-interference. But the times are against her and her Thursday salon, for her ex-son-in-law Gettner, having stirred up a revolution, has now deserted from the Hungarian rebel army and seeks protection and hiding. The Countess offers him sanctuary, and her daughter's second husband is taken prisoner in his place. Gettner repays the hospitality by making love to his former wife, and then shooting the Countess's son in a duel and wounding him. But none of this, or the fact that because of her action the Countess has been turned by the rebels out of her home and is forced to live in the stables, influences the Countess's belief in human charity. Gettner is eventually converted to her philosophy, and before the play ends the political fortunes have turned, the rebel colonel is given shelter by the Countess, who, dying, summons up her strength for her last Thursday salon.

The play may be regarded as a commissioned work for Dame Edith Evans, who played the part most beautifully in the London production. The play, consequently, has the appearance of being contrived rather than natural, and it is difficult to believe that Fry wrote it because he felt compelled to do so, or because he had left unsaid something he felt essential. It is merely the repetition of a mood, more sombre, with his language held in check and used more cautiously. It is a monologue for Dame Edith, and the other characters are the merest puppets. If Fry is to remain a poet in the theatre he will in the future have to find more dramatic material than that of the theme of non-intervention; the idea of shaking your head at the way of the world and philosophising in long, unoriginal platitudes may be the stuff twentieth-century idealist dreams are made of, but it is unlikely to prosper or be very healthy for the theatre. His growth of vision seems to have remained where it did when he wrote *A Phoenix Too Frequent,* and his inability to make head or tail of this poor world of ours is no excuse for dramatic paralysis (*The Dark is Light Enough* can hardly even be called a play in the accepted sense). Fry has had a great influence in the English theatre by creating a public favourable to poetic ventures; this can only be maintained with something more dramatic than his present attitude of mind. Max Reinhardt once wrote: "We carry within ourselves the potentialities of all passions, all fates, all forms of life...."

Perhaps in the comedy of high summer which remains to complete his four-season cycle, Fry will consider the dramatic "possibilities of love, hate, rejoicing and sorrow that we are born with" at the same time as he continues to contemplate the marvel of creation.

(II) GRAHAM GREENE

Sooner or later a successful novelist will turn his eyes to the theatre. Graham Greene has written three plays, *The Living Room* (1954), *The Potting Shed* (1958) and *The Complaisant Lover* (1959); an adaption of his novel *The Power and the Glory* has also been successfully produced. As a novelist Greene is one of the few important contemporary figures, in the cinema he is a master of suspense in such films as *The Third Man*, but in the theatre the technique seems to stifle his broader vision — and the ability to carry us with him.

In *The Living Room* Graham Greene makes his own variations with stock characters — the two elderly sisters, the one terrorised by the other; the innocent (but soon not-so-innocent) Rose, who is unable to find happiness because she is the mistress of a married man (who is also a psychiatrist for the sake of the play) and cannot find absolution for her affair from a priest (because, for the sake of the play, he is her uncle). Now all these characters and the strange house which they inhabit bear no relation to life in general nor human beings in particular. Apparently neither psychiatry nor religion can save Rose from suicide, and we are left with the impression that it was no one person's fault, but a general despair and failure of the world. For those who like to put a premium on failure in life, Graham Greene's play suits the prevalent mood of despair; this is not because a suicide is in itself unlikely — of course not — but because the situations are so painstakingly contrived and never ring true.

The same weakness is apparent in *The Potting Shed*, where the plot takes on the character of a religious who-dunnit, with a detective played by a thirteen-year-old girl, a defence lawyer, and clues lying in the potting shed waiting to be unravelled in time for the final denouement. Instead of a murder we have a suicide, instead of a doctor to examine the body we have a priest, who as he leans over his young nephew who has just hung himself in the potting shed, begs God to let him live, adding "Take away my faith, but let him live." All this happened many years before the play opens. Henry Callifer, a well-known Rationalist, is dying, and all his family, except James — who is asked to stay downstairs, for fear that the miracle of his life might upset his father in his last hours. It was in fact his miracle which destroyed his father's faith in aetheism as much as his uncle priest's faith in God. The development of the play is an exercise in psychological suspense as the truth and reality of the miracle is argued and explained. But although Greene attempts to bring his characters to life they remain the stock protagonists of his own invention. Maybe a Claudel or some other great poet could convince us that you can bargain for a miracle, but the naturalism of Greene's theatre is all against our belief. Like Alice's pudding, or after reading an ingenious murder-story, we feel that it was merely a clever thing to invent.

The Complaisant Lover is a very different type of play, or one might even say two plays in one, for there is an abrupt change of tempo from the first half, which has all the ingredients of a French bedroom farce, to the second, where the hilarity ends and we are reminded that there is a serious problem of human relations to be solved. Victor Rhodes is not the tiresome practical-joker or the unromantic and insensitive dentist husband he appears to be in act one; this facade is shattered, the reality revealed when he discovers his wife's infidelity at the beginning of act two. His emotional breakdown comes as the climax and transitional turning point to what went before and the subsequent *denouement*. Had we really been so unkind as to laugh at the situation in the Amsterdam hotel bedroom where unsuspectingly he confronts his wife with her lover (instead of old school friend Jane Crane who should have been there) without realizing that anything is amiss? Even his Dutch dental colleague who couldn't speak English probably understands more than the wronged husband.

Nevertheless a way out must be found, and it is here that Rhodes, the practical joker now turned moralist, suggests an English compromise. He will allow what he cannot prevent on condition that his wife keeps the home together. Moreover the husband knows that eventually the lover will tire of his wife and leave her, so that this unconventional design for living turns out to be a feasible and practical solution. The husband is at the end of the play, a wiser, if a sadder, man.

In its leap from farce to serious comedy Greene does not achieve a compromise as easily as do his characters. As an experiment in entertaining techniques, with the undertones of a religious conscience, I am not sure that Greene has yet mastered the art of the theatre as he has the novel. He would seem now to be striving, not unsuccessfully, after popular success, but his novels have another dimension which is as yet absent from his stage work.

ELMER RICE

J. B. PRIESTLEY

SEAN O'CASEY

CHARLES MORGAN

MARCEL PAGNOL

CLIFFORD ODETS

MAXWELL ANDERSON

ROBERT EMMET SHERWOOD

(*Above*) Ugo Betti

(*Left*) Gabriel Marcel

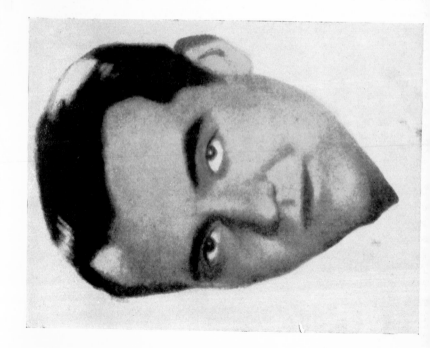

(III) JAMES BRIDIE

If we were to arrange this credit list of British playwrights in some order of merit, the place to be occupied after Christopher Fry (assuming his name is allowed to go first) would offer a promising field for controversy. We have Eliot and Fry, it is true, but where are the white hopes of the British theatre? Where indeed! It seems prudent at this stage, rather than consider young but inexperienced playwrights such as John Whiting and others, to return to the theatre of the 'thirties and 'forties, when the English comedy was saved by a Scotsman, James Bridie. But Bridie was not like the bagpipers who in the 1940 American-organised Carnival for Britain piped "There'll always be an England"; it was as a Scot with the Scottish dry sense of humour and philosophical wit that Bridie crossed the Border and saved the West End from stagnation.

The plays of James Bridie present an optimist's window on the world; he is a tolerant moralist little concerned, unlike his Yorkshire contemporary J. B. Priestley, with social propaganda. Bridie, an acute observer of man, shows a shrewd sense of character throughout his work, a sense developed, no doubt, by the experience he gained when he was a medical practitioner. At any rate, he delights in poking fun at our foibles without preaching. His characters are without exception interesting people, the good are never too good and the bad are always human. "I find a few facetiae light this wilderness of a world like glow-worms", exclaims Dr. Angelus after he has finished poisoning his wife and mother-in-law, and goes on to confide with the audience that he is a rare combination, a man of science and a philosopher. In his characters Bridie has a bond of understanding and sympathy, and transfers this to the audience even for characters they would not normally feel affection for at all (i.e. John Knox, or the Wee Free minister in *Mr. Bolfry*).

Throughout his work — some thirty plays — Bridie shows an innate sense of theatre, and even in his poorest plays he never bores and even offers just a wee dose of idiosyncrasy which is the signature of Bridie's own civilised intellect. They are always interesting but often slap-dash. It was as if he had so many ideas in his fertile imagination that he rushed on to the next one without doing justice to his last one. As so many critics have complained, a play by Bridie has the appearance of being unfinished. It is more like a first draft, often in urgent need of revision and structural alteration. His refusal to take pains is regrettable, but fortunately a born playwright does not depend on that.

One can do him more justice by attempting a general picture of his work than by presenting a classification of his plays starred according to an A.A. handbook. Bridie never gave us a masterpiece by which he may be remembered by succeeding generations, but there is no reason why his themes should date. For he delighted in using the fantasies of a biblical story to give flight to his own wit and flow of language, and he thus finds himself perfectly at home in such plays as *Tobias and the Angel* and *Jonah and the Whale*. And surely the body-snatching of Burke and Hare which is described in *The Anatomist* will never fail to hold an audience.

Among Bridie's other works perhaps the best known is *The Sleeping Clergyman* (1933), where heredity and the way in which it is affected by environment is traced over three generations. In the third generation Bridie maintains his belief that however true it may be that the worst features of heredity are passed on, at the same time no man is wholly evil and the genius that is the better self may also grow stronger and defeat evil. A word perhaps also on the theme of *Mr. Bolfry*, where Bridie asks us to imagine the possibility of a group of young people who, in the severe atmosphere of a Free Kirk manse in the Western Highlands, decide one night for want of entertainment to experiment in witchcraft, and with the aid of an old book on the subject, to the accompaniment of thunder and lightning the Devil arrives, dressed as a minister of the Church of Scotland. On the morning after the visitor has departed, all think it was an ugly nightmare, until they discover the proof, Mr. Bolfry's umbrella, which walks out of the house on its own, to their amazement.

The typical approach of Bridie can best be described by examining his treatment of a theme like *John Knox*, one of his lesser known plays, which was written for production at the Edinburgh Festival by the Old Vic, but which had to be abandoned owing to casting difficulties and was produced instead in 1947 at Bridie's own Glasgow Citizens' Theatre. Bridie presents the career of Knox episodically, linking the sequences together through a commentary provided by a present-day divinity student and his girl, who see Knox and other historical characters of the period as ghosts on Hogmanay. In the final episode Bridie reconciles the two. Mary sympathises with Knox, because to this day he is regarded as a villain, but when she suggests that they're really lucky to be dead, Knox explodes in anger and starts preaching at her once more — even in heaven!

Yes, Bridie came to the rescue of the English theatre when there was

no one left after Shaw who could write the polished and witty conversation pieces which English audiences had grown to admire and
demand instead of tragedy. It is ridiculous to call Bridie the Scottish
Shavian (just as it is to call Edinburgh the Athens of the North or
Amsterdam a northern Venice); his plays have an atmosphere of their
own. But his imagination, the sharpness of his intellect, the flow of
language (he often makes his characters slightly tipsy in order to
encourage the whirlwind of words to come more naturally!) and the
roundness of character surely give Bridie (or Dr. Osborne Henry
Mavor, if we prefer his real name) a place of honour in the theatre
since Shaw.

(IV) SEAN O'CASEY

At one time in his career, after the productions of *Juno and the
Paycock* (1924) and *The Plough and the Stars* (1926), Sean O'Casey
would have been described as the most exciting dramatist in the contemporary theatre, and certainly these two plays are among the few
outstanding works in the theatre of the inter-war years. Unfortunately
the tragedy of Ireland was to become the tragedy of Sean O'Casey
himself when he turned his back on Ireland and settled in England, for
unlike his fellow Irishman Shaw, O'Casey was a foreigner exiled from
his own land, and in his new home his genius turned to bitterness, his
poetry to politics, his nationalistic hopes became hopes for a Communist international and his "darlin' son" was born a Red commissar.
There can be no better example of how art dries up when even in
absolute sincerity a writer endeavours to help the Communist cause.
O'Casey has never been able to write a heartfelt tragedy since leaving
Dublin, even *Red Roses for Me* falls considerably short of his tragedies
such as "Juno".

Born in a tenement house in the back streets of Dublin, O'Casey had
a harsh upbringing. His father died when he was three and his mother
(who undoubtedly inspired the character of Juno) had to provide for
the family as best she could. At fourteen O'Casey became a manual
labourer, and in his spare time taught himself to read and spent his
earnings on books (though he had since childhood been nearly blind).
After a strenuous day's work and though he had never known good
health, O'Casey took to helping the causes of Irish nationalism and the
Irish Labour struggle. In the 'twenties, however, he became disillusioned, and when, after his early theatre successes, the Abbey
Theatre rejected his *The Silver Tassie* (1928) he decided to leave Ireland

and settle for good in England. He has continued playwriting, bu
has not been able to find roots in England, as was evident in the firs
play he wrote away from Ireland, *Within the Gates* (1933). Here th
better part of his genius is absent, and even in the characters such as th
Cockneys who might have replaced the Irish brogue, O'Casey is fa
from home. In both *The Star Turns Red*, a confused piece of propa
ganda, and in *Red Roses for Me* (1943), a play which has considerabl
merit, O'Casey writes as an exile, while if *The Bishop's Bonfire* con
tains flashes of brilliant comedy, as a play it never comes alight. It i
doubtful if his old genius ever will.

We shall not attempt to deal with any of O'Casey's plays in partic
ular; his two masterpieces are too well known to invite approval at thi
late date, and in the others the failings do not require to be analysed a
any length. In his early (and best) work, *The Shadow of a Gunmar*
(1923), and in *Juno* and *The Plough and the Stars* O'Casey was a
realist, but in *The Silver Tassie* he turns to expressionism. There is a
different and more bitter mood in this study of the football hero whc
returns from the war maimed to live in a society itself a cripple. The
method of expressionism and symbolism (which had been used as a
contrast to realism in *The Silver Tassie*) is carried to greater extremes ir
Within the Gates, where his poetry deserts him and becomes as insipid
as the characters are cardboard. Poetry returned, if we bypass anc
quickly forget the naive Communism of *The Star Turns Red*, writter
for Unity Theatre in 1940, in a rich fantasy of life in *Red Roses for Me*
(1943) reminiscent of his earlier writing. O'Casey was inspired here by
the Irish railway strike of 1913, and by his own memories of the period
The central character is Ayadmonn Breydon, a young railway worke
who loves life and art and who dies under fire from the police at th
head of a worker's rally. O'Casey has recreated in this play not only th
past but also his present hopes. Yet in spite of the sweep of its action and
tragic understanding which suggested that O'Casey had at last suc
ceeded in re-establishing his contact with his own countrymen, the play
was only a moderate success.

Oak Leaves and Lavender (1946) was a salute to our Soviet ally when
already the cold war tide was encroaching, but *Cock-a-Doodle Dandy*
(1949, produced at the Edinburgh Festival ten years later) is a satire
full of gusto for Irish rural life, with its rival team of killjoys, in
cluding the village priest and policeman, and the young of heart who
flout them. But somehow this type of play is limited in its appeal to
those who can appreciate the significance of what to those unfamiliar

with Irish temper and idiom might seem a rambling and parochial allegory.

Managers in the West End cannot really be blamed for hesitating to produce these pieces. Even the best and most human of his plays written in exile, *The Bishop's Bonfire*, would be largely meaningless before an audience unfamiliar with the religious framework and practice in Ireland. The problem is a peculiarly nationalistic one, for it is the Irish interpretation of the Roman faith which has led to criticism, such as the burning of books, which is the symbolism of O'Casey's bonfire. Religious fanaticism is the theme of the play, but it is more the study of character types that makes the play come from time to time alive. A village awaits the coming of its bishop (he never appears in the play) and to this plot are allied a number of sub-plots — the frustrated love affair because of class, the frustrated love affair because of faith and the vow to virginity, the priest whose interpretation of Christianity differs from that of his immediate superiors. Frustration, drunkenness, cynicism, and yet *The Bishop's Bonfire* rises above the level of defeat because its characters reveal O'Casey's ability to depict in passages the richness of Irish humour which is sufficient to banish despair. Arguments become less tedious when Irish eyes are smiling.

O'Casey was both discovered and rejected by Dublin. He understood and had the genius to give expression to the feelings of the Irish people. He is a national writer who has been thwarted when attempting to follow the dictates of an international creed. It is only when O'Casey forgets theories that he is able to understand humanity, for, as one of the characters observes in *The Bishop's Bonfire*, "Even the Book God is writing will have very little meaning for us till it's finished".

(v) J. B. PRIESTLEY

If Bridie is a Scot, Priestley is a Yorkshireman, which means that we must come down to brass tacks when we discuss his contribution to the British theatre. This is perhaps a rather convenient moment to take stock of Priestley's work, for he has now ceased being a Labour Party champion and seems to have lost the ardent faith he once had in Socialist utopias and the ideals which he propagated in many of his plays. The vision he believed so easy and common sense is no longer to be reached by party politics; The City where his characters once went is now nothing more than a symbol, and viewed from the wilderness, he is no longer certain that it is practical. After being for so long a man who knew the answers, he is now a man of doubts. He still has his pipe in his mouth, but it has gone out. After a misadventure, *The White Countess* (written in collaboration with Jacquetta Hawkes), even his broad Yorkshire humour deserts him in *Mr. Kettle and Mr. Moon*.

Humour is Priestley's forte. How robust is the humour of *The Good Companions*. And it seems to this writer that Priestley has never bettered the North-Country farce *When We Are Married*, with its Yorkshire fun and games. Even his more sophisticated comedies such as *Ever Since Paradise* are extremely competent and entertaining. But these are not the plays that interest Priestley, and the larger part of his theatrical writing has been bound up either with the time theories of Dunne and P. D. Ouspensky's *A New Model of the Universe*, or his social propaganda pieces where the new utopia is identified with Labour policies. The time plays included *Time and the Conways* and *I Have Been Here Before*, both written in 1937, but it is his social plays that have been most discussed since then, and with which we shall concern ourselves in this short comment on his plays. In this group there are three important examples, *They Came to a City* (1942), *The Linden Tree* and *An Inspector Calls* (both 1947). In *They Came to a City* Priestley was fortunate in writing a topical play which expressed the hopes of a nation; it reflected the political idealism of the time which was argued in down-to-earth common sense. It was a political play of the first order, but whether it was a good play is quite another thing. A group of people divided into two caricatures, the privileged conservative classes of yesterday and the ordinary man and woman of the street who shall have their lives to live to-morrow — these people find themselves unaccountably outside the walls of an unknown city. The capitalists of yesterday are afraid to enter the city and horrified with what they see when they do venture inside; but the younger generation and also members of the working class have no fears — and find the city answers their dreams. After a quick look round at the show places (like a conducted party in the Kremlin or Peking to-day) they return and must decide individually whether they wish such a city or not. Two of the younger generation decide to leave the city behind, like the horrified capitalists, in order that they may teach others the truth of this city:

Not every man, not every woman, wants to cry out for it, to work for it, to live for it and if necessary to die for it — but there's one here, one there, a few down this street, some more down that street — until you begin to see there are millions of us — yes, armies and armies of us — enough to build ten thousand new cities.

But in spite of this impassioned rhetoric — and also perhaps because of its electioneering spirit — the play is no more than well-intentioned. Priestley has failed because his characters are no more than types and his city is only a political city. It is doubtful whether Priestley would be so easily thrilled with the idea of such a community city to-day — would he not wish to remain in the wilderness there also? But the real failure of the play is not character or language, but the lack of any spiritual power and mystery which alone would make a theme of this magnitude a work of art. Materialism seems an unpromising end in itself, however much the commissars may insist.

In *The Linden Tree* Priestley is still overtly political, but he is writing here not about another utopia, but about how the silent revolution during the years of the Labour Government from 1945–1950 has affected the lives of a middle-class family in a drab north of England town. Mrs. Linden, who is worn out after the war years and discontented with the continuation of rationing and restrictions, longs to get away from the environment, while her husband Professor Linden feels it his duty to stay on at the university, although he has now reached retiring age. The professor's son, who has made a fortune during the war, wishes them to settle in a large country estate he has just bought in the south of England, and the Linden's second daughter feels that her parents should come and share her privileged aristocratic life in the south of France, where she has married a Frenchman and is in the process of accepting a way of life which is out of touch with the world. The eldest daughter is equally uncompromising on the other side, as a Communist materialist, and only the youngest daughter believes in her father and urges him to stay on. The theme is therefore a reflection of the dilemma felt by many middle-calss families, but again — though less marked than in *They Came to a City* — Priestley has selected characters almost too black and white, and in their clash of political and ideological beliefs he makes a plea for a better understanding of post-war England and all that it stood for.

Only in *An Inspector Calls* does Priestley really come to grips with his theme; here all his characters are responsible for the death of a poor girl. They have not murdered her according to the law, but they have killed her nevertheless through the inhumanity they have shown her.

The father has sacked her from his works, the daughter had her dismissed from a shop (merely because she was feeling grumpy and was jealous of the poor girl's smile), her fiancé had had the poor girl as a mistress and then deserted her, while the son had given her a child and had then disowned her, and the mother had refused her application for charity. The year is 1912. The inspector who calls and makes the enquiry is not a real police inspector, but as one of the characters describes him, "he was our police inspector all right". And there remains the description of him by the father, a rich industrialist: "probably a Socialist or some sort of crank — he talked like one".

Priestley is a playwright who has attempted to break out of the conventions of the naturalistic drama, tending sometimes towards a modified form of expressionism, at other times breaking up the illusion of the box-realism deliberately, as in *Ever Since Paradise*. He would fly if he could, but he has not the power of poetry to sweep him over and beyond the immediate present. His blunt Yorkshire idiom and common-sense outlook make this alien to his character. Although an idealist, he is most successful when he realises his limitations; an intelligent thinker, he has not a serious mind. But he has a flare for the theatre, masterly in his technique, generally topical, and a writer to whom good humour comes naturally. Where his experiments in the wilderness may lead him is an open question, especially for a man with such diverse activities. For the first time Priestley realises that the future is full of uncertainties.

(VI) CHARLES MORGAN

Although better known as a novelist, Charles Morgan wrote three plays for the theatre, *The Flashing Stream* (1938), *The River Line* (1950) and *The Burning Glass* (1954), each play presenting an intellectual situation which depends on the choice of a course of action. In *The Flashing Stream* the decision requires singleness of mind and spiritual purpose. This play, the most successful of the three, takes place in the Falkland Islands just before the outbreak of the second world war (the play was produced in 1938). Edward Ferrers and Karen Selby are two of the world's greatest mathematicians working on a secret weapon for the Admiralty known as "Scorpion", which is a device to shoot down enemy bombers and thus save Britain from air attack. Both Karen (who has been called to assist Ferrers after the death of her brother in an experiment) and Ferrers find they are in love, but for the importance of their experiment they decide to lead a celibate existence. The singleness of mind which their work demands must link them together. Unfortunately the other characters in the play become mere types, and threaten to destroy the very serious conception of the play.

Morgan's failure to make a play satisfactory on all levels is evident even more in his other two plays. There is, moreover, in all these plays, a selection of character types almost restricted to those of the upper-class south of England society. It was a Dutchman who once wrote a book asking whether the English were human, and from the characters in these plays one begins to wonder. If we consider, for example, his most recent play *The Burning Glass*, Morgan makes no attempt to dramatise his situation with characters who convince as human beings. Instead we meet the family on their country estate, with the aristocratic mother who knew the Prime Minister from balls of old, and is thus able to contact him privately when her genius of a son discovers a means which can destroy any city in the world. At this stage the enemy agent appears, a spy posing as a spiv and with heavy foreign accent (we don't trust these foreigners, never did) and the son is rather too obviously kidnapped. All is well, however, for his wife also knows the secret, and when the enemy discover this they promptly return the scientist and all ends well. In fact, the play never disturbs at any time and such an idea is lost unless we feel the fear of the characters. Everyone in the play is too sure of himself.

The issues raised, however, are on a very different level from such improbable melodrama. The discovery of a weather control machine which can focus the sun's rays in the upper atmosphere in such a way that any spot or city on earth can be burnt up like paper under a magnifying glass held to the sun, such a discovery presents the scientist's anguish, whether he should withhold its powers until science is used by all to benefit mankind instead of destroying humanity, or permit the discovery to be made available to all. Morgan makes his scientist withhold its uses even for peacetime purposes, though he promises to give it to his country in the event of a national emergency. The argument is debatable, but that is the strong point of the play. The failure is its treatment.

There is a strange contradiction in both the plays and novels of Morgan which is not resolved; he is almost a writer for the 18th century *salon*, a philosopher who has to explain the mysteries of the universe to old ladies delicately balancing a cup of tea, or at a week-end house dinner party before the port wine stage is reached. There is a condescendence on his part to speak simply on these lofty matters which by ourselves we would never understand. And when a difficult question is posed, he seems to prefer philosophy as an escape to the commonplace reality. The truth is that in his philosophy Morgan was a popularizer of an accepted tradition; in other words he was not himself a philosopher. It is unlikely that his work will long survive his death.

(VII) BRENDAN BEHAN

Some are born rebels, certainly Brendan Behan. And on the strength of two plays, *The Quare Fellow* (1956) and *The Hostage* (1958) this ebullient, glass in his hand, tongue, fire and justice in his cheek Irish poet looks like one day filling the mantle left vacant by O'Casey. His first play ("quare fellow" is prison slang for the "condemned man") takes us inside prison walls to meet the inmates, wardens, governor, each drawn with a human authenticity that could only come from someone who had lived, worked and suffered with them. Behan has spent eight of his thirty-six years in prison for "terrorist" activities on behalf of the Irish Republican Army. While the play lacks form, the brute force of the dialogue sustains the action, which passes on the eve of a hanging. Here we are, listening almost to a tape recorder which had been left running, much in the same way as in his autobiography *Borstal Boy* Behan left nothing to be added by way of a commentary. And this same impartiality is present in *The Hostage*. If he can sustain it and develop his poetic vision on the frontiers of tragedy and comedy there is little doubt that the English theatre will have added another Dubliner to its history.

Behan has arrived too late for the great days of the Abbey Theatre, too late for nationalism. Gone are the figures from Yeats and Synge to O'Casey. It is fitting that Behan should have found his way to London through Theatre Workshop. Here he can be at home as he could never be in respectable Dublin, where to-day he is regarded as something of an *enfant terrible*. It is the dusty counter, the riff-raff, the honest swear word that Behan delights in; not for him polite drawing-room fare. He would like the audience to spend an "Irish" evening with him, not merely to watch a play. The actors must improvise ("The author should have sung that one — that is if the bleeding thing has an author") or, after a devastating satire

"But praise God that we are white
And better still are English."

he adds "Well, that's brought the show to a standstill". All this seems much nearer the Commedia dell'arte tradition, with actors talking to one another, addressing the audience, enjoying the bawdy song and Irish jig, than to the Brechtian influence which many London critics have recognised. In fact the Brechtian overtones in Joan Littlewood's Theatre Workshop production are used to suit Behan's, and not Brecht's, purpose. As an artist Behan would not accept any of Brecht's tenets, he probably couldn't care less.

The theme of *The Hostage* concerns a young Cockney national serviceman whose life is in danger when he is held hostage for an I.R.A. man in Belfast who is to be hanged. Nobody in the play wants this to happen, but all things are possible, tragedy can lead to tears, fate may decide as easily as you can dance an Irish jig.

As an observer of ordinary people in extraordinary circumstances Behan has the rare gift of dialogue and creating characters. Out of such material is great writing possible.

(VIII) JOHN WHITING

It is doubtful if new dramatists are ever discovered by play competitions — certainly John Whiting found that winning the prize of the Arts Theatre competition did him more harm than good, for he had already been discovered by the critics with his earlier play *A Penny for a Song*. The damning notices of *Saint's Day* (which must have been the worst press in English dramatic criticism) might well have ended his career. For to speak no plainer than the other critics have done, *Saint's Day* is a piece of confusion which requires not apology but explanation. Whatever its streamers of symbolism may have meant (and its supporters have offered no clue) it makes no effort to be intelligible, and surely a play which cannot be understood by an average intelligent audience is very seriously wrong. Yet, in spite of this failure, there remained somewhere the conviction that in John Whiting there was a playwright with ambitions as yet beyond his means of expression. His latest play *Marching Song* has given proof of this hope.

The atmosphere of *Marching Song* reminds one of a play by Ugo Betti — only with something missing. *Marching Song* has neither Betti's dramatic drive, nor his skill, but the theme of a man who is a prisoner both in fact and also inwardly of his own conscience, is one Betti could also have developed with penetrating exposure. But Whiting is more interested in ideas as ideas, and less in ideas as spiritual significance as in Betti; nor has he the economy of words in the delineation of character — Whiting's prose is verbose and his characters two-dimensional. He has the structure of the play, but he has as yet to bring it to life.

Marching Song, though not an important play, is nevertheless an interesting one. A general of a defeated army is released from prison in order to face a trial where he will be a scapegoat for the humiliation of a nation. In order to preserve the unity of the nation, however, the Chancellor tries to persuade the general to commit suicide, and it is this choice which the play develops in its conflict — for the punishment requires the general's disgrace. The general's conscience forces him to relive the horror when he ordered his mechanised brigade to mow down a swarm of children who had blocked their way in an attack. The general had made his choice then, and in the horror of the deed immediately afterwards, he had been unable to continue the pre-arranged attack. His pride for war had overlooked humanity, and for victory was substituted his defeat. In the decision he has to take after release from the prison, he has to find his own way out. For neither the woman he no longer loves nor the young girl whom he has just met and who momentarily inspires him with confidence can answer for him.

It will be seen that Whiting has here a promising work, but he has far to go before he can be considered an influence in the British theatre. He has, however, made a start, and he seems to have left behind, where it ought to be forgotten and buried, *Saint's Day.*

(IX) PETER USTINOV

Peter Ustinov is the Orson Welles of Shaftesbury Avenue. In his career to date there has always been something of the boy wonder about him, and in his unflagging energy he seems to dissipate his talent in a round of acting, films, producing, television and, last but not least, playwriting. He is a little too much the jack of all trades. Still in his early thirties he has written ten plays or so, from his early *House of Regrets,* which gained him considerable esteem, to *No Sign of the Dove,* which *The Times* critic described as not merely one bad play, but three — a bad play in each act. But if this last play received a storm of adverse notices, Ustinov had known critical and box-office success in his *Love of Four Colonels* (1951) and *Romanoff and Juliet* (1957); he is an uneven writer who either succeeds or fails. In *House of Regrets* he was able to portray a group of Russian émigrés in a London boarding house (a set Ustinov knew so well), living on the memories of their past, and where only the younger generation realised that their place was to live the present as members of their adopted country. *Blow Your Own Trumpet*, produced by the Old Vic the following year, was a complete failure, but with *The Banbury Nose* (1944) Ustinov gained his first long run. This play is a biography spread over three generations of life in an army family, the military tradition defeating each generation. The technique of the play follows the quotation "Life must be lived forwards, but it can only be understood backwards". Ustinov, in telling the story backwards, uses this trick successfully.

Among the plays which followed in quick succession are *The Tragedy of Good Intentions*, *The Man behind the Statue*, *The Indifferent Shepherd*, and *The Love of Four Colonels*. In this last play Ustinov takes us to the four-power occupation of Austria and in doing so offers a lively satire on the national characteristics of each nation as depicted by their four respective colonels. The colonels are led by two immortal spirits, representing good and evil, to a deserted castle which turns out to be the traditional home of the Sleeping Beauty. Each colonel sees in the figure of the sleeping princess his own ideal, and the transposition of the castle into a stage enables each colonel to enact his chosen scene and period with the princess of his heart. Each man thus reveals in his conception of love his hidden self. The Frenchman chooses to play a scene in the tradition of Marivaux, the Englishman naturally chooses the Elizabethan drama. It is left to the American to turn missionary and rescue the fallen princess from the hands of a gangster on the run, while the Russian prefers of all times the Czarist days and Tchekhovian chatter. Each little play within the play provides Ustinov with a magnificent opportunity to parody literary styles, which he does in the best tradition of the *New Statesman* competitions. It is entertaining and should not be judged too critically. But a light and frivolous satire on national behaviour is unlikely to be confused with serious drama.

Whether Ustinov will ever discipline himself to succeed in a serious work, or whether the present difficulties of securing West-End production for such efforts will make him continue playwriting as one of his many diversions, cannot be answered. As it is, Ustinov has had a long flirtation with the theatre, both as actor and playwright. Will he be content to let that be?

(X) TERENCE RATTIGAN

As a highly successful playwright whose plays offer entertainment to large numbers of people, Terence Rattigan may be said to have found the recipe for producing box-office hits, and it is perhaps ungrateful to sound carping here because he only treats the theatre for entertainment. Rattigan does not believe in the so-called play of ideas, but that "the character makes the play". And he contends that this is true not only of his serious plays, but also of farce. He believes in "the farce of character". "Plot", he continues, "in a farce is necessarily so extravagant that it is usually believed impossible for the author to introduce even the elements of characterisation without destroying the illusion and killing laughter. But if the plot, however extreme, is at the very beginning rooted in character, it is possible with a little forcing, to mould the plot into the most extravagant and farcical shape without exciting the audience's disbelief."

There is no reason to doubt that this is the reason for the success of his farces such as *French Without Tears* and *While the Sun Shines*. Rattigan's failure is not when he writes a farce of character, but a serious play of character. In his farces we do not ask that his characters should be complete individuals, whereas in a serious play the character must be a creation. The main criticism of Rattigan's work, then, is a fundamental criticism, namely, that his characters are wishy-washy creatures with neither nobility in their thoughts nor individuality in their actions. They are types we know exist, and though we might recognise them, they are certainly not people we would want as our friends. Nor is it true that it was the characters who made *The Winslow Boy* a worth-while play, but the concept of freedom which the Archer-Shee case presented. That Rattigan altered the historical facts to suit his characters makes no difference to the contention that it was the topical idea which was responsible for the great success.

It is a *coup de théâtre* that makes for the success of *The Deep Blue Sea,* a play which compels admiration in performance but which does not bear examination in reading, for we can have no admiration for his characters. The story of a lonely, sex-starved woman who tries to commit suicide and is eventually reassured that life is worth living (though we have our doubts as far as she is concerned) is a tragedy only of twentieth-century drabness; if the character makes the play here, we have a drama of the sickly minded. In *Separate Tables* Rattigan takes us to a Bournemouth boarding-house for two one-act studies of loneliness which hardly rise above the level of a plot formulated "magazine story". The usual jokes are made at the expense of the intellectuals and Left-wing journalists and politicians, and the dialogue throughout is insipid. If this is Rattigan attempting to be serious, let us long for an

early return to the happy-go-lucky *French Without Tears*. For his limitations as a dramatist were surely proved in *Adventure Story*, where
Rattigan chose his most ambitious character, Alexander the Great.
When critics complained that the subject matter was beyond his powers,
Rattigan replied in a short article in the *Radio Times* that the fact remained "that neither Shakespeare nor Shaw has written a play about
Alexander the Great and I have; and as this is, they say, a free country it
is hard to see why a subject should be banned to a playwright, however
humble, merely because two great dramatists might have chosen that
subject themselves, but did not." From such a statement Rattigan would
have us believe that a critic should praise him when he tackles a gigantic
theme and fails, just as when he tackles a light-weight comedy and succeeds. No critic is banning Rattigan from writing about Alexander the
Great, but Rattigan in his turn must not ban criticism, and the more ambitious the play the higher always are the critical standards. A play beyond an author's power may be well meant, but it is never good theatre.
Adventure Story might have suited Bridie very well, or one can think of
several French dramatists who would at any rate have brought their
philosophy and classical education (as well as their dramatic power)
to bear on the treatment, but Rattigan is only a theatre craftsman.
However hard it may seem for experiments to be abused and takings at
the box-office diminished, any playwright worth the theatre must make
the attempt. In Rattigan's effort we realise that masterpieces can never
be written by a playwright of talent only.

(XI) SHELAGH DELANAY

When Shaw wrote of "the incomparable Max" that the younger
generation were knocking at the door, he made his exit as a critic
without protest. But then this was before the "junior miss" invasion of
the literary world, which has inevitably reached the theatre. Miss
Shelagh Delanay was aged nineteen when she wrote *A Taste of Honey*.
Coming from Salford, Lancashire, she claims that she is the antithesis
of London's "angry young men", for "she knows what to be angry
about and what to laugh at". Her anger is the teen-agers' revolt against
the mother and environment, a fact which is the rule rather than the
exception in all levels of society. The implicit tragedy is, as Simone de
Beauvoir observes in *Le Deuxieme Sexe*, that the teen-ager can neither
accept nor repudiate the destiny nature has allotted her, for "she is
inwardly too mixed up to try and fight the world. She has to content
herself with flights from reality or merely to face things symbolically."

Here then is the teen-ager theme treated by a teen-ager, the relationship of mother and daughter, a girl starved of love by her ageing
prostitute mother. The girl is left alone for Christmas when the mother
goes off with her latest partner. She dreams her adolescent dreams, of a
prince from darkest Africa, the symbol of sex perfection. She meets a
coloured sailor from Cardiff, Wales. Never mind, there's still "a bit of
jungle somewhere in the embraces of the boy". Nor does she reproach
him later for leaving her stranded bearing his child.

In the second part of the play Miss Delanay introduces a "queer",
who in a brother to sister relationship shields the girl from her fears
of pregnancy. But too soon the mother returns and the "queer" is
sent packing. The old bickering is resumed, the wheels have turned full
circle and we are back where we were, only with the feeling that in
another generation's time the pattern will again be repeated.

When Theatre Workshop brought the play up to the West-End
there was a lot of ballyhoo publicity comparing Miss Delanay to
Sagan, which is nonsense, apart from suggesting that Miss Delanay
cannot stand on her own feet. Far better to have placed her among the
exotic disciples stemming from the work of Tennessee Williams. As
for the future let us hope that the taste of success as well as honey will
not make Miss Delanay forget that a young playwright of promise has
still to cross the tight-rope.

(XII) AUDEN AND ISHERWOOD

It is strange how heroes of the Left-wing intellectuals (and how few
intellectuals were not Left-wing in the 1930's!) such as W. H. Auden
and Christopher Isherwood, should now have become mere names, as
dated as the title of any pre-war song hit. Their three plays, *The Dog
beneath the Skin* (1935), *The Ascent of F.6* (1936) and *On the Frontier*
(1937), were products of their time and for immediate consumption;
they reflected the disillusionment and despair of man, whom they did
not believe could survive the horrors which in fact he did. Their
technique in these plays was taken from the German expressionists, and
they did not bring anything new to the theatre. Of the plays, *The
Ascent of F.6* is the most acceptable, possibly because the theme of a
British expedition sent by the Government to hoist the imperial banner
over a mountain marked F.6 — hitherto unconquered — has a dramatic appeal in spite of the politics. But these plays are now blunt in their
satire and they no longer concern us. Their authors have both deserted
them as they searched for different gods in America.

(XIII) THE OLD AND THE NEW

A list of all the playwrights who have met success or provoked discussion in the last thirty years or so would make for dull reading, and can be found in reference books. The balance sheet, however, is not complete without a word on Noël Coward and Emlyn Williams, although both these popular playwrights seem to have been in eclipse these last years. When in the 'twenties Noël Coward arrived and took the West End by storm he might almost have been accepted himself as one of the bright young things of the 'twenties, and *The Vortex*, *Fallen Angels*, *Hay Fever*, *Private Lives* and *Cavalcade* take us up to 1931. This seemed to be the culmination of his career, and during the rest of the 'thirties he was less productive, though such plays as *Design for Living* and his one-act collection "Tonight at 8.30" earned him Miss G. B. Stern's comment that he was "permanently potential". *Blithe Spirit* (1941) reminded us that he had lost none of his polish in the field of sophisticated comedy and slick dialogue and repartee, while the film, *Brief Encounter*, taken from his one-act play *Still Life* from "To-night at 8.30", is a delicate study of human relationship and the best writing that Coward has done in his career.

Since *Blithe Spirit*, however, Coward has given little indication of his 'potential' genius, for his star no longer seems to be able to capture the spirit of the age. One feels to-day that he searches in vain for what should be the mood, escapism, ultra-patriotic sentimentality, and so on, and the result is such anaemic plays as *Quadrille* (where his sparkle has gone and the jokes fall flat), *Peace in our Time*, *Relative Values* or *Nude with Violin*. We can but shake our heads, and remark that Coward was lucky to have lived in the 'twenties, for his period pieces from that decade admirably reflected society.

Emlyn Williams has also been out of touch with the theatre in recent years; his greatest successes were just before the second world war, with his expert thriller *Night Must Fall* (1935), and his sentimental tale of the scholarship boy from a Welsh mining town, *The Corn is Green* (1938). His most interesting play, however, is *The Wind of Heaven* (1945) where Williams chose the theme of the return of the Messiah in the form of a boy to a Welsh village which had been stricken with plague during the time of the Crimean War. In attempting such a dangerously ambitious subject Williams has given us a play of significance, and his highly developed sense of the theatrical hides his other shortcomings. Williams is too often sentimental, he is not a philosopher and his characters are rather surface figures, but his plays are effective theatre. Indeed he has a sense of Victorian melodrama in his writing

*

Of the new playwrights who have attracted notice in the post-war theatre in London, the names of N. C. Hunter, Denis Cannan and Bridget Boland may be mentioned. N. C. Hunter has been described as Tchekhovian, and in his leisurely portrayal of typically English characters in a country-house atmosphere he has been fortunate in having as his actors some of the outstanding names of the British stage. Both in *Waters of the Moon* and *A Day by the Sea* Hunter writes parts which can be made to live in performance when acted by such artists as Dame Sybil Thorndike, Dame Edith Evans, Sir Ralph Richardson, John Gielgud, Sir Lewis Casson, and others. But the characters cannot be enjoyed in reading the script any more than the play would lend itself to a provincial repertory.

More interesting as playwrights are Denis Cannan, whose *Captain Carvallo* showed promise, and Bridget Boland, whose play *Cockpit* deserved a better fate than its West-End failure. More recently she had a moderate success with *The Return*. Robert Bolt's *Flowering Cherry* is an English variant of Arthur Miller's tragedy of the common man theme. Here are dreams of ideals and escape from a world of reality through the bottle. The children are no happier than their parents. The Somerset orchard which is the ideal is unobtainable, and in vain does the wife cling to her illusions of hope and pride up to the final moment of decision and truth.

The Royal Court venture of the English Stage Company is beginning to show results, though John Osborne remains their only really promising discovery. But the *Observer* play competition prize-winner *Moon on a Rainbow Shawl*, by Errol John, and *Each in his own Wilderness*, by Doris Lessing, have been among the new plays which show talent. The Belgrade Theatre in Coventry is responsible for the production (and their subsequent presentation in London) of two of Arnold Wesker's plays, *Chicken Soup with Barley*, and *Roots*. Mr. Wesker has now completed a third play of this trilogy *I'm Talking about Jerusalem*, while an earlier play *The Kitchen* has been produced at a Sunday night performance of the Royal Court. Wesker is a young writer with a real ability for dialogue in the social realist school. *Roots* for example concerns a so-called prodigal's return home and failure to stir the family to action; all his plays present a working-class world.

While there is no doubt about their effectiveness, this would seem to be the type of documentary writing which television can handle so well, but which in the theatre leaves little room to the free play of the imagination which is so essential in moments of great drama.

Industrialists have also been coming forward to help subsidize the Royal Court venture, even though one of them did express his concern over the *avant-garde* choices (described as "a kind of hoola hoopism"), and pleaded for a "new Shakespeare without sex". There are many other names one could mention at the expense of this becoming a mere list of prospective talent. It is for theatrical managements to continue to prospect, to see that in the future young writers do not turn their backs on the theatre and to remember that in the theatre, like anything that lives, there is always cause for alarm, and no room for complacency.

SIXTEEN

U.S.A.

Elmer Rice; Robert Emmet Sherwood; Clifford Odets;
Maxwell Anderson; Philip Barry; Thornton Wilder;
William Saroyan; William Inge; Archibald MacLeish.

THE brightest prospect for the American theatre is that the
stage is set, and, as showmanship would put it, the potentialities are tremendous. Eyes look not on the achievements of the
past — for there are few worth looking at — but on the future, the
period in which the new 100 per cent. American drama will grow to
maturity. Up to the present American playwrights have learnt the lessons of European masters, first O'Neill and more recently Tennessee
Williams and Arthur Miller, though the plays of these last two writers
are more than merely works of disciples, their steps are surer and the
immigrant strain less conscious. The playwrights, then, are coming,
the stars have had their names glittering in lights for some time, and
there is money in the Broadway till. But when will Broadway (and
Broadway *is* the American theatre) become a centre of good theatre
and the cultural leader in world drama?

Whereas America has been forced to assume her rôle as leading
power in the free world, there is no such urgent necessity for her to play
such a missionary part in the theatre. That she will do so one day, if the
theatre survives, is almost inevitable, but in the meantime American
drama has hardly had time to have reached a golden age; it is sufficient
that each decade since the 'twenties has been an advance on the previous
one. Had the theatre been capable of organising itself like Hollywood as
a centre of dream-producing products it would be very different, but
there are no short cuts to success in the living traditions of theatre.
Can we really expect a drama to flourish when subjected to the exploitation of the 'box-office or bust' rule?

Since the 1914–1918 war, the American drama has been brought into existence from scratch. The Theatre Guild, for example, when it was founded in 1918, had only $19.50 for its second production (apart, of course, from the idea which had led to its formation), yet from importing foreign plays to begin with it soon encouraged American authors to write directly for their own theatre, and thus it found its playwrights. Yet even so, the Theatre Guild has not developed into an Old Vic or a Comédie Française, and at the time of writing all attempts to set up a permanent American National Theatre (A.N.T.A.) have not proved too successful. Moreover, in the 'thirties the Left-wing Group theatre may claim to have done as much for American drama as did the Theatre Guild, which had modified its policy. We are not concerned here with elaborating the politics of the American theatre, nor to give more than a glimpse of the background of its organisation, without which it would be almost impossible to view a list of its better known playwrights in perspective.

The American dramatist has not equalled the standard of the novelists in modern American literature, but in the long run the theatre would seem to offer to-day more promise than the novel — and this in spite of the fact that in order to mount a play on Broadway a fantastic fortune has to be invested (this is equally true of the West End) with the result that theatre-backers cannot afford to nurse a play to success (again true in the West End); a play is either a hit or a miss. During the war years the theatre in New York was largely escapist, until towards the end came the production of O'Neill's *The Iceman Cometh*, the discovery of Williams and Miller, and the production of a number of social-purpose plays, such as *Deep are the Roots* by James Gow and Arnaud d'Usseau. If to-day much of the post-war impetus has been spent, the hope for to-morrow continues and new playwrights have appeared to follow the trail led by Williams and Miller. A decisive force is undoubtedly Elia Kazan, a director whose style is admirably allied to Williams or a play like *J.B.*, Archibald MacLeish's morality play about a present-day Job.

Are Broadway audiences more discriminating than West-End playgoers? It seems that in the case of an importation of plays from London, audiences find themselves at a loss in many cases to explain why such a mediocre play should have proved such a stir in London (one can name, for example, *Escapade* which was well received by critics and public in the English production, or Charles Morgan's *The Burning Glass*). Eliot and Fry have found favour, and many Continental plays,

including those by Giraudoux, but not Anouilh. American tastes ar
inevitably national, but in the theatre the American critic plays a fa
more responsible part than most of his British opposite numbers. Th
audiences themselves treat the theatre as more of an occasion than d
London playgoers, and it must be remembered that the Road ha
almost gone out of existence in America, with the result that the theatr
is centralised in Broadway, and most Americans who want to see a show
must go there. The playgoers are of course a small part of the theatre
going public, and no doubt most provincials prefer the latest Osca
Hammerstein or Cole Porter musical — but not all. There is in Broad
way, as in other theatre centres in Europe, a small but discriminating
public for serious plays, and this can and has often led a larger public t
enjoy good theatre.

Broadway now and again shows a faith in the drama which probably
astounds itself. There are backers who prefer good theatre to sound
investments. Writing in *Theatre Arts* after the failure of Truman
Capote's *The Grass Harp*, the producer Saint-Subben refers to a
"small island of idealists who help to finance theatre ventures of high
aims". He goes on to declare: "I could name many investors in the
theatre who have never, to my knowledge, refused to back a script that
had quality or merit, even if the financial risks were great." Whether
this is always so definitely the case or not, and whether patrons' tastes
are always so impeccable as Mr. Saint-Subben believes or not, that one
or two such backers may exist would give cause for faith in the commercialised playbills of Broadway, and faith that the theatre will be
kept alive there.

Meanwhile let us return to our consideration of what has been
accomplished and examine some of the playwrights Broadway has
produced in the last twenty years or so.

(1) ELMER RICE

We shall not attempt in the following comments on American playwrights to suggest a merit-order, but even were this the case it would
not be improper to consider Elmer Rice first of all. He is a dramatist of
the inter-war years, when his plays *The Adding Machine* (1923) and
Judgment Day (1934) proved him to have a fine sense of rhetoric and
debate which he made good use of in the theatre. Rice graduated from
New York Law School in 1912 and for a while he practised at the Bar,
but the success of his first play *On Trial* (1914) made him desert law for
the theatre. His decision was more than justified when in *The Adding*

Machine he introduced to American audiences the expressionistic technique which Toller and Kaiser were working on in Germany. Rice brought consummate skill to his innovations of the technique. The following year came his exciting melodrama *Street Scene,* which gained him a Pulitzer Prize. The entire action of this play takes place in front of a New York tenement. Rice's growing interest in social problems is also reflected in *We, the People,* where the theatre was turned into a meeting hall. *Judgment Day* was a topical reminder for American audiences of what had just happened when the Nazis burned the Reichstag.

Unfortunately Rice has not succeeded in any of his later plays in rising to this level, and plays such as *Flight to the West* — really little more than an anti-Nazi debate — *A New Life* or *Dream Girl* have been but a pale pastiche of his earlier work. Perhaps after all he should have retired as he threatened to do after the failure of *Between Two Worlds,* at which time he had already written his interesting plays, and he would have been remembered just the same as he is now for his interest in the social-purpose play, and his desire to win his argument with credit to his legal training.

(II) ROBERT EMMET SHERWOOD

Like Elmer Rice, Robert Sherwood was attracted by the so-called play of ideas, the desire to impart a message in his plays, which often deal with the fears let loose in the morning papers. The subjects discussed are vital as long as they remain topical, and in his plays we have a considerable variation in the solution of the problem according to how his own conscience reacted to each new crisis in an age of crises. Returning gassed and wounded from the first world war, Sherwood turned pacifist, which lasted up to his writing of *Idiot's Delight* in 1936. *Idiot's Delight,* however, was not only a protest against war, but also against Fascism, and this protest led eventually to his own abandonment of pacifism. Faced with the evils of dictatorship, pacifism was no longer valid, for it was more important to safeguard freedom. Thus his mood changes and in *There Shall Be No Night,* written at the time of the Russian invasion of Finland, he takes for his theme that of a scientist who believes in pacifism, but who in the end decides to fight. It was an ironic comment that the country he wrote it for soon found itself on the enemy side, and for the London production Sherwood changed the country from Finland to Greece. The change did not really matter, for the theme was applicable to any small nation invaded by the crushing power of a military dictatorship, and Sherwood had very great sympathy for a little nation fighting for its freedom. He helped America to realise that she could no longer stand by and watch while the tyrant was triumphant.

There Shall Be No Night, together with *Idiot's Delight,* is Sherwood's great theatrical success, but he is also known for *The Road to Rome* (1927), *Reunion in Vienna* (1931), *The Petrified Forest* (1935), *Abe Lincoln of Illinois* (1938) and *The Rugged Path* (1945). Of these others, *The Petrified Forest* is perhaps the most interesting, introducing us to characters who symbolise the disillusionment of an age, but who at the same time seem real people. A greatly depressing play, it is nevertheless expert in its theatrical tension. These plays have earned Sherwood a place in the history of the American theatre, for his success as a playwright lay in the fact that he was a first-rate theatrical journalist in the very best sense, and he wrote with the zeal of a man who had a mission to fulfil.

(III) CLIFFORD ODETS

The idea that our actions are governed by our economic circumstances is stressed in all the plays of Clifford Odets, an angry Left-wing social writer discovered by the Group Theatre, and at the same time a playwright of vitality, conviction and passion. His dialogue knocks hard and achieves its aim without resort to clichés; his characters are complex individuals caught up in the system, and not merely cardboard puppets with a system to present or defend. Odets' plays are gloriously partisan and biased, but propaganda is not substituted for good theatre.

His first attempt at playwriting was an out-and-out political piece which nevertheless showed that here was a playwright in the making. In *Waiting for Lefty* (1935) Odets turned the theatre into a hall and assumed that the audience were strikers listening to their leaders on the platform debating whether or not the taxicab drivers should strike or not. The same year Odets wrote his first full-length play *Awake and Sing,* which portrayed a Jewish family circle at the time of the depression. It is a study of each member of the family, who meet their own disillusionment, but the bitterness of the mood and the revolutionary nature of its intent is made moving by the warmth of the humanity in his characters. Odets' next important play was *Golden Boy,* where the struggle of a man's soul between ambition and material wealth becomes the decision that Joe Bonaparte, a young American of Italian origin, has to make between his ambition to be a violinist and the prize purse of the ring. He chooses the ring and wins his riches, but he also kills a man here and can no longer continue fighting. His hands are now ruined; his life has been frustrated through his thirst for money; he ends up by meeting death in a motor accident.

For a while Odets left Broadway for Hollywood, and did not return until 1949, when his play *The Big Knife* was produced. This is a savage picture of the inhuman set-up in Hollywood which makes slaves even of its leading stars and where frustration is everywhere. The play has been severely attacked by such American critics as John Gassner who, writing in *Theatre Arts*, complains that it is "a plain case of misty motivation and misplaced sympathy". Gassner goes on to suggest that "the unemployed on Broadway must find it curious that Odets should suffer for an actor who has a fourteen-year contract and 3,500,000 dollars thrust upon him". But surely this is to miss the whole point of Odets' protest. It might be curious, but it is true. In her anthropological study of *Hollywood, the Dream Factory*, Miss Hortense Powdermaker emphasises that it is the social system under which film stars have to work that makes for such a high degree of frustration, and which, incidentally, it also passes on in the false glitter of so many Hollywood products. *The Big Knife* may be unpleasant, it may seem excessive, but I am sure that for Odets it is an honest view of the way he felt in Hollywood. So his return to Broadway is celebrated in *The Country Girl* (produced in London under the title "Winter Journey") where Odets makes amends to the theatre by writing a success story for Broadway. All is forgiven. Taking for his leading character a once famous actor now gone to seed through drink, Odets says that he "wanted to accomplish something in particular". (I quote his own words) "I wanted to take simple elements and make something sharp and theatrical out of them. I stated a fact, the story of these people, rather than speculated about the fact." This is an Odets far removed from the playwright we knew as critic of society; the dramatic instinct is still there but much of the purpose is missing.

If we turn to *The Flowering Peach* (1954) Odets retells his version of Noah and family in the contemporary idiom. Odets, very much at home in portraying the dissensions of Jewish family life in the Bronx, fails completely to come to terms with the biblical theme, a theme which he recognises with all its deadly seriousness — concerned as it is with the relationship between man, God, and the extinction of the world as a punishment for allowing sin to run riot. When disaster happens, Noah cannot understand why God has chosen him to be saved, for his house, rather his ark, is witness to the same sins that

R

brought about the floods on earth — adultery, greed, drunkenness. Yet they have been spared to rebuild the world, the future is in their hands and is their responsibility, they have been spared but they have not been redeemed, for neither they nor Odets are any nearer to understanding what they ought to believe. And the confusion in the writing is a match for the confusion in the thinking.

The Flowering Peach was too large a theme for Odets; but within his limitations he is undoubtedly one of the most forceful American writers to-day.

(IV) MAXWELL ANDERSON

Like O'Neill, Maxwell Anderson approached the theatre with a roaming eye for expression and with ambitions which would have required genius and not talent, however gifted. But at least he aimed high, and his efforts to discover a harmony between modern poetry and ordinary conversation have produced a style which, though hardly what the blank verse was to the audience of Shakespeare, can be described as a twentieth-century exposition suited to the drama. Maxwell Anderson is not, of course, a poet like Eliot, nor does he even have the fluency with words that Fry possesses, but he likes the sound of words and his plays are always pleasant to the ear. A prolific writer, his successes have included *Elizabeth, the Queen, Mary of Scotland, The Masque of Kings, Key Largo, The Eve of St. Mark, Joan of Lorraine* and more recently, *The Bad Seed.* But better than any of these is his gangster tragedy *Winterset* (1935) where his theme is one of injustice. A son believes his condemned father is innocent and sacrifices his own life to prove it. There are passages where the verse rises to deep imaginative insight, and the atmosphere of squalor and frustration is enlarged through the emptiness of Maxwell Anderson's own spiritual power. The lack of faith seems to make the tragic concept of the play fall short in what should have been its moment of greatness. Neither O'Neill nor Maxwell Anderson (nor, for that matter, Arthur Miller) has found the answer for modern tragedy, but both attempted its creation. They wished to make traditions of permanent values available to the shifting and sophisticated audiences in Broadway.

(V) PHILIP BARRY

Highly regarded as a writer of light comedy, Philip Barry has made several unexpected and unconventional ventures into fantasy and plays of more serious purpose, including *Here Come the Clowns, The Joyous*

Season and *Hotel Universe*. This latter is his most ambitious work, and as can be seen from the title, it unfolds itself on a symbolic plane. It is a rendezvous where several souls, brought together in anguish, undergo a kind of expiation for their sins in such veiled significance that the play baffled its audience. Barry is really a writer of comedy, and it is in plays such as *The Philadelphia Story* or *The Animal Kingdom* that he reaches his public and has had success. In spite of his other ambitions, it is in the comedy of manners that Philip Barry's talent lies.

(VI) THORNTON WILDER

Philip Barry did not succeed in his experimental work, whereas Thornton Wilder has achieved fame on the result of two extremely unusual and ingenious plays, *Our Town* and *The Skin of Our Teeth*. Both these plays overthrow the conventions and limitations of modern naturalistic theatre, though they owe a good deal to the German expressionistic techniques for their success. *Our Town* is the story of Groves Corner, a small New England town, the story of its inhabitants, the living, loving, dying. The play is presented on a bare stage without scenery, and the characters are introduced by the stage manager, all in order to make the audience realise that the play is attempting to make them participate in a story of American life. In *The Skin of Our Teeth* Thornton Wilder surveys a kind of allegory of man through the ages and the disasters he overcomes. From an allegory of ordinary folk in *Our Town* we move to an allegory of mankind. Thornton Wilder presents his plays in the form of modern moralities, but recently his plays, such as *The Match-Maker* or *A Life in the Sun* (written for the Edinburgh Festival), have not added to his reputation, though he enjoys a vogue in certain circles.

(VII) WILLIAM SAROYAN

Another playwright who has attempted innovations from the normal is William Saroyan; indeed, with his work experiment seems to become too often an end in itself. His plays present a hymn of optimism in ordinary people, "the beautiful people", to quote the title of one of his plays. Saroyan caused an immediate stir when the Group Theatre produced his first play *My Heart's in the Highlands* in 1939. The play may be described loosely as a fantasy, or perhaps as Brooks Atkinson has so aptly worded it: "A prose poem in ragtime with a humorous and lovable point of view". The play gained the Critics' Circle Award in New York and the Pulitzer Prize the following year. His experiments, which included *Love's Old Sweet Song*, *The Beautiful People*, *Across the Board on To-morrow Morning* continued until the production of *Get Away Old Man* in 1943. Since then no new Saroyan play has been produced on Broadway, though in November, 1952, *Theatre Arts* published the text of a new play *The Slaughter of the Innocents,* but which remains unproduced. The theme of this play is that of the traditional freedoms of democracy in face of the pressure of events.

Saroyan is a convinced and sometimes facile optimist (which is at least a change from the dismal jimmies) but his experiments do not result in clarity, and he certainly has not fulfilled the promise of his first play.

(VIII) OTHER WRITERS

Even more than in the British theatre, it is impossible to mention the numerous playwrights in the American theatre who have had success, and in a survey which attempts to place modern world drama in perspective, it is increasingly difficult with minor writers to decide whether they should be included or not. America has produced many competent craftsmen (and the schools of playwriting in American universities have had their results here) but if the standard of Broadway, like Hollywood, is technically efficient, the content of most of her plays is mediocre.

There are a number of playwrights, however, who might have been included here, were not we forced to restrict our company. Lillian Hellman, for example, has produced several impressive works, including *The Little Foxes* and *The Children's Hour,* and during the war, while America was still neutral, wrote the anti-Nazi *Watch on the Rhine.* Other playwrights might have included George S. Kaufmann and Moss Hart, Sidney Kingsley and the late Sidney Howard, author of *They Knew What They Wanted* and *The Silver Cord.* But by way of ending this credit list I prefer to draw attention to two new playwrights, first William Inge, whose *Come Back, Little Sheba* seems to follow the *Death of a Salesman* school. The characters are a middle-aged couple wondering what they have done with their youth, and memory of the past is presented in contrast to how the youth of to-day live and love. Inge does not wish the play to be regarded as a tragedy, for though melancholy in mood there is no suicide, and it has been described as "a pathetic comedy". The characters of the middle-aged couple are likeable human beings, but not tragic heroes, and yet the sense of their tragedy is implicit in their survival. We find other plays in this style appearing fairly regularly, such as the problem of old age as presented in *The Wooden Dish* by Edmund Morris (produced in London, 1954).

(IX) ARCHIBALD MACLEISH

Man's relation to the unknown external forces of the universe, such is the ambitious theme of the most discussed play (and one of the most highly praised) in the American theatre for many years. Archibald MacLeish's tragedy of a modern American Job in report to God, *J.B.*, is a morality play which comes to grips with the modern tempo and the bewilderment of our age, more than any other. The new American drama seems to take for its hero the little man, the tragedy of ordinary people caught in the labyrinth of a civilisation and system that challenges and threatens. So MacLeish takes Job as his representative because he believes "the myth of Job is a myth for our time because this is the answer also: the answer that moves so many of us who, without the formal beliefs that supported our ancestors, nevertheless pick up our lives again after the vast disasters and go on — go on as men". J.B. is a prosperous American businessman, "big, handsome, sanguine, vigorous in his middle thirties," who is shortly to see his prosperity taken from him, his home broken up as disaster strikes each member of his family, until his wife, at the end of her strength, tells him

> "I cannot stay here—
> I cannot stay here if you cringe,
> Connive in death's injustice, kneel to it,—
> . . . .
> We have the choice to live or die
> All of us."

and standing over J.B. she exclaims in horror "Curse God and die". But J.B. replies "Blessed be the name of the Lord" and she abandons him. J.B. beaten down by the elements, beseeches God to show him his guilt. But there is no answer. He does not know if he is being punished for his sins, if he has offended God, to these questions there is no reply.

As in the Old Testament Job's worldly possessions are restored and increased, his only comfort is

> "What's the future but the past to come
> Over and over — love and loss —
> What's loved most, lost most.

MacLeish has set his play inside the tent of a travelling circus "once splendidly gilded and painted but now worn, tattered and patched from year after year after year on the roads of the world". The stage is occupied by two intersecting circus rings, and there is a wooden platform surmounted by a high perch of the kind used by acrobats. The audience, entering, sees the circus as it was at the end of the previous performance, and into this setting come Nickles and Mr. Zuss, both circus employees, who put on the masks of God and the Devil so as to play their play. And soon we realise the circus has been transformed to the universe, the platform becomes Heaven, the bare stage earth. After momentary doubts as to whether they should as it were meddle with the unknown, the play within the play begins.

This mechanism seems to me unworthy of the theme. The German expressionists might have made use of this device, but never, for example, the subtle mind of a Pirandello who was so occupied with the same question of the aesthetics of theatre and reality. As such when MacLeish's characters come forward they are mystical beings, human but not individuals. The world is a far simpler scene than would have been presented by European dramatists, who have had less reason to accept the confident idea that this is the best and happiest of worlds or, to quote Roosevelt, that "man is only prisoner of his own mind". *J.B.* is a play which could not have been written by a European, or rather, a continental writer would have treated the subject in a very different form.

Where does the American Theatre go from here? One should mention the name of Elia Kazan, who directed *J.B.* among many of the other prominent Broadway productions in recent years, as one of the dynamic forces of their theatre. With men like Kazan, and writers like MacLeish, Miller and Williams the American theatre is suddenly aware that it has grown up, that it has its own tradition which from now on will influence, rather than borrow from, Europe.

SEVENTEEN

FRANCE

Henry de Montherlant; Albert Camus; Gabriel Marcel;
André Obey, Emmanuel Roblès, Georges Bernanos;
Marcel Pagnol; Georges Soria; Felicien Marceau.

IF history has been unkind to France in the twentieth century, it has
given her outstanding men in the arts and has enabled her to have a
very real resurgence in the theatre. We have already considered at
length the contributions of Claudel, Giraudoux, Cocteau, Jean-Paul
Sartre, Salacrou, and Anouilh, and in this credit list there remains a
number of other playwrights and plays to demonstrate the more than
ordinary vitality there has been in the French drama in the last thirty
years. Paris is a city for playgoing. Not so large as London, the theatres
are within easier reach of the suburbs, but this is not a reason for its
being a theatre centre. It is a habit, a part of the French way of life,
which starts generally in childhood at the classical matinées given by
the Comédie Française on Thursday afternoons. In the war years
under the strain of the German occupation the theatres became the
heart of the nation, where neither lack of transport and heating, nor a
clumsy censorship nor the stamping of the German patrol made any
difference to the playgoers. Not only did the theatre survive, it rose to
the occasion, found new dramatists and produced such ambitious
works as Claudel's *Le Soulier de Satin,* which had lain unproduced and
considered unproduceable throughout nearly twenty years of peace.

Towards the end of the Fourth Republic the French theatre also
underwent a crisis, from which it has not yet emerged. If the public
turned more towards the boulevards and away from the small Left-
bank *avant-garde* theatres (both the Noctambules and the Théâtre de
Babylone have closed, though a new theatre, the Récamier opened in

the autumn of 1958) the trend towards lightweight was reflected even in the Comédie française. M. Malraux, when he announced the Malraux Theatre Plan in 1959, complained that out of a total of 556 performances at the Comédie française, Racine had been played only six times, while in comparison the works by Labiche had received 113 performances. Greek tragedy had been ignored. Malraux believed that the Comédie française should be built on "the unquestioned patrimony of French genius, neglected masterpieces, major modern works, translations of outstanding foreign plays and the creation of plays rejected by the commercial theatre."

To remedy this the Comédie française has been deprived of its second theatre, the Salle Luxembourg, which is to be directed as a separate concern by Jean-Louis Barrault. Of the two new experimental theatres promised, one, the Récamier, is to be directed by Jean Vilar, who remains head of the Théâtre National Populaire, the other by Albert Camus. All this will require a large subsidy, considerably more than the present one which to Anglo-Saxon eyes already seems extremely generous (about £340,000 was given by Comédie français in 1953). M. Malraux has also asked for plans to be drawn up for the construction of a mobile stage structure for theatrical performances at the new Palais de la Défense building on the western outskirts of Paris, thus converting into an amphitheatre with a capacity of from 5,000 to 25,000 spectators. A production of the *Antigone* of Sophocles directed by Jean-Louis Barrault will open this "Grand Théâtre de France".

Another important recent event in the French theatre, however, is the creation of five dramatic centres in the French provinces, the Centre dramatique de l'Est, with its headquarters at Strasbourg, the Comédie de St. Etienne, the Centre dramatique de l'Ouest at Rennes, the Comédie de Provence, and the Grenier de Toulouse. These centres, established between 1947 and 1952, have brought a theatre of quality to areas where many had never seen a straight play — previously the monopoly of Paris. The centres are subsidised both by the State and the local municipality, the grants range from 29,250,000 francs (£29,000) to 11,000,000 francs (£11,000). There can be no doubt as to the success of these experiments, for an audience has been found for all that is best in the modern repertoire, including Pirandello, Lorca, Giraudoux, Synge, Strindberg, Tchekhov and other leading writers. An interest for the theatre has been created. It is hoped to build up in time regional theatres, with local authors and actors, of a standard to equal the best that Paris can present, and to further this aim drama schools have been founded to work alongside the professional players.

As in other countries, the French theatre to-day lacks giants. Perhaps it has passed its zenith, but the effects of the theatrical renaissance are still being felt and, indeed, reflected in other countries. Meanwhile an annual harvest continues, even though vintage years in the theatre are considerably less frequent and more unpredictable than in the vineyards.

(I) HENRY DE MONTHERLANT

If so many contemporary French dramatists are slaves of their time, Henry de Montherlant is in opposition; he wishes to have nothing to do with his time. He has been described as a 'man of the Renaissance', which is perhaps as misleading as suggesting that Fry is a 'modern Elizabethan', but it is true that Montherlant inherits the great French classical tradition and the eloquence and rhetoric of the masters of the French language. No modern writer is nearer the style of Corneille or Racine, no writer so recaptures a tradition which had been considered lost. Montherlant is not concerned with the great *débâcle* in the modern world, or ephemeral politics; neither does he serve the cause of philosophy or religion. If Montherlant chooses a religious subject, such as that of *Le Maître de Santiago,* he does so that he might explore the inner drama of the human soul, in other words, he chooses to portray a holy ascetic as he might a murderer. He would claim that he was not a Christian but an artist. His is a study not of creeds, dogmas or manifestoes, but of character and conflict. The character must not be cut to shape, and the conflict must not make a character coherent for the sake of dramatic unity. Here we have Montherlant's first quarrel with the theatre, for he believes that "the theatre, like the novel, has only importance to the extent it penetrates the study of man, that is, the study of some being who is neither 'determined' nor 'well drawn' . . ." He protests against the idea that the theatre obeys laws different from other literary forms; for him — he goes so far as to confess — it is the theatre which interests him least. Do you, he asks, think of theatre when reading Shakespeare and Racine?

The argument has quite a few flaws, and the literary value of Racine and his attachment to the French language may well be the reason why Racine does not take the side of Shakespeare outside France. Montherlant's own literary approach will prevent his works finding a large public in English-speaking countries, where audiences are less disciplined than in France to listen to the flow of language which takes the place of dramatic action. Nevertheless, in spite of himself, or perhaps because of his classical heritage, Montherlant does conceive his conflict in dramatic terms, and the force and vehemence of his language suit the intensity of the situation. His fine prose style is far removed from the banalities of every-day conversation, and this presents difficulty in translation, though Montherlant has been more widely and more successfully translated than Claudel or Giraudoux.

The plays of Montherlant are original and in striking contrast to the narrow horizons of the spirit of the age. For they are concerned with eternal problems of the human soul which present the sweep of human aspirations and reveal the dignity of the inner man. There is a pause for reflection, and an appeal is made to our intelligence to applaud the valour of his characters, however much we may detest the principles they represent. Montherlant does not present the uncertainties and *inquiétude* of other modern writers; he is a satisfied man. In 1930, he tells us, he found what he calls his equilibrium. "Since 1930 I have been happy . . . This happiness did not fall from heaven: it is my work and, besides, it is my acquisition since I have paid for it."

Montherlant is first and foremost an aristocrat, and seeks in his work to convey the nobility which is his possession. His own pride is the least appealing aspect of his work, and at the same time the most important motive in all his writings. His ancestors came from Catalonia and settled in Picardy in the sixteenth century. It is perhaps the great Spanish pride which explains Montherlant's own passion. As an aristocrat he is removed from the world in which he lives, and the temptation to infuse his works more and more with the egoism of character is his most serious danger. Montherlant's Spanish ancestry, however, has no doubt led to the inspiration of his two outstanding plays, *La Reine morte* and *Le Maître de Santiago,* set in the Spain of the Middle Ages and the Golden Age respectively. The severity of these plays, the violence of their conflict and the power of their conception are the very tones of the Spanish temperament.

The life of Montherlant presents some curious asides, such as his addiction to bull fighting (until in 1925 he was tossed by a bull and had a horn thrust into his side), his enthusiasm for running the 100 metres and for playing association football, in spite of having been severely wounded in the war. Among his many novels he wrote in 1930 *La Rose de Sable,* which because of its anti-colonialism he refused to publish for fear of hurting French prestige. Montherlant has also gained many celebrated prizes: in 1934 he received the Grand Prix de Littérature de l'Académie Française and sent the prize money to the Moroccan Red Cross, stipulating that it was to be divided between French soldiers and the conquered Moroccan rebels. When he won the Northcliffe prize, Montherlant presented it to the hospitals of London, and the Grand Prix Colonial he refused in order to safeguard his independence as a writer on the colonial question.

It was in 1942 that Montherlant turned to the theatre (if we exclude a piece written when he was eighteen called *L'Exil*) when Jean-Louis Vaudouer, the *administrateur* of the Comédie Française at that time, suggested a subject which he thought Montherlant might make into a play for his players. *La Reine morte* was the result, and must be one of the few commissioned plays which have found a place in literature as well as theatre. Since then Montherlant has written several other plays, including *Fils de Personne* (1943), *Le Maître de Santiago* (1945), *Malatesta* (1946) *Demain il fera Jour* (1949), *Celles qu'on prend dans ses Bras* (1950), *La Ville dont le Prince est un Enfant* (1951), *Port Royal* (1954) and *Don Juan* (1958). His two most important (and successful) works are *La Reine morte* and *Le Maître de Santiago* which illustrate admirably Montherlant's rôle in the theatre.

The idea of *La Reine morte*, set in the Portugal of the Middle Ages, immediately appealed to Montherlant, though he took great liberties in his interpretation of the historical facts relating to Alphonso IV and Inès de Castro, and in order to have freedom to make his king an individual he changed his name to Ferrante. The plot is a simple one: King Ferrante is anxious to marry his son Pedro to the Spanish Princess of Navarre for political reasons. But, unknown to him, Pedro has already secretly married one of the young ladies of the Court, Inès de Castro, with whom it was known he was in love. The King is perfectly willing to let Pedro have Inès as his mistress, but when Pedro does not co-operate he askes Inès to help him in his task. But Inès then confesses her marriage to Pedro. One of the King's ministers, Egas Coelho, urges the King to kill Inès, but the King hesitates. He eventually decides on killing her, not because he wants to, but to demonstrate to his ministers that he is hard and not weak, and because some power compels him to do so. No sooner has he given the order than he himself dies.

There are, then, four characters in conflict with each other, and out of the clash of their convictions comes tragedy. King Ferrante represents order, the safeguarding of public interest, and the terrible necessity that he must see done. Pedro, his son, represents the right of the individual to make his own choice. Inès represents fidelity, she is Montherlant's happiest female creation. She has done no harm, she will not run away or save herself by being unfaithful to her husband and sacrificing her unborn child. She is caught up in events she has no experience of. Finally there is Egas Coelho, the political realist, who sees for political necessity only one possible action. Thus in his characters Montherlant has the opposition of character which leads incisively to the final tragic scene which has the full grandeur of the classical style, with the brush strokes that are the characteristics of great Spanish artists, such as Velazquez.

Compared with *La Reine morte*, it may be suggested that *Le Maître de Santiago* resembles more a painting by El Greco, harsh and mystical in its effect, simple and overpowering in its design. Here we have a portrait of a man who has rejected the world. It is a short, intense drama which turns in its closing scene to a ritualistic chant of religious fervour — and yet a religious inspiration by a man who is himself without faith! We are in Spain, the Spain of the period of the development of the colonies; the idea of the play came to Montherlant during his first visit to Barcelona in 1933 when he read the sentence: "Some years after the discovery of America, there were a number of old Spaniards who believed this discovery was a disaster for Spain." So the character of the Master of Santiago, Don Alvaro Dabo, was born, a man who in his religious exactitude demands the total renunciation of the world, not only for himself, but also that his daughter, who is in love, should sacrifice herself for him. No wealth in the New World for him, no marriage and happiness for her; it is a total refusal, urged on by a kind of sadistic romanticism for purity. He is not a king who must kill his daughter-in-law out of necessity; he is a man aspiring to his idea of the good life who is determined to shut the outside world out of his vision and make his daughter renounce the world as a supreme sacrifice with him.

The Master, as Montherlant stresses, is not an example of a model Christian, for his egoism, cruelty, and all his actions have a dreadful inhumanity. Mariana does not follow her father because of the love of God. And the Master delights in making her suffer, as, for instance, on the renunciation of life by his daughter he asks her, "And yet no tears? Wrestle and suffer more. Where there is no fight there is no redemption." Tempting her with the picture of her lover, she betrays herself when she replies, "Because of him I know the full force of sacrifice. How else would I have been able to have loved him for it for ever?" There is in the religion of the Master that curious Spanish fanaticism. Consider how Alvaro gloats over his victory and rejection of life:

ALVARO With our blood no other blood shall mingle. No other man shall turn and turn you again in his arms. And no children, nobody shall besmirch me, nobody shall betray me; with you my race ends clean through and through. The last! We shall be the last! What power in that word, the last — opening out on to the void sublime.[1]

The love of Alvaro is a love of extermination, he has a hardness which is only explained by his pride. (The French word 'dur' rhymes with 'pur' and Montherlant here equates the two.)

Has one the right to choose a Christian theme when one does not believe in the theme? Montherlant defended himself against critics (Julien Green in his *Journal*, in particular) when in an article which appeared in *Combat* he pleaded his case on artistic grounds. If you can invent a king, a queen, a mother or a murderer, why not a man who believes? He concluded that whereas for Green "sympathy and respect do not replace faith", for Montherlant they could do so.

Numerous critics have found contemporary allusions in *Le Maître de Santiago*, but apart from an unintentional one against colonialism (we recall the novel Montherlant never published on this subject) it would be wrong to imagine that Montherlant saw the play in a contemporary framework. He seems highly amused that some have found the play belonging to the literature of the Resistance and others have named it belonging to the literature of opposition (to the Resistance), while yet a third has found a Communist thesis therein. Montherlant's character in this respect is not unlike his hero, Don Alvaro, turning his back on the lesser men.

The third part of the Catholic trilogy, which started with *La Ville dont le Prince est un Enfant* and *La Reine morte*, is *Port Royal* (1954), a study of the Port Royal nuns who were in 1664 accused of Jansenist heresies and isolated in different convents and deprived of the sacraments by the Archbishop in an effort to make them change their beliefs. Yet this play, written in Montherlant's fine style, is only half a success, and perhaps only half a play, it being almost uncompromisingly undramatic. His *Don Juan* (1958) proved a lamentable failure.

See original on p. 295.

Montherlant has turned to the theatre at a time when the great revival of French drama was beginning to ebb (a theatre without Claudel, Giraudoux, and where even Anouilh and Sartre have fallen by the wayside). Though he is hardly a man of the theatre, his revival of genuine tragedy in the classical tradition, drawing on the resources of human qualities, has a very positive value in the theatre to-day.

(II) ALBERT CAMUS[1]

At the time of the Liberation of France, when the existentionalism of Sartre reached its zenith, the name of Albert Camus was associated with his new French school. Very soon, however, we were able to revise such arbitrary pigeon-holing of his work, for not only was Camus an independent thinker, but a writer who was quite capable of taking over from Sartre. As a philosopher his works *The Myth of Sisyphus* and *L'Homme revolté* have established him in his own right, while the novels *L'Etranger* and *La Peste* would be among any half dozen titles of outstanding post-war fiction. Although also a dedicated *homme de théâtre*, Camus has never achieved the same distinction in this medium. More recently he seems a better adapter, of Faulkner's *Requiem for a Nun*, for example, than in his original works, such as *Le Malentendu, Caligula, l'Etat de siège* or *Les Justes*.

It is possible to see in his novels a kind of signposting which could lead to an exit from the existentialist gloom, whereas his plays appear too much like skeletons to make this road seem worth while. Devoid of any theatrical illusion, through very obvious symbolism and painstaking abstraction his plays are contrived to represent philosophical ideas, no matter how artificial and lifeless may be the result. Yet they do remind us of the loneliness of man and the misunderstanding that seems incurable between man and the very nature of existence. This is the absurd reality which man meets in the theme of *Le Malentendu* ("Cross Purpose"). It is founded on the misunderstanding of an old lady and her daughter who murder a wealthy traveller who comes to their inn, only to discover that he is in fact their son and brother, returning home after making his fortune. This slick little magazine-story plot is the starting point for an angry and despairing question mark for man's relation to the universe, and in the last act all pretence at being a murder story — or any kind of illusory fiction — is dropped. Martha, the accomplice of her brother's murder, confronts her brother's wife with these revealing words:

[1]Albert Camus was killed in a road accident on 4 January 1960, as this book was going to press.

MARTHA Realise that neither for him nor for us, neither in life nor in death, is there fatherland or peace. (*Laughing scornfully*) For you can hardly call it a fatherland, can you, this heavy earth deprived of light, where you go about feeding sightless animals ... That great call of the human being, that awakening of souls, what's the good of it? Why cry out to the sea or to love? It is laughable ... Remember that your sorrow will never equal the injustice done to man.[1]

The play has a certain dramatic drive which compensates to some extent for the plot which is too slender to sustain a full-length play, even when used as an illustration of philosophical intentions. But neither in *Le Malentendu* nor in his best-known play *Caligula* has Camus expounded his philosophy as successfully as Sartre has done in his plays such as *Les Mouches* or *Huis Clos*. The figure of Caligula, the model emperor turned tyrant, committed to wickedness and his own isolation, should have admirably served Camus in search for a theme to express the maladjustment of the communion between man and the world we live in, but while there are many notable passages in the dialogue, the play hardly survives as a unity. The observations, such as "Men die and still they are not happy", or "Everything around me is lies, and I want to live in the truth", or Caligula's realisation after killing his mistress that "killing isn't the solution" and his question "Who would dare in this world to condemn me without a judge, where no one is innocent?" compel our attention, even though they lead to the cul-de-sac of nihilism. Caligula cannot understand, and his own humility is the saving grace of Camus, which, even when he leads the race towards pessimism, makes his company far preferable to the dogmatism of Sartre. "What matters is truth. And I call truth everything that is matter", Camus wrote in *Noces* at the beginning of his career. His honesty made him rebel against society, made him write his famous editorials in *Combat*, but it was merely an honesty which reflected the times through which France was suffering during and shortly after the liberation. *Le Malentendu* dates from 1943, *Caligula* from 1945.

If his recent work has disappointed those who had such high hopes of the author of *La Peste*, it would be wrong to discard Camus as a writer content to rest on the laurels of a Nobel Prize. It would be surprising if in his new post as head of an experimental theatre under the

Malraux Theatre plan we do not hear more, much more, of Camus as
dramatist in the future.

(III) GABRIEL MARCEL

Just as once upon a time we were all socialists (if Sir William
Harcourt's observation was true), so the modern French theatre assumes
that we are all philosophers now. All plays, of course, have presented
some kind of a philosophy even though it was no more than the
expression of the author's temperament, a kind of philosophy of the
theatre — to use Cocteau's terminology — whereas the modern French
theatre introduces the philosopher into the theatre. We have already
seen in the case of Sartre how a philosopher has found a large public
by becoming *un homme de théâtre*, a public which is willing to accept
that existentialism rather than the play is the thing — even though they
would never dream of studying existentialism in *L'Etre et le Néant*.
Gabriel Marcel, unlike Sartre, can hardly be described as a man of the
theatre, for although he has always from childhood been attracted by
the theatre, he has remained strictly a philosopher. His plays, so rich in
philosophical content, are often stimulating and profound, but they can
also appear contrived, artificial and, alas, monotonous. They are not,
heaven forbid, the type of *pièce à thèse* which Marcel also detests, but
somehow his attempt to expound complex philosophical conflicts in
terms of commonplace character types and every-day conversational
dialogue just cannot ring true. His plays have a dimension which requires some kind of symbolism and stylisation to simplify for the
audience the reality of the conflict, but Marcel rules out these devices
and relies on natural dialogue. The plays are of interest more for their
ideas than as good theatre, and it is for this reason that Marcel — in
spite of the moderate success he has achieved in France — is never
likely to find the wider and international public that Sartre (much less
a philosopher, but much more a playwright) enjoys. We shall not,
therefore, attempt in this outline a study of the theatre of Marcel and the
development of the philosophical background, since such a task would
be out of all proportion to his status in the modern drama. The theatre
for him is a subsidiary interest, as is mnsic, and although he recognises
the importance of the drama as second to none in the arts, he approaches
it like a surgeon does a patient, not as an artist does life.

Gabriel Marcel is a philosopher, not a prophet, and consequently he
is honoured in his own country. His plays are philosophical conflicts,
they do not present ready-made solutions and they are never dogmatic.

Nothing could be further from his intentions than the existentialist drama of Sartre or Camus, with which his name is so often carelessly associated. It has been convenient for French critics to pigeon-hole Marcel as the leader of the Christian wing of the existentialist school (which has led Sartre to emphasise that his atheistic type of existentialism is the only coherent and logical analysis), which Marcel himself denies. In a talk given at the Institut Français in London in July, 1950, (and subsequently translated by Rosalind Heywood and published in the introduction to *Three Plays* by Gabriel Marcel) he defines his plays as the drama of the soul in exile: "For me, the soul in exile is the soul who has become a stranger to itself, who can no longer understand itself, who has lost its way. . . . But we are *not* alone, and only too often our uncertainty takes the virulent form of misunderstanding our own intentions and our own behaviour to other people. Once this happens, our misunderstanding inevitably becomes contagious and tends to spread misery and bewilderment." For his drama of the soul in exile Marcel takes ordinary characters and leaves them to fight out their situation in ordinary conversation; they do not fully understand themselves, nor do others their situation. His conflict becomes an intellectual challenge, running through all his works from *Le Seuil invisible*, written in 1914, up to the present. Among his best known works are *La Chapelle ardente* ("The Funeral Pyre") produced in 1925, *Un Homme de Dieu* from the same year, and *Le Monde cassé* (1933). No satisfactory account can be given in a few lines of the ideas implicit in these plays, the *angoisse* provoked by their inner conflict. Perhaps a suggestion of these features may be found if we recall the theme of *Rome n'est plus dans Rome*, produced at the Théâtre Hébertot in 1951, and one of the most actable of Marcel's plays.

In *Rome n'est plus dans Rome* Marcel confronts a problem which is one of the most disturbing anxieties for all Europeans, and especially those who have suffered German occupation: whether when threatened with Russian occupation and the dictatorship of the Communist Party, one should escape while the going is good, or stay and fight. Can the flight to freedom, like those who escaped to London in the last war, be the solution for the next war? Should those who know that they are on the extermination list dare to stay? It should be remembered that at the time the play was produced it was a known fact that Russia could have overrun Europe in a few days had the cold war turned hot.

So the stage is set. A French professor is known to be on the Communist black list, and his wife, thinking of their children, has secured

S

for him — against his wishes — a chair in French literature in a South American Dominican university. We also meet the professor's nephew, Marc-André, who having left school asks his uncle whether he should flee to a job he has heard about in Equatorial Africa, or stay. If he stays Marc-André fears that he must become a Communist in order to save himself, although he does not believe in Communism. The professor gives in to his wife's wishes, and they all sail for South America. But it turns out to be a reactionary university where the professors must be actively engaged in turning their subjects to suit the ends of propaganda. Too late the professor realises his mistake: the duty of Frenchmen is to remain in France. When asked to speak over the radio and give a message to those who remain in France, he denounces the lines of Corneille:

> Et, comme autour de moi j'ai tous les vrais appuis,
> Rome n'est plus dans Rome, elle est toute où je suis.

"That is false", he exclaims through the microphone, Rome must remain in Rome: "We were wrong to leave; we should have stayed and struggled on the spot. The illusion that you can take your country with you is only the origin of pride and foolish presumption. You who are perhaps hesitating before the threat of to-morrow, remain, I implore you, and if you do not feel able . . . if you have not the strength . . ."

His speech ends uncompleted, but we know his message is complete. Faith is the only way to fight the menace.

Such is the type of 'lounge-suit' tragedy which Gabriel Marcel describes in the tragedy of the soul in exile. Perhaps Marcel holds a position in the French theatre similar to that held by Charles Morgan in Britain; true, Marcel is a professional philosopher, but both writers in their 'theatre' appeal to the mind rather than the emotions, and if the characters are far too often types, puppets reacting to the liberties of their author's mind, they offer a promising evening's debate for those theatre-goers who are more interested in the argument than in the importance for a play to reveal an imaginative vision of life.

(IV) MAINLY ABOUT INDIVIDUAL PLAYS

With Gabriel Marcel we come to the end of the modern French dramatists we have selected, but there remain a number of individual plays which deserve special mention, though inevitably we cannot pretend to attempt to list all the worth-while plays in the modern French repertoire. For the main part they are works which have caused very great interest in recent years, with the exception of the early work of André Obey which showed such promise back in 1931 in the days of Copeau's Compagnie des Quinze, and whose subsequent work has been a sad disappointment. A word too on Marcel Pagnol and Jean Giono, though their plays date from the 'thirties and are now better known for the film version of the *Marius* trilogy and also of Giono's *La Femme du Boulanger*. From the post-1945 theatre, there is Emmanuel Roblès prize-winning *Montserrat,* where the subject with its challenging theme at once engaged the audience's attention, as did the two religious plays which ran throughout the 1952–1953 season in Paris, *Dialogues des Carmélites* ("The Carmelite Story") by the famous French novelist Georges Bernanos, and *Sur la Terre comme au Ciel* ("The Strong are Lonely" in London) by the Austrian dramatist Fritz Hochwalder. There remains the boulevard theatre, where the plays of Marcel Achard and André Roussin constantly remind us that the French are still masters of wit and farce, and those saving graces which are so essential after an overdose of existentialism. Of course, were we even to consider all the plays which might possibly be included, this chapter would become a mere list of names, and while figures such as Thierry Maulnier, Claude-André Puget, Maurice Druon, Clavel . . . testify to the vigour of the French theatre, they are still figures of promise rather than achievement. Shortly before the war Mauriac turned to the theatre, and his *Asmodée* still deserves attention. In this story of a tutor's influence over the woman of a household in the Landes we have much of the stifled passions of a Mauriac novel, with the sun beating relentlessly on the shutters, while all is dark and claustrophobic within. Another novelist Julien Green, an American born in Paris and who writes in French, achieves a similarly remarkable atmosphere in plays such as *Sud* and *L'Ombre*, though here, as in his novels, there is a touch of the more frigid puritanism of the New World.

Farce, perhaps should be wicked. Felicien Marceau, like Marcel Aymé, believes this. In *l'Oeuf* (1956) le petit Parisien Emile Magis sets out to defeat the "system". As long as he remains pure he cannot penetrate the egg. When he compromises, that is, plays the rules of the game like everybody else, steals, lies, and so on, then he is accepted. By conniving with society, society will give him a job as civil servant, a wife, and protection, even when he murders his wife. Magis, once he has penetrated the shell, cannot be harmed. It is a fierce biting play which cannot be really understood outside France; like a local wine it does not travel, and the play did not take on in London. Marceau has repeated his success in *La bonne Soupe* (1958) though this play is less damaging to our morale.

It was in 1931 that Jacques Copeau and the Compagnie des Quinze presented three plays by André Obey at the Vieux-Colombier, and hopes were raised that an important new dramatist had been discovered. His three plays, *Le Viol de Lucrèce* ("The Rape of Lucretia"), *Noé* ("Noah") and *La Bataille de la Marne* ("The Battle of the Marne") gave indications of wild ambitions which had been almost forgotten in the French theatre in the years of its decline. Of the three plays *Noah* is perhaps the most successful, and while the play is not sustained on the level of its lofty theme, there are certain scenes which do justice to the intentions. Obey has attempted to call on all the resources of theatrical imagination, only without the ability to achieve his aims. It was left to a writer like Giraudoux to show him how this could be realised. Obey has continued writing, but we no longer expect him to give us the masterpiece that was once awaited from his pen. In a recent play of his, *Une Fille pour du Vent* ("Sacrifice to the Wind"), we find little originality in his adaptation of classical legend to express pacific sentiments. The burst of applause in the Comédie Française every night when the line came "It's never too late to stop an imbecile war" (this was during the fighting in Indo-China) showed that the play was too blatantly discussing actuality. Giraudoux's *La Guerre de Troie n'aura pas lieu* is an example of a pacifist play which has application to our own struggles but not identification.

From time to time the French take a holiday away from classical and philosophical texts and enable us to enjoy the unsophisticated and good-humoured way of life under the Midi sun. For a portrait of Provence we have but to turn to Jean Giono whose *La Femme du Boulanger* has so admirably captured the mood of the region, while Marcel Pagnol holds the mirror to the comings and goings in the old port of Marseilles (before it was destroyed) in his *Marius* trilogy. In both Giono and Pagnol we have the different generations, the old cronies gossiping in the bistro drinking their pernod, the schoolmaster determined to get the better of Monsieur le Curé, the Lyonnais gentlemen trying to convince César that Paris is larger than Marseilles, while the young Marius is torn between the desire for adventure and his love for Fanny. These plays come gloriously alive, there is a down-to-earth humanity which makes us feel the characters exist and we know them out of the theatre. The part of César was created by the late Raimu in the original production of *Marius*, and his performance has been magnificently recorded in the film version — how seldom can such acting be enjoyed these days. How can we ever forget the tender affection he shows for his son when he reminds Marius of his duty to marry Fanny: "Honour, Marius, is like matches: it is only any good once."

It is perhaps dangerous to choose a subject of topicality, though Georges Soria rises above the journalistic level in *L'Etrangère dans l'Ile* (1958), which is set in Cyprus. Pygmalion and Demetrios are two Cypriots who have been educated in England. Pygmalion is a lawyer, his brother a surgeon. Both have learnt to admire the English cultural tradition, the English language, and Pygmalion has married an English woman doctor. As long as they live together in London they understand one another. It is only when Alicia arrives in her husband's native Cyprus that she knows she is a foreigner, and as the climate of hate is more oppressive then the climate she had been willing to bear they have to realise that they are of necessity separated, that one must choose the heritage to which one belongs.

An exciting new play was the discovery of *Montserrat* by Emmanuel Roblès. This was chosen out of 188 manuscripts in a new play competition (only one other play was retained) and not surprisingly, for it is the very material of drama, a virtuoso performance by the author of tension, intensity, horror and conflict of duty and humanity. Montserrat is an officer in the Spanish army which is fighting the Venezuelan insurrection led by Simon Bolivar. Montserrat is led to disgust of his own side by the excess of cruelty they inflict on the rebels, and secretly he warns Bolivar that he must flee before capture. His treachery is discovered by his own side, and Izquierdo, who commands the garrison, has him and six innocent passers-by in the street arrested. These six innocent victims will be held as hostages and shot unless Montserrat discloses the hiding-place of Bolivar. One by one the innocent characters are dragged to their execution, to the horror of Montserrat. The repetition of this scene six times does not lead to monotony, but such is the dramatic skill of Roblès that the terror increases death by death. When Montserrat faces his own, it is with final relief that we know the revolution will succeed, and that the sacrifice has not been in vain.

It is a play with a message for our own times, as has the story of the *Dialogues des Carmélites* by Bernanos, which has been such an outstanding success in the French theatre (as well as in Germany and Austria). The story of the martyrdom of the Carmélites of Compiège, in order that through offering their lives they may help to end the massacres of the French Revolution, is true, but the subject was borrowed by Bernanos from a short story by the German novelist Gertrud von le Fort, and Bernanos might never have come across it at all had he not been asked to write the dialogue of a film scenario on this subject. Bernanos, then in ill health, felt a spiritual necessity to write the dialogue, finding in the story of these nuns the same fear of anguish in an age of revolt as he suffered in his own spiritual faith. The climax of the play is when the Carmélites, dressed in the robes the revolutionary authorities have forbidden them to wear, walk bravely the one behind the other to the guillotine chanting "Laudate Dominium omnes gentes"—and the play thus enacts their martyrdom in a religious ritual. The communion of fear becomes a testament of the nobility of the human soul. As a play, however, the final exultation so overpowers the earlier structure that, in spite of having been carefully directed to this end, the first half of the play moves at a very different level from the second part — and is not made easier with disconcerting changes of scene. But no one can forget the triumph of the final scene.

Will these religious plays be followed up by more? They have been more than a counterblast to atheistic works, for they have expressed the need for faith felt by a large section of the French people. There seems no doubt that the French theatre alone is in the fortunate position of having a public willing to accept serious work: a theatre where audiences want to be both entertained and treated as adults. There is vitality, vigour, a spirit of adventure in the French theatre to-day; the nation presents divisions in religion, philosophy, politics which, however regrettable they may be in other spheres, stimulate each other to action. There is a wealth of talent among young French writers, and it is likely that the French theatre will be a centre of good drama for many years to come. Let us hope so. But genius . . . Ah, that is a more serious matter. Perhaps after all they are born, and not made. . . .

EIGHTEEN

OTHER COUNTRIES

Spain: Jacinto Benavente — Austria: Fritz Hochwälder —
Switzerland: Friedrich Dürrenmatt — Denmark: Kaj
Munk: — Italy: Ugo Betti

P ARIS, London, New York — but theatre and playgoing are
not, we hope, to be restricted to the big three. Many of the
masters of the modern theatre would be excluded were plays
only produced in these cities — in fact, the modern theatre would
probably not exist at all. Ibsen was a Norwegian, Strindberg a Swede,
Pirandello an Italian. And a theatre-going public is to be found in most
of the European capitals, often more enlightened than those who consider themselves the élite among playgoers on the boulevards, Broadway,
or Shaftesbury Avenue. The rising playwrights as well as those who
have made their name, in Scandanavia, Spain, Italy and other countries,
would require a section which would fill the larger half of this volume,
and we shall have to restrict our wanderings rather than obscure our
perspective of the contemporary theatre with a long list of interesting
playwrights who, for the most part, have not (in some cases we should
add "not yet") made any significant contribution to the trends of world
drama, and whose work has not found an audience beyond their own
frontiers. The only figures who do not deserve to be grouped with the
average are Ugo Betti, Jacinto Benavente, and possibly Kaj Munk and
Nordahl Grieg.

Moscow, of course, is a great theatre city, and many of the capitals
of her satellites have also a flourishing theatre, so far as the theatre can
be said to flourish under the yoke of 'socialist realism' (or should we
say 'Soviet realism'?). But this book is not impressed with the theatre
used as an instrument for blatant propaganda, bound to the canons of
the Marxist dogma. "The point of view of art for art's sake is regarded

as at best futile and at worst decadent", wrote Mordecai Gorelik on the Polish Theatre in 1950. Since then Poland has been the one satellite to free herself from the iron grip of the censor, with the result that her theatre is very lively and Western plays, particularly *avant-garde* writers such as Beckett, very popular. But for the rest of the Communist world Gorelik's official policy dictum still holds sway and when applied to Russia as well, it reads like some frightsome epitaph on the modern drama.

From Russia to Spain, from revolution to reaction, and yet Fascist Spain has produced in literature and the arts a continuation worthy of the heritage of Spain, while Soviet Russia has sunk to the level of Hitler's Reich. In the theatre Spain has given us García Lorca, and also her only Nobel Prize winner Jacinto Benavente. Benavente had the fecundity of the great Spanish dramatists, though he did not capture their spirit half so successfully as did Lorca. For Benavente was not only a Spaniard, but also a European; he had translated into Spanish, Shakespeare and Molière, was a student of Ibsen and had read Freud, and had a general admiration for and understanding of the ways of the West. All this he introduced in his volumes of plays, produced over a period of more than sixty years, and which ranged from satire and comedy of manners to the drama of ideas and the philosophy of scepticism; from realism to fantasy there seemed no end to Benavente's industry to cover the whole field of modern dramatic experiment. His theatre is consequently too diverse to attempt any satisfactory short study, and all his plays together do not seem to this critic to have anything like the merit of Lorca's half-dozen folk dramas. Europe and Spain is somehow an unsatisfactory hybrid, and while all of us must admire the civilised intellect of a man like Benavente, his plays do not come across to us as fresh and powerful in their interpretation of the Spanish soul as might have been hoped. It is almost as if Benavente was concerned in introducing from abroad the attitude of mind to enable Spain to become part of the West; he was not caught up, as, for example, Pirandello was, in the creation of his own imagination; for Benavente (unlike Pirandello) passion did not need to be brought to bear on intellect — ideas could walk perfectly well by themselves. Benavente has had one success in translation, his famous *Los Intereses Creados* ("The Bonds of Interest") written in 1907, but it is questionable whether his plays will ever be widely known abroad. Far more likely that he will be remembered in histories of the drama as a Spaniard who let loose modern European movements in Spain, delighted in exposing the foibles of Spanish society and survived his satires to find himself a national hero, worshipped by all.

Since Benavente's death in 1953 the Spanish theatre continues with what might be called 'caretaker playwrights', if this term may be used to suggest mediocre playwrights who carry the theatre on until such time as an important new dramatist arrives. The time is not yet, but it is possible that one day we may hear more of such names as Luis Escabor, Agustín de Figueroa, Alfonso Sastre, Antonio Buero Vallejo, José Suarez Carreño and Victor Ruiz Iriarte.

FRITZ HOCHWÄLDER

The name of the Austrian dramatist Fritz Hochwälder first attracted attention when his play *Sur la Terre comme au Ciel* ("The Strong are Lonely" in its London version) was one of the successes of the 1952 Paris season, due no doubt to the then topical controversy of the "worker priest" movement. Here we have a group of priests also carrying out a brave experiment, although the action passes in a Jesuit college at Buenos Aires in the year 1767. The Jesuit fathers are building in Paraguay a kingdom of Heaven on earth. With the arrival of the King of Spain and, as it turns out, the Pope's representative, they have to decide between abandoning their work in Paraguay or to defy their instructions and follow their individual consciences "for the greater glory of God". It is a case of submission or open rebellion. One of the fathers refuses to submit, suggesting that perhaps for a long time they had all ceased to be Jesuits. The same father, when later brought to face face a Spanish firing squad, submits and receives absolution. Duty demands obedience, but in their hearts the question remains unanswered "what shall it profit a man to gain the universe if he should lose his soul. . . ?"

At the 1959 Salzburg Festival *Donnerstag*, a modern miracle play by Hochwälder written in the hope that it might replace *Jedermann*, proved a disappointment. The theme is of a salesman employed by "Belial Inc" who is commissioned by the "Grossingenieur" (the devil) to find a man dead, though physically alive. A famous architect Promfrit, who has lost faith, hope and charity, is engaged as candidate. He is promised bourgeois comfort, space travel and the most beautiful blonde in the world—in return for his own soul. The pact is in the end violated and the architect prays to a God he does not believe in, so that "man in his final hour has freedom of choice". Like Cocteau's *Bacchus* Hochwälder would seem to use a religious theme as providing the drama between opposing forces of good and evil, but he does not himself take sides.

FRIEDRICH DÜRRENMATT

Borne near Berne, Switzerland in 1921, Friedrich Dürrenmatt has already proved himself to be the most original and promising play-wright in the German language since Brecht. His own masters seems to be Wedekind and Pirandello. His name first came to notice in Britain when the Lunts toured the provinces in a play of his called *Time and Again,* which was subsequently presented on Broadway as *The Visit.* There is a grisly and gruesome touch of the older Expressionists in his theme of a wealthy old lady's return to her native town where the villagers are expecting her to donate her fortune to the local community without suspecting her sinister condition: that first they must kill the man who had wronged her so many years ago. Lynn Fontanne discovered a role which provided her with an admirable *tour de force,* though Alfred Lunt was less happily cast, and the audiences who were more accustomed to seeing the Lunts in the sophisticated naturalism of Coward, Rattigan or Robert Sherwood, were somewhat bewildered.

An Angel Came to Babylon is an allegory set in the kingdom of Nebuchadnezzar in which the author ridicules the hollowness of society and civilisation. Dürrenmatt's theatre has been called "cosmic", and living in Switzerland he sees the world as "something monstrous; an enigma of calamity that has to be accepted, but to which there must be no surrender". The unexpected always happens, from outside, the outlaw intrudes to shake the complacency of the secure. Thus in *The Marriage of Mr. Mississippi* (produced London 1959) the Public Prosecutor calls on the widow to express his condolences, but also for something else. He knows her husband was having an affair with his wife. He knows she murdered her husband, but he has not called as the public prosecutor but a suitor. He has executed his wife for the adultery, he has punished her for breaking the Mosaic law which he wishes to reinstate in modern life, whereas the widow has murdered for passion. In marrying the Public Prosecutor she will be able to expiate her sin.

This revolt against conventions and society is also asserted in *One Evening in Late Autumn,* a radio play which won the *Prix Italia 1958.* Korbes, a Nobel prize winning novelist is visited by an amateur detective, a retired civil servant who has discovered that the murders Korbes writes about are factual dossiers of the murders Korbes has committed. He is as great a murderer as he is a novelist. Now the time has come for Korbes to find material for another book and another murder, and here the detective has underestimated Korbes, who is absolved from the rules and conventions of the bourgeoisie. No one will listen to the old man's scream for mercy.

Life in Switzerland has undoubtedly moulded Dürrenmatt's own revolt and protest. At any time the anarchist may enter and throw his bomb on what we all take far too much for granted. Dürrenmatt is a great shatterer of myths and revealer of the moment of truth; he is a dramatist to remember.

KAJ MUNK AND NORDALH GREIG

In Germany interest rests more on the technique of *mise en scène* than in writing; there remains Scandinavia, where several playwrights appeared in the inter-war years giving promise of hope, but alas, the war prevented a harvest. The most famous was Kaj Munk, a Dane who, like Lorca, was one day suddenly snatched from his home and family, driven away secretly, and his bullet-riddled body thrown into a way-side ditch. Munk was a Lutheran pastor, in fact priest, politician and playwright. He wrote some twenty plays, among which the best known are *An Idealist*, *The Word*, *Cant*, and *The Elect*. Had he lived there is reason to believe that he would have become a considerable figure in European drama, but his work up to the time of his martyrdom in 1944 was a powerful attack on dictatorship and a trumpet call to action, perhaps too *engagé* to have permanent value. One of his last works was *Niels Ebbeson*, based on the life of Denmark's national hero who himself resisted the invaders of his day. No wonder the Nazis were after Munk's blood, for he could not be silenced any other way and in his plays there is the testament of a man who suffered for his faith, for truth and freedom, and who knew that he had defeated his murderers.

Another victim of the war was Nordalh Grieg, who was killed in a Royal Air Force raid over Berlin. His most important work was *Nederlaget* ("The Defeat") set in the Paris Commune, but very definitely featuring contemporary society in its implications. The conviction of right and the ardour of faith in face of the darkness of defeat is the theme, and the result is a political drama of white heat. Again we have the death of a young dramatist who would almost certainly have developed had he lived.

In various countries it is possible to select playwrights here and there who have given or are giving indications of better things to come. In

Italy, for example, where the theatre has such a fierce struggle against the material superiority of the Italian cinema, there are a number of playwrights of interest, though only Ugo Betti has achieved eminence and had success beyond Italy's frontiers. The other playwrights have yet to suggest that the theatre in Italy has the vitality (however much it may lack the prosperity) of the cinema. It seems the Italians have so much a sense of the dramatic in everyday life that the theatre is super-fluous; Italy has, however, given the modern theatre both Pirandello and, more recently, Ugo Betti, who demonstrate how the theatre of passion and ideas can be interwoven. It is with Ugo Betti that we shall close this present stock-taking of the credit list of playwrights in the modern theatre. But, as with all such inventories, the theatre is in a constant state of flux, for playwrights (and the public and the players) are all, like the theatre, mortal.

UGO BETTI

Inevitably after the death of a great dramatist the mantle of his fame is assumed to fall on a playwright of the younger generation, as for a time Ibsen's was said to have fallen on Helge Krog. Pirandello's mantle has not fallen on Ugo Betti, for this is a dramatist with his own vision of a world on trial, a vision which avoids the innate pessimism of the great Italian master. Ugo Betti (1892–1953) was a High Court judge, and an acute observer of the reaction of those condemned. As a philoso-pher of man, Betti realises the transcending quality of human courage and the need for Christian charity in a world where social conditions and upheavals make us all in some degree condemned, and even the best of us incompetent to judge other men. His characters long for a recon-ciliation with God, so that they can reveal the nobility of their souls. Betti is not a dramatist of pessimism, far from it, but living through an era of Fascism and disaster for Italy, Betti could not help being a wiser and a sadder man than others.

His first play *La Padrona*, produced in 1927, attracted attention by the force and even violence of his theme and writing. Twenty-five plays have followed, as well as short stories and a novel. Among his plays are *Frana allo Scalo Nord* (1935), *Notte in Casa del Rico* (1942) and *Ispezione* (1947), the last one having affinities with Priestley's *An Inspector Calls*. But we shall consider here three more' recent works, *Corruzione al Palazzo di Giustizia* ("Corruption at the Palace of Justice" — broadcast by the B.B.C. under the title "The Sacred Scales") produced in 1949, *Delitto all'Isola delle Capre* ("Goat's Island") produced in 1950, and his last play *La Regina e gli Insorti* ("The Queen and the Rebels") produced 1953.

In *Corruption at the Palace of Justice* Betti contemplates the possibilities of the discovery of corruption in high places, and the miscarriage of justice which could be worse than the corruption. Ludvi-Pol, a man of great power and evil repute, commits suicide in the law chambers, and the scandal of his death causes consternation among the judges, since nearly all have been involved in corruption to suit Ludvi-Pol's intents. The guilty party is known to one man who, mortally sick, takes the guilt upon himself, and leaves the guilty member to seek his own salvation in the knowledge of his rival's gesture, and in the suicide of a young girl caused through the case.

Goat's Island is a very different type of play, wild and pagan in its tempo, for it is set in that part of Italy beyond the Eboli Christ stopped at. The action takes place in an isolated farmhouse in the midst of marshland and far from the nearest town. Here Agata with her daughter Silvia and her sister-in-law Pía have gone to live after Agata's husband has left her. Life there is like the title of the play, for they are cut off as it were on an island living with their goats. The life is dreary, for the three women are not peasants, until one day a stranger arrives carrying a sack and announcing that he was an intimate friend of Agata's husband. It is soon obvious that he has come to stay and take the place of the husband who had once said to him "Angelo, go to my home and find my wife. Take my place, and you'll be night and day the master of the house." So he sits down with the three women to dinner. He is at home and helps himself to wine:

Drink then, my friends. Ah! You were a little flock without a shepherd: just notice how a man's voice livens thing up! What excellent cheese! And what nice goats! Do you know what people say about goats and shepherds in my country? A tall story but true . . . they say that shepherds, because they have to remain alone for such a long time with the company of their beasts, forget the language and customs of men . . . when they believe no one is present, they bleat "beeh" . . . they don't boast about it, but they have been caught out . . . and then you can guess the rest without difficulty. . . . That is why in the villages of my country the best guardian of goats is a devil. . . . Come on, all of you, why aren't you drinking?

Angelo stays, an absolute parasite, but a passionate lover of Pía and Agata, much to Silvia's disgust. She is driven to desperation and attempts to kill him, but Agata warns him just in time. Angelo realises that he has to make her happy like the other two.

The final act is an act of fate. Angelo goes down the well one day where Agata's husband used to store his wine (the well has dried up) and the ladder falls, imprisoning him there. Gradually he realises that the women don't intend to rescue him. There is an unknown power which prevents Silvia and Pía from doing so. They leave for the town, and Agata remains behind, so as to be beside the memory of Angelo "until the beginning of eternity".

In his last play Betti returns to a Christian theme which we can all accept, the dignity of the human soul in face of martyrdom. In *The Queen and the Rebels* we are in a world of rebellion, a world where ordinary people all try to be on the side of the law but where always the unfortunate and innocent are convicted. Argia, a prostitute, is taken captive along with other travellers during a period of internal revolution, on the pretext that the ex-Queen is in the neighbourhood. Argia discovers the identity of the ex-Queen among the travellers and discusses with one of the guards (who has been her lover) how they can sell her to the authorities. But on meeting the ex-Queen alone, Argia takes pity on the poor girl who is terrified of everyone and only wants to be allowed to live in peace:

ARGIA   What do you want?
THE QUEEN   To be left alive. Nothing else. Unknown, far away. And
            to sleep, night after night, in peace.

To be Queen is Argia's desire, to be what she never can be, because she is so common. But soon the tables are turned, the Queen dies and Argia is accused of being the Queen. She appeals to the guard, her lover, to save her, but he no longer comes to her aid. There is no way out for Argia but to be Queen:

Now every eye shall look to the ground. There shall still be someone to stand before you. Yes, I am the Queen!

Her courage is equal to her rôle, a prostitute can be queen, for the object of life is to be lived regally.

Two years after his death the plays of Ugo Betti had been discovered, and in the autumn of 1955 three of his plays were running in the West End. Introduced by the B.B.C. Third programme, *L'Aiuola Bruciata* was presented by the Arts Theatre Club, *The Queen and the Rebels* offered Irene Worth a chance in an actress's lifetime at the Haymarket, while *Summertime* was a reminder that Betti was a versatile playwright and could laugh as well as be a philosopher in the theatre. *Summertime* is an unimportant piece, the mildest of light comedies, but sharing with the serious works that unique sense of theatre which was Betti's great understanding. His death is a serious blow for the modern theatre, for his work brought to the theatre the outlook of a philosopher and a humanist, to say nothing about the Italian love of all that is dramatic in life.

NINETEEN

DRAMATIC HORIZONS:
STAGE, SCREEN AND T.V.

"When a nation is strongest, physically and spiritually,
its people delight most in tragedy. When a nation is
weakest, physically and spiritually, its people will not
listen to tragedy, but demand what is called light entertainment: comic plays, spectacular pieces, trivial shows."
ST. JOHN ERVINE, *The Organised Theatre* (1924)

OURS is an age of miracles in science and mediocrity in the
arts; the miracles of science have been and are being put to
evil uses and their destruction of man is reflected for man in
the arts. Man has surpassed his own imagination, discoveries are made
faster than intelligence can appreciate their significance; yet far from
living in an age of great adventure, watching new horizons opening up
before us as they must have done in the days of the Renaissance, our
eyes are turned inwards towards the terror and confusion which surround the modern tempo. What should have been the greatest adventure of all turns to criminal disillusionment; the pace has made us lose
control and instead of nations uniting to rise together on the synthesis
of human achievement they turn on one another, dog eats dog, and in
their madness threaten the extinction of existence. What a fiasco! No
wonder artists cannot reveal the hopes when man has not the courage
to realise them. The spirit of the age is something completely alien to
the delight of discovery of the Renaissance or Elizabethan man, who
celebrated the crescendo of his excitement in poetry, drama and the
arts. To-day we all know that the individual no longer exists — as
one wit once noted, there is even a society of individualists — and man

has been replaced by machines which operate without thinking. The spirit of the age is anxiety, confusion, despair, and a desire to escape from the responsibilities of man's genius and folly without being able to do so. For the easy solution of the 'twenties 'to eat, drink and be merry' is no longer possible to-day; the artist is committed to intervene directly in the lives of the people and prick their conscience by holding a mirror to the turmoil. We enter here a maze from which there is no escape.

The drama, more than the other arts, is influenced most directly by the spirit of the age and the intellectual level of the playgoer. The theatre does not exist for plays meant only to be read, and a play which does not immediately communicate with an audience and hold their interest while in performance ceases to be a play, or to belong to the drama. The novelist can write for an individual reader and invite him to enter alone into his world of imagination; the artist can paint for an individual viewer and even the pianist can perform as well in rehearsal as in recital. The theatre, on the other hand, is quite different, for it is a collective whole. The audience, the actors and the playwright are its three essential creators, and they cannot be separated. It has often been said that a play always finds the audience it deserves (though in the long run), and so why should not the reverse be true, that audiences find the play they deserve (and in the short run)? If so (as I believe) we can explain the mediocrity of so much in the contemporary theatre through the social conditions engendered by an age of crisis; either the desire is to escape or one becomes over-serious through deliberate reminders of the hunger-march in the 'thirties, the swish of the swastika in the 'forties, and the menace of the atom to-day.

There is a danger that the so-called serious theatre will become a literary critics' theatre, written for the critic rather than the public. (The new school of critics in America with their ultra-academic language has already penetrated the frontiers of dramatic criticism, and crossed the Atlantic into English academic circles — its influence on literature and the drama is already having effect, one fears). There is little hope for artistic freedom in this atmosphere where the English language itself becomes something only understood by other critics — to say nothing about critics having to explain the meaning of symbolism as a kind of grammatical key to the universe. The art theatre should not be for academic experiment, but to give the new writer in the theatre an opportunity to have his work produced and to experiment before he is ready for the public.

T

We have seen in the course of this study that a handful of men have risen above the spirit of the age and entered the living traditions of the drama. On the whole, however, the serious theatre to-day is not one of illumination, but of reflection. If we divide dramatists, like the famous art critic Bernhard Berenson once divided men, into 'life-enhancers' and 'life-diminishers', then we realise that the modern dramatist, with the notable exceptions, falls on the side of 'life-diminishers'. Perhaps the claustrophobic atmosphere of the naturalist drama is partly to blame for the modern inability to see dramatic horizons, but only the three-dimensional stage set. The life-diminisher at any rate sees no further than his own age, and often with the best of intentions he produces confusion and calls it order, despair and calls it realism, materialism and calls it faith. The life-diminishers have succeeded so well in their task that they have wrecked the very aesthetics of the drama, and have so blinded the audience to the living traditions of the theatre that they threaten the very continuation of dramatic values. Ivor Brown, writing of the results of the Festival of Britain play competition sponsored by the Arts Theatre Club, commented that "in a fairly long career of playwatching I have never known such a diversity of opinion as now exists about artistic values". The winning play of the competition had been John Whiting's *Saint's Day*, which had completely failed to make itself intelligible to either audiences or critics and had ensured a deluge of adverse criticism. The play had failed in its primary duty, to create within the dramatic framework an order out of confusion, and no amount of excusing by the distinguished panel who selected the play (Messrs. Ustinov, Clunes and Fry) will help the baffled playgoer in his bewilderment. We can accept Eliot's dictum quoted in the days of *The Criterion* that "if you can keep the bloody audience's attention engaged, then you can perform any monkey tricks you like when they ain't looking, and it's what you do behind the audience's back so to speak that makes your play immortal" as one way (but not the only way) of creating appeal at different levels and on different planes (it is questionable whether the plays which are immortal have played tricks of this nature), but even this dictum for a theatre of ambiguity demands that the impact of any play must be felt at once collectively by the audience. Any other type of communication simply is not theatre, and it is precisely this failure in so many so-called uplifting plays that makes the gap widen between the public and the new playwright.

Must our theatrical entrepreneurs continue to believe that when we are tired of trivial flights of fancy, either anger and self pity or obscurist drama venturing far beyond our understanding is the remedy? Cannot we be taken out of ourselves by good drama? Why should this age with its infinite possibilities present confusion only, as if it was nothing but a conglomeration with scissors and paste of screaming headlines, jabbering politics and the wailings from the existentialist menagerie? Ah yes, but of course the contemporary theatre must be the theatre of to-day (must it?). The argument can be continued on these lines: the life of the average citizen in London, Birmingham, Lyons or Milwaukee is dull, but he is aware of the fear of what is reality.

Why, we may ask, should the life of the ordinary citizen who does not end up in a Siberian labour camp be dull? Because he is protected by the Welfare State, and knows that in his old age he will be cared for and that his children need not want for food or clothes, why should this be dull? The popular press would have us believe that morals have fallen, that crime is rampant, that juvenile delinquency and child neglect is out of hand, yet sociologists beg to differ. Much of the morbid preoccupation with crime is the effort of the ordinary press to take the public out of themselves. The community prospers even though the threat of another war is never absent, the ordinary business of life continues, with more time than ever before for leisure, for people to take an interest in the world outside their work. In Britain and America a large percentage of the population switch on their television sets nightly to be entertained, and a surfeit of non-stop TV is as good a way as any to blunt a desire to be taken out of oneself. For life is still dull, for neither television nor the average play or film offers, any more than the evening paper, a coherent picture of life.

It is in the revelation of life that the drama, as an art, can continue to survive against the entertainment factories of cinema and television. And it can never be even challenged in this field, for the theatre alone requires participation. A member of the audience knows that his support, which becomes the collective will of an audience, determines the performance. Television can be turned off with a switch, but a play is live and the magnetism between actor and audience has a communicative power unknown to filmgoers or television watchers. The conventions in the drawing-room are not those of the auditorium.

Television and the theatre are, of course, bound to overlap, and West End successes will be adapted for TV, when they are not brought direct from the stage of a London theatre. But this is far from the television ideal, it comes surely from the lack of suitable original material written direct for the medium. Up to the present television has not offered much incentive for playwrights to write directly for it, since the new writer, and often experienced writers, receive only £250 for a play of one hour. As Mr. Ted Willis, himself well-known as a writer both for TV and the legitimate theatre has commented, the TV playwright "has the largest public of any dramatist in history and the smallest audience". But as opposed to the lack of remuneration relative to the size of an audience which would bring him a fortune in the theatre, even with a choice of programmes the TV public does not select, in the way that we choose our theatre or cinema. "Play of the Week" or "World Theatre" are turned on (or kept on) regardless of writer and often cast; viewing is passive and participation unshared. It is courageous for the B.B.C. to even try putting across for example Lorca to this giant public, but how can his *duende* be communicated across the screen?

Perhaps Hollywood will eventually "by-pass" cinema palaces through an unscrambling device. This method has been used in the States for the television relay of top sporting events, and to ensure that the promoter does not sustain a loss from the fall in attendance due to television, TV audiences can only receive the programme by placing a coin in a slot by their set, which immediately "unscrambles" the picture and enables them to see the event. Meanwhile many Hollywood companies are producing direct for television; the capital of entertainment cannot ignore the appeals of the greatest medium for entertainment. But as well as entertainment, television is also like an evening paper, it lives on topicality and information; theatre on the other hand is just theatre; the one is a craft like journalism, the other an art.

Television then, cannot kill the drama, for it is merely a new form of daily journalism. If the drama dies — and it is often forgotten that it is mortal — it will be through its failure to give the public what television cannot provide, a theatrical experience. And it is a failure to be theatrical that is the danger of much of the new serious drama. Plays which can only be understood on careful reading and mean nothing at first performance, plays which interpret life in the chaos of Orwellian 'doublethink', where ambiguity becomes a kind of crossword for the author's own enjoyment, such fancies and fashions can no longer be afforded if the theatre is to keep open in an age of mechanical entertainments. No more can the slick, tailor-made, triangular light comedy be allowed to monopolise the boards, for rather than see a second-rate play the public will remain by their TV sets. If the theatre tries to fight TV by imitating it, it is lost. It is within the living traditions of the drama that the theatre can offer something different and continue its existence.

Television can affect the theatre, just as the cinema has already influenced the theatre, but neither medium can kill it of its own free will. Television has already its own heroes, and will doubtless reinforce the pervading star-conscious complex of theatre managers. In English-speaking countries the star is often the *raison d'être* of the play, the name of the playwright means nothing to the audience. Faced with competition from the cinema, theatre managements found that a popular star, or better still, a 'star-studded' cast, could make even an indifferent play or any old revival succeed, and so the fashion caught on and seems here to stay. In France the author is more honoured, in London and New York it is the star who is box-office. The system is financially deplorable and disastrous for the unknown playwright and player, but no doubt advertising, press and television will all do their worst to perpetuate what Mr. Peter Cotes calls the 'nonsense'. Recently there have been signs that things are changing, but we have not yet reached the position in Devine's Royal Court Theatre like that under the Vedrenne — Granville-Barker management when a playgoer wanted to know what a notice, announcing that Granville-Barker was unable to play the part of Tanner in *Man and Superman* meant. The box-office attendant explained, and the playgoer merely asked. "But I suppose someone will play it?" On being assured of this he impatiently banged down his half-crown, telling the man not to make such a fuss.

Television can be said, like the sound radio before it, to have created an audience for drama by bringing plays regularly into homes which never before went to the theatre. But this audience will still have to be tempted away from their TV sets and help fill the theatres along with present playgoers, who must not desert it. The theatre has never been a mass medium, and can never hope to have the numbers who regularly watch TV each night. But although a minority, there must be a playgoing public, and there are comparatively few cities in the world where there is a playgoing public of sufficient strength to keep the theatre living.

If the theatre is to survive, the *ersatz* material and the complacent acceptance of the second rate will have to be rejected, and an early return to traditions made. For if we are content with inferiority, the second rate will give way to the third rate until the theatre of compromise becomes the theatre of the lowest common denominator. Taste is what is so lacking to-day, and a nation which finds margarine indistinguishable from butter, and which produces newpapers in which the junior supplements are of a slightly higher intelligence than the adult part, will willingly declare that Shakespeare is a bore and that tin-can musicals compare favourably with classical composers. An age without taste is unlikely to discover works of art.

Who cares if the theatre dies? Perhaps its corpse won't quite lie down, but will go on giving the pretence of life with 'safe box-office propositions' and with a 'glittering' cast, and many playgoers will continue to take the theatre for granted. But if we return to an earlier proposition, that the contemporary theatre is the theatre of to-day, we realise that here is the fallacy of so many playwrights. The contemporary theatre should not only be the theatre of to-day, but part of a tradition which can continue for posterity. The difficulty with such a word is that so many so-called 'highbrows' seem to know what will be accepted by posterity, and consequently such an attitude is a delicious target for Noël Coward's fashionable actor in *Present Laughter* when he tells an insufferable young 'highbrow' who has dared to criticise him: "I don't give a hoot about posterity. Why should I worry about what people think of me when I'm dead as a door-nail anyway?" Surprisingly Noël Coward's plays have become period pieces reflecting the 'superficial, frivolous' mood of the 'twenties, and his recent failures in the theatre indicate that he can no longer capture the same mood to-day. It no longer exists.

In the course of this survey of the development of the modern drama since the days of Ibsen and Shaw we have noted the desperate search for every kind of artistic expression since the dramatist, starting with Pirandello, broke free from the naturalistic straight-jacket. The only mood one can be certain of is uncertainty, and no amount of scientific investigations through graphs of supply and demand curves could prove that the future of the theatre lay in the anti-naturalistic camp any more than in the naturalistic, the play of emotions or ideas, epic theatre or theatre in the round, the *théâtre engagé* or the *théâtre libre*. The question mark is whether there will be a theatre of to-morrow at all, and it is in an effort to make the living traditions of the drama apparent in our own times that this survey has been attempted to view the modern theatre in some kind of perspective.

The question remains, from Pirandello to whom? Who, indeed, of the living dramatists are the 'life-enhancers', among whom we may include Pirandello, Claudel, Giraudoux, Lorca from yesterday. Alas, so many writers to-day are 'life-diminishers'. Will they continue in fashion, or is there already a stir which promises to be a prelude to a revival in the life-force of the arts, and indeed a new hope for the world? Are we beginning to build up from the debris, to reconsider our definitions and beliefs? The very concept of good and evil, so upset by our existentialist moralists and our great dictators, continues to play its rôle with certain modern dramatists as it has done, unchanging in its laws, throught the centuries of dramatic history.

We want to know about this place man occupies in the universe. We want the theatre to be our revealer and to be able to approach, at the frontiers of theatre, the great unknown. For in the supreme moments of theatre there is a collective communion which can give life itself a meaning. The theatre in the living tradition of the drama gives man hope, faith and courage in fellow-man. The world in any age is as exciting or as terrible as man makes it, and according to the spiritual level at which man wishes to live — for since the beginnings of drama the theatre has been associated with religion. "Who shoots at the midday sun, though he be sure he shall never hit the mark, yet as sure he is he shall shoot higher than he who aims at a bush", wrote Sir Philip Sidney in the true spirit of the Elizabethan age. Have we the courage to aim likewise? Making the theatre live means making the theatre part of our existence and an expression of the continuity of the life-force.

BOOK LIST

The following selected books are those most likely to be of interest and help to readers of the present volume; the list does not aim at being exhaustive. Ibsen and Shaw are not included, and the choice of other works has been restricted to those easily obtainable in libraries and bookshops. Fuller bibliographies will be found in those volumes marked with an asterisk.

I REFERENCE BOOKS

The Oxford Companion to the Theatre, Edited by Phyllis Hartnoll. (Oxford University Press. Second edition 1957.)

World Drama, by Allardyce Nicoll (Harrap, 1949).

Who's Who in the Theatre, Edited by John Parker (Pitman, 10th ed., 1957).

European Theories of the Drama, by Barrett H. Clark (editor) (New York, 1918. Revised 1947).

Masters of the Drama, by John Gassner (New York, 1940. New ed., 1954).

II THE WORLD'S A STAGE

Le théâtre Moderne — hommes et tendances (ed. Jean Jacquot: Centre national de la récherche scientifique, Paris, 1958).

Théâtre et collectivité, A symposium edited by André Villiers (Paris, 1953).

Frontières du théâtre, by Paul Arnold (Paris, 1946).

Playgoing, by James Agate (Jarrolds, 1927).

Le théâtre et son double by Antonin Artaud (Paris, 1944).

Réflexions sur le théâtre, by Jean-Louis Barrault (Paris, 1949. Translated and published by Rockliff, 1951)

The Playwright as Thinker, by Eric Bentley (Published in London under the title *The Modern Theatre,* 1948).

In Search of Theatre, by Eric Bentley. Collected essays. (New York, 1953. London, Dobson, 1954).

Métamorphose de la littérature (de Proust à Sartre) Volume 2, by Pierre de Boisdeffre. Essays on Cocteau, Anouilh, Sartre and Camus (Paris, 1952).

Animateurs de théâtre, by Robert Brasillach (Paris 1936. Revised ed., 1954).

On the Art of the Theatre, by Edward Gordon Craig (London, 1911. New edition as *Dramatic Scene*, 1923).

Edward Gordon Craig — Designs for the Theatre, by Janet Leeper (Penguin Books, 1948).

A Study of the Modern Drama, by Barrett H. Clark (New York, 1934. Revised ed., 1938).

The Actor and his Audience, by W. A. Darlington (Phoenix House, 1949).

Drama and Life, by Roger Dataller (Nelson, 1938).*

Tragedy, by W. Macneile Dixon (Edward Arnold, 1924).

Souvenirs et notes de travail d'un acteur, by Charles Dullin (Paris).

Drama, by Ashley Dukes (London, 1926. Revised ed., Home University Library, 1936).*

The Organised Theatre, by St. John Ervine (Allen & Unwin, 1924).

Poetry and Drama, by T. S. Eliot (Faber and Faber, 1951).

The Three Voices of Poetry, by T. S. Eliot (National Book League, 1953).

Selected Prose, by T. S. Eliot (Penguin Books, 1953).

The Idea of a Theatre, by Francis Fergusson (Princeton University Press, 1949).

L'art du théâtre, by Henri Ghéon (Montreal, 1944).

New Theatres for Old, by Mordecai Gorelik (New York, 1940. London, Dobson, 1947).

L'essence du théâtre, by Henri Gouhier (Paris, 1943).

The Use of the Drama, by Harley Granville-Barker (London, 1946).

The Theatre in our Times, by John Gassner (New York, 1954).

Life and the Theatre, by Lynton Hudson (Harrap, 1949).

Théâtre et vie intérieure, by Georges Jamati (Paris, 1952).

Témoignages sur le théâtre, by Louis Jouvet (Paris, 1952).

The Theatre of To-morrow, Kenneth Macgowan (New York, 1922).

Continental Stagecraft, by Kenneth Macgowan and Robert Edmund Jones (New York, 1922).

Dramatic Values, by C. E. Montague (Chatto & Windus).

The Poet in the Theatre, by Ronald Peacock (Routledge, 1946).

Les deux cent mille situations dramatiques, by Etienne Souriau (Paris, 1950).

La mise en scène théâtrale et sa condition esthétique, by André Veinstein (Paris, 1955).

The Stage is Set, by Lee Simons (New York, 1932).

My Life in Art, by Constantin Stanislavsky (London & New York, 1938).

Notes sur un tragique et une tragédie, by Paul Valéry (Paris, 1946).

La psychologie de l'art dramatique, by André Villiers (Paris, 1951).

Drama from Ibsen to Eliot, by Raymond Williams (Chatto & Windus, 1952).

European Drama, by N. Scarlyn Wilson (London, 1937).

The Art of Drama, by Ronald Peacock (Routledge & Kegan Paul, 1957).

The Producer and the Play, by Norman Marshall (Macdonald, 1957).

Index to the Story of My Days, by Gordon Craig (Hulton, 1957).

III THE DRAMATISTS
LUIGI PIRANDELLO

Luigi Pirandello, 1867–1936, by Walter Starkie (London, 1926. Revised 1936).

The Drama of Luigi Pirandello, by Domenico Vittorini (Philadelphia, 1935).

Pirandello by Guy Dumur (Collection "les grands dramaturges", Paris, 1955).

JEAN GIRAUDOUX

Le théâtre de Jean Giraudoux, technique et style, by H. Sörensen (Denmark, 1950).

L'oeuvre de Jean Giraudoux, by Gunnan Host (Oslo, 1942).

Giraudoux par lui-même (Pictures and texts presented by Christian Marker. Paris, 1952).

Jean Giraudoux et "Pour Lucrèce" (Cahiers de la Compagnie Madeleine Renaud — Jean Louis Barrault, 1953).

Le théâtre de Giraudoux et la condition humaine, by Marianne Mercier-Compiche (Paris, 1954).

The Making of a Dramatist, Jean Giraudoux, by Donald P. Inskip (Oxford, 1958.)

Louis Jouvet, Man of the Theatre, by Bettina Knapp (Columbia, 1957).

PAUL CLAUDEL

Le drame de Paul Claudel, by Jacques Madaule (Paris, 1947).

Introduction à l'oeuvre de Paul Claudel, by Sainte-Marie-Perrin.

Paul Claudel, by Georges Duhamel.

Paul Claudel and "The Tidings Brought to Mary", by Kathleen O'Flaherty.

Paul Claudel et "Christophe Colomb" (Cahiers de la Compagnie Madeleine Renaud — Jean-Louis Barrault).

The Poetic Drama of Paul Claudel, by Joseph Chiari (The Harvill Press, 1954).

The Theme of Beatrice in the Plays of Claudel, by Ernest Beaumont (Rockliff, 1954).

Paul Claudel by Jacques Madaule (Collection "les grands dramaturges" Paris).

Claudel, aujourd'hui (Cahiers de la compagnie Madeleine Renaud — Jean-Louis Barrault, Dec. 1958).

T. S. ELIOT

Most of the critical studies of T. S. Eliot concern his verse, and only passing reference is made to his drama. For the development of his dramatic style, nothing could be more revealing than Mr. Eliot's own self-criticism in *Poetry and Drama* (Faber & Faber). The British Council pamphlet on T. S. Eliot by M. C. Bradbrook (revised 1951) gives the essential background to Eliot's writing.

BRECHT

Brecht by Geneviève Serreau (Collection "les grands dramaturges" Paris, 1955).

The Theatre of Bertolt Brecht by John Willet (Methuen, 1958).

Theaterarbeit (Berliner Ensemble productions. 1954 Dresdner Verlag).

Parables for the Theatre (two plays, "The Caucausian Chalk Circle", and "The Good Women of Setzuan", New York, Evergeern).

Brecht: A Choice of Evils, by Martin Esslin (Eyre & Spottiswoode, 1959)

GARCIA LORCA

Lorca, the Poet and his People, by Arturo Barea (Faber, 1944).

Lorca, An Appreciation of his Poetry, by Roy Campbell (Bowes & Bowes).

García Lorca, by Edwin Henig (London, 1944).

Three Tragedies of Lorca translated with introduction (New Directions, New York).
Lorca by François Nourissier (Paris, 1955).

JEAN COCTEAU

Jean Cocteau, by Margaret Crosland (Peter Nevill, 1954).
Dramaturgie de Jean Cocteau, by Pierre Dubourg (Paris, 1954).

EUGENE O'NEILL

Eugene O'Neill, the Man and his Plays, by Barret H. Clark (New York, 1926. New ed. and revised, 1947).
The Haunted Heroes of Eugene O'Neill, by Edwin Engel, (Harvard 1953).
Eugene O'Neill and the tragic vision, by Doris V. Falk (Rutgens Univ. Press, 1958).

JEAN-PAUL SARTRE

L'homme Sartre, by Marc Beigbeder (Paris, 1947).

ARMAND SALACROU

Armand Salacrou, by José van den Esch (Paris, 1947).

JEAN ANOUILH

Jean Anouilh, by Hubert Gignoux (Paris, 1946).
A la rencontre de Jean Anouilh, by Jean Didier (Brussels, 1946).
Jean Anouilh, Poet of Pierrot and Pantaloon, by Edward Owen Marsh (W. H. Allen, 1953).

EUGENE IONESCO

Special number devoted to Ionesco of "Cahiers des Saisons" (Paris, Winter, 1959).

HENRY DE MONTHERLANT

Notes sur mon théâtre (Paris, 1950).
Le théâtre de Montherlant, by Jacques de Laprade (Paris, 1950).

IV NATIONAL DRAMA

THE BRITISH THEATRE

Dobson's Theatre Year Book, 1948, Edited by John Andrews & Ossia Trilling (London, 1949).

No Star Nonsense, by Peter Cotes (Rockliff, 1949).
The Unholy Trade, by Richard Findlater (Gollancz, 1952).
Christopher Fry, by Derek Stanford (Longmans, 1954).
James Bridie and his Theatre, by Winifred Bannister (Rockliff, 1955).
The Other Theatre, by Norman Marshall (John Lehmann, 1947).
British Theatre, by Peter Noble (British Yearbooks, 1946).
Theatre Outlook, by J. B. Priestley (Nicholson & Watson, 1947).
Theatrical Cavalcade, by Ernest Short (Eyre & Spottiswoode, 1942).
Modern English Drama, by Ernest Reynolds (1949).
Drama since 1939, by Robert Speaight (The Arts in Britain series, London, 1947).
Theatre of Two Decades, by Audrey Williamson (Rockliff, 1951).
The Fugitive Art, by T. C. Worsley (John Lehmann, 1952).
Le théâtre contemporain en Grande-Bretagne et aux Etats-Unis (Etudes Anglaises Paris, October-December, 1957).
Actress, by Yvonne Mitchell (Routledge, 1957).

THE AMERICAN THEATRE

The Fervent Years, The story of the Group Theatre and the 'thirties, by Harold Clurman (Dobson, 1946).
American Playwrights 1918–1938, *the Theatre Retreats from Reality*, by Eleanor Flexner (New York, 1938).
The American Drama since 1918, by Joseph Wood Krutch (New York, 1939).
'Modernism' in Modern Drama, by Joseph Wood Krutch (New York, 1952).
Modern American Drama and Stage, by Boyd Martin (Pilot Press, 1943).
The Theatre Guild Anthology (New York, 1936).
Best Plays of the Modern American Theatre, Edited and introduced by John Gassner (Two volumes, New York, 1947).

THE FRENCH THEATRE

Le théâtre des années folles, by Pierre Brisson (Geneva, 1943).
The French Theatre of To-day — An English View, by Harold Hobson (Harrap, 1953).
Le théâtre en France depuis 1900, by René Lalou (Paris, 1951).
La galerie dramatique, by Francis Ambrière (Paris, 1949).
Anthologie du théâtre français contemporain, Edited by G. Pillement. (Three volumes, Paris, 1945–1948).

Le théâtre français contemporain, by Edmond Sée (Paris, 1931. New ed., 1951).

The Contemporary French Theatre, by Joseph Chiari (Rockliff, 1958).

V THEATRE JOURNALS

Theatre Arts Monthly (U.S.A.)

World Theatre (Le Théâtre dans le Monde); published occasionally for UNESCO.

The Stage (London, the theatrical profession's weekly newspaper).

Theatre World (illustrated monthly dealing with current West End productions).

Plays and Players (A monthly illustrated magazine published in London).

Drama (The quarterly published by the British Drama League).

Paris Theatre (monthly, containing playscript of current production).

L'Avant-scene (Paris, bi-monthly with text of current productions).

Théâtre d'aujourd'hui (Paris, illustrated every two months).

Arts-Spectacles (Paris, right wing weekly devoted to the arts).

Encore (London, every two months; accent on theatre of ideas).

La Revue Théâtrale (Paris, occasional review).

VI ANNUALS

Theatre World Annual, ed Frances Stephens (Barrie & Rockliff).

International Theatre Annual, edited by Harold Hobson (John Calder).

Théâtre de France.

ORIGINAL TEXT OF PASSAGES
QUOTED IN THE BOOK

(The translations from the following passages have been made by Lothian Small)

Quotation A: Siegfried, by Jean Giraudoux

ROBINEAU . . . Qu'as-tu fait pourtant depuis ces douze ans, Zelten? Toi qui aimais le printemps, la musique, la joie, la paix, qu'as-tu-fait?

ZELTEN   La guerre! La guerre contre trente-cinq nations. Le combat contre une seule. . . . Et toi, le porte-lunettes, le démocrate paisible des bibliothèques royales et impériales, toi, mon ami le plus cher, depuis douze ans, qu'as-tu-fait?

ROBINEAU La guerre, contre toi . .

Quotation B: Siegfried, by Jean Giraudoux

LEDINGER   Revenez avec nous, mon ami. Vous souffrez. Vous avez maigri. Revenez.

SIEGFRIED Oui, j'ai maigri, Ledinger. Mais, autant que de la grandeur de la perte, c'est de la grandeur du cadeau que j'ai souffert ces nuits dernières. Un convalescent, comme moi, aurait plutôt besoin en effet d'une patrie minuscule. Celui qu'on ampute subitement de l'Allemagne et sur lequel on charge la France, il faudrait que les lois de l'équilibre fussent vraiment bouleversées pour qu'il n'en éprouvât aucun trouble. Je vous dirai que j'ai songé, avant-hier, à disparaître, à chercher un asile dans un troisième pays, dans un pays que j'aurais choisi autant que possible sans voisins, sans ennemis, sans inaugurations de monuments aux morts, sans morts. Un pays sans guerre passée, sans guerre future. . . . Mais plus je le cherchais sur la carte, plus les liens au contraire qui m'attachent aux nations qui souffrent et pâtissent se reserraient, et plus je voyais clairement ma mission.

Quotation C: Siegfried, by Jean Giraudoux

SIEGFRIED Je vivrai, simplement. Siegfried et Forestier vivront côte à côte. Je tâcherai de porter, honorablement, les deux noms et les deux sorts que m'a donnés le hasard. Une vie humaine n'est pas un ver. Il ne suffit pas de la trancher en deux pour que chaque part devienne une parfaite existence. Il n'est pas de souffrances si contraires, d'expériences si ennemies qu'elles ne puissent se fondre un jour en une seule vie, car le coeur de l'homme est encore le plus puissant creuset. Peut-être, avant longtemps, cette mémoire échappée, ces patries trouvées et perdues, cette inconscience et cette conscience dont je souffre et jouis également, formeront un tissu logique et une existence simple. Il serait excessif que dans une âme humaine, où cohabitent les vices et les vertus des plus contraires, seuls le mot "allemand" et le mot "français" se refusent à composer. Je me refuse, moi, à creuser des tranchées à l'intérieur de moi même. Je ne rentrerai pas en France comme le dernier prisonnier relâché des prisons allemandes, mais comme le premier bénéficiaire d'une science nouvelle, ou d'un coeur nouveau . . . Adieu. Votre train siffle. Siegfried et Forestier vous disent adieu.

Quotation D: Pour Lucrèce, by Jean Giraudoux

LUCILE   Sans recours? Quelle erreur! Il est là, dans ma main, mon recours. Je riais de vous tout à l'heure, quand vous m'appeliez vaincue, car il y était déjà. Je le tiens d'une petite fille, qui avait mon nom, mon âge, et qui s'est juré, quand elle avait dix ans, de ne pas admettre le mal, qui s'est juré de prouver par la mort s'il le fallait, que le monde était noble, les humains purs. Cette terre est devenue pour elle vide et vile, cette vie n'est plus pour elle que déchéance, cela n'importe pas, cela n'est pas vrai, puisqu'elle tient son serment!

Quotation E: Pour Lucrèce, by Jean Giraudoux

BARBETTE   Tu as bien été violée. Pas par Marcellus, cela on en guérit, cinquante en ont guéri. Tu le sentais bien toi-même. Tu t'en serais remise. Mais par la bêtise des hommes, la grossièreté des hommes, la méchanceté des hommes. Elle t'est apparue d'un coup. C'était trop. Douce comme toi, on en meurt.

Quotation F: L'Echange, by Paul Claudel

Le théâtre. Vous ne savez pas ce que c'est? — Non — Il y a la scène et la salle.

Tout étant clos, les gens viennent là le soir et ils sont assis par rangées les uns derrière les autres, regardant,

. . . Ils regardent le rideau de la scène.

Et ce qu'il y a derrière quand il est levé.

Et il arrive quelque chose sur la scène comme si c'était vrai.

. . . Je les regarde, et la salle n'est rien que de la chair vivante et habillée.

Et ils garnissent les murs comme des mouches jusqu'au plafond.

Et je vois ces centaines de visages blancs.

L'homme s'ennuie et l'ignorance lui est attachée depuis sa naissance.

Et ne sachant de rien comment cela commence ou finit, c'est pour cela qu'il va au théâtre.

Et il se regarde lui-même, les mains posées sur les genoux.

Et il pleure et il rit, et il n'a point envie de s'en aller.

Et je les regarde aussi et je sais qu'il y a là le caissier qui sait que demain

On vérifiera les livres, et la mère adultère dont l'enfant vient de tomber malade,

Et celui qui vient de voler pour la première fois et celui qui n'a rien fait de tout le jour.

Et ils regardent et écoutent comme s'ils dormaient.

(Théâtre, III, pp. 195–196).

Quotation G: Partage de Midi, by Paul Claudel

YSÉ   Non, non, il ne faut point m'aimer. Non,
Mesa, il ne faut point m'aimer.
    Cela ne serait point bon.
    Vous savez que je suis une pauvre femme.
Restez le Mesa dont j'ai besoin.

. . . . .

Dites que vous ne m'aimerez pas. Ysé, je ne vous aimerai pas.

Quotation H: Partage de Midi, by Paul Claudel

YSÉ   Et que nous font les autres? mais tu es unique et je suis unique.

Et j'entends ta voix dans mes entrailles comme un cri qui ne peut être souffert,

Et je me lève vers toi avec difficulté comme une chose énorme et massive et aveugle et désirante et taciturne.

Mais ce que nous désirons, ce n'est point de créer, mais de détruire, et que ah!

Il n'y ait plus rien d'autre que toi et moi, et en toi que moi, et en

moi que ta possession, et la rage, et la tendresse, et de te détruire et de n'être plus gêné

Détestablement par ces vêtements de chair, et ces cruelles dents dans mon coeur,

Non point cruelle!

Ah, ce n'est point le bonheur que je t'apporte, mais ta mort, et la mienne avec elle.

Quotation I: Partage de Midi, by Paul Claudel

MESA   Dis, Ysé, ce n'est plus le grand soleil de midi. Tu te rapelle notre Océan?

V

Mais la lampe sépulcrale colore ta joue, et l'oreille, et le coin de
votre tempe,

Et se reflète dans vos yeux, vos yeux dans le miroir . . .

Il souffle la lampe

La petite lampe est éteinte. Et il est éteint en même temps,

Ce dernier soleil de notre amour, ce grand soleil de midi d'août

Dans lequel nous nous disions adieu dans la lumière dévorante,
nous séparant, faisant de l'un à l'autre désespérément

Un signe au travers de la distance élargie.

Adieu, Ysé, tu ne m'as point connu! Ce grand trésor que je porte
en moi,

Tu n'as point pu le déraciner,

Le prendre, je n'ai pas su le donner. Ce n'est pas ma faute.

Ou si! c'est notre faute et notre châtiment.

Il fallait tout donner,

Et c'est cela que tu n'as pas pardonné.

Silence

Quotation J: Le Soulier de Satin, by Paul Claudel

Et crois-tu donc que ce soit le corps seul qui soit capable d'allumer
dans le mien un tel désir?

Ce que j'aime, ce n'est point ce qui en elle est capable de se
dissoudre et de m'échapper et d'être absent, et de cesser une
fois de m'aimer, c'est ce qui est la cause d'elle même, ce qui
produit la vie sous mes baisers et non la mort!

Si je lui apprends qu'elle n'est pas née pour mourir, si je lui
demande son immortalité, cette étoile sans le savoir au fond
d'elle-même qu'elle est,

Ah, comment pourrait-elle me refuser?

Ce n'est point ce qu'il y a en elle de trouble et de mêler et d'in-
certain que je demande, ce qu'il y a d'inerte et de neutre et de
périssable,

C'est l'être tout nu, la vie pure,

C'est cet amour aussi fort que moi sous mon désir comme une
grande flamme crue, comme un rire dans ma face!

Ah, me le donnât-elle (je défaille et la nuit vient sur mes yeux!)

Me le donnât-elle et il ne faut pas qu'elle me le donne,

Ce n'est point son corps chéri jamais qui réussirait à me contenter!

Jamais autrement que l'un par l'autre nous ne réussirons à nous
débarrasser de la mort,

Comme le violet s'il fond avec l'orange dégage le rouge tout pûr!

Quotation K: Le Soulier de Satin, by Paul Claudel

PROUHÈZE Eh quoi, noble Rodrigue, aurais-tu donc voulu que je remette
entre tes bras une adultère?

Et plus tard quand Don Pélage est mort que je t'ai jeté cet appel
   à toi,
Oui, peut-être il vaut mieux qu'il ne t'ait pas atteint.
Je n'aurais été qu'une femme bientôt mourante sur ton coeur et
   non pas cette étoile éternelle dont tu as soif.

Quotation L: Le Malentendu by Albert Camus

MARTHA   Comprenez que ni pour lui ni pour nous, ni dans la vie ni dans la
mort, il n'est de patrie ni de paix. (*Avec un rire méprisant*) Car on
ne peut appeler patrie, n'est-ce pas, cette terre épaisse, privée de
lumière, où l'on s'en va nourrir des animaux aveugles. . . . A quoi
bon ce grand appel de l'être, cette alerte des âmes? Pourquoi crier
vers la mer ou vers l'amour? Cela est dérisoire. . . . Comprenez
que votre douleur ne s'égalera jamais à l'injustice qu'on fait à
l'homme.

Quotation M: Les Mouches, by Jean-Paul Sartre

JUPITER   Imaginez qu'il se présente un jour aux portes de cette ville. . . .
Je dirais donc: "Jeune homme, allez-vous-en! Que cherchez-
vous ici? Vous voulez faire valoir vos droits? Eh! vous êtes ardent
et fort, vous feriez un brave capitaine dans une armée bien batail-
leuse, vous avez mieux à faire qu'à régner sur une ville à demi
morte, une charogne de ville tourmentée par les mouches. Les gens
d'ici sont de grands pécheurs, mais voici qu'ils se sont engagés
dans la voie du rachat. Laissez-les, jeune homme, laissez-les,
respectez leur douloureuse entreprise, éloignez-vous sur la pointe
des pieds. . . . Bon voyage, jeune homme, bon voyage; l'ordre
d'une cité et l'ordre des âmes sont instables: si vous y touchez,
vous provoquerez une catastrophe (*Le regardant dans les yeux*)
Une terrible catastrophe qui retombera sur vous.

Quotation N: Les Mouches, by Jean-Paul Sartre

ELECTRE   Il faut que j'éclaire ton visage, car la nuit s'épaissit et je ne te vois
plus bien. J'ai besoin de te voir: quand je ne te vois plus, j'ai peur
de toi; il ne faut pas que je te quitte des yeux. Je t'aime. Il faut que
je pense que je t'aime. Comme tu as l'air étrange!

ORESTE   Je suis libre, Electre; la liberté a fondu sur moi comme la foudre.

Quotation O: Le Maître de Santiago, by Henry de Montherlant

ALVARO   A notre sang nul sang ne viendra se mêler. Il n'y aura pas d'homme
qui te tournera et te retournera dans ses bras. Et pas d'enfants,
personne pour me salir, personne pour me trahir: avec toi je
m'éteins dans toute ma propreté. Les derniers! Nous serons les
derniers! Quelle force dans ce mot de *derniers,* qui s'ouvre sur le
néant sublime.

INDEX